SPEAKING OF
THE FANTASTIC III

Borgo Press Books by Darrell Schweitzer

Conan's World and Robert E. Howard
Deadly Things: A Collection of Mysterious Tales
Exploring Fantasy Worlds
The Fantastic Horizon: Essays and Reviews
Ghosts of Past and Future: Selected Poetry
The Robert E. Howard Reader
Speaking of Horror II
Speaking of the Fantastic III: Interviews with Science Fiction Writers

SPEAKING OF THE FANTASTIC III

INTERVIEWS WITH SCIENCE FICTION WRITERS

DARRELL SCHWEITZER

THE BORGO PRESS
MMXII

I.O. Evans Studies in the
Philosophy and Criticism of Literature
ISSN 0271-9061

Number Fifty-Seven

SPEAKING OF THE FANTASTIC III

Copyright © 2004, 2005, 2006, 2007, 2008, 2009,
2012 by Darrell Schweitzer

FIRST EDITION

Published by Wildside Press LLC

www.wildsidebooks.com

DEDICATION

For Oz Fontecchio,

Patron of the arts,
A faithful and tireless
Friend of science fiction.

CONTENTS

ACKNOWLEDGMENTS 9
INTRODUCTION 11
GEORGE R. R. MARTIN 15
JAMES MORROW 26
JACK DANN 42
GEOFFREY A. LANDIS 61
JOE W. HALDEMAN 74
ZORAN ZIVKOVIC 86
ESTHER M. FRIESNER 97
KRISTINE KATHRYN RUSCH 115
HARRY TURTLEDOVE 128
GREGORY FROST 139
TOM PURDOM 153
D. G. COMPTON 176
ROBERT J. SAWYER 189
CHARLES STROSS 202
BRIAN HERBERT and KEVIN J. ANDERSON 223

HOWARD WALDROP. 249
ABOUT THE AUTHOR 267

ACKNOWLEDGMENTS

THESE INTERVIEWS WERE previously published as follows, and are reprinted (with minor editing, updating, and textual modifications) by permission of the author:

George R. R. Martin originally appeared in *Weird Tales* #344, April-May 2007. Copyright © 2007 by Wildside Press. Copyright © 2012 by Darrell Schweitzer.

James Morrow originally appeared in *Orson Scott Card's Intergalactic Medicine Show* #7, January 2008. Copyright © 2008, 2012 by Darrell Schweitzer.

Jack Dann originally appeared in *The New York Review of Science Fiction* #212, April 2006. Copyright © 2006 by Dragon Press. Copyright © 2012 by Darrell Schweitzer.

Geoffrey A. Landis originally appeared in *Science Fiction Chronicle* #245, March 2004. Copyright © 2004, 2012 by Darrell Schweitzer.

Joe W. Haldeman originally appeared in *Orson Scott Card's Intergalactic Medicine Show* #12, May 2009. Copyright © 2009, 2012 by Darrell Schweitzer.

Zoran Zivkovic originally appeared in *Orson Scott Card's Intergalactic Medicine Show* #8, April 2008. Copyright © 2008, 2012 by Darrell Schweitzer.

Esther Friesner originally appeared in *Orson Scott Card's Intergalactic Medicine Show* #9, July 2008. Copyright © 2008, 2012 by Darrell Schweitzer.

Kristine Kathryn Rusch originally appeared on the DNA

Publications website in 2009. Copyright © 2009, 2012 by Darrell Schweitzer.

Harry Turtledove originally appeared in *Orson Scott Card's Intergalactic Medicine Show* #10, December 2008. Copyright © 2008, 2012 by Darrell Schweitzer.

Gregory Frost originally appeared in *Orson Scott Card's Intergalactic Medicine Show* #13, July 2009. Copyright © 2009, 2012 by Darrell Schweitzer.

Tom Purdom originally appeared in *The New York Review of Science Fiction* #208, December 2005. Copyright © 2005 by Dragon Press. Copyright © 2005, 2012 by Darrell Schweitzer.

D. G. Compton originally appeared in *The New York Review of Science Fiction* #232, December 2007. Copyright © 2007 by Dragon Press. Copyright © 2012 by Darrell Schweitzer.

Robert J. Sawyer originally appeared in *Orson Scott Card's Intergalactic Medicine Show* #6, October 2007. Copyright © 2007, 2012 by Darrell Schweitzer.

Charles Stross originally appeared in *The New York Review of Science Fiction,* #248, April 2009. Copyright © 2009 by Dragon Press. Copyright © 2009, 2012 by Darrell Schweitzer.

Brian Herbert and Kevin J. Anderson originally appeared in *Orson Scott Card's Intergalactic Medicine Show* #14, September 2009. Copyright © 2009, 2012 by Darrell Schweitzer.

Howard Waldrop originally appeared in *Postscripts* #7, Summer 2006. Copyright © 2006, 2012 by Darrell Schweitzer.

INTRODUCTION

I've been interviewing for most of my life now, and so most of what I have to say about interviewing I have said before, in introductions to books like this one, beginning with the original T.K. Graphics version of *SF Voices* in 1976. I did my first interview in 1973, which involved a very young Gardner Dozois, an even younger version of myself, and a college chum who came along to make sure the borrowed tape recorder kept working. The result, which appeared underneath a photo of a long-haired Gardner glaring down from a height and alongside (in the other front-page column) a photo of David Bowie at his most androgynous, appeared in 1973 in a Philadelphia "underground" newspaper called *The Drummer* (as in "a different drummer") which was given away on campuses and sold on newsstands as a supplement to a larger publication called (I kid you not) *The Daily Planet*. Yes, like Clark Kent I really was a (presumably) mild-mannered reporter for *The Daily Planet*.

Even then I instinctively grasped the basics of a good interview, which may be summed up in the following rather run-on sentence: Find someone interesting and articulate, ask just enough questions to get them talking, then point the microphone, shut up, and, oh, by the way, make sure your equipment works.

After that early success I have hopefully improved my technique over the years and learned to ask more intelligent questions, but the basic principle has remained the same. I am not the star of the interview. The interviewee is. Interviews are not *news*, and therefore do not lose their inherent interest as soon as the forthcoming books the author is talking about have come out, but are instead informal moments in time, captured in context. In an earlier introduction like this I compared it to catching Homer right after he had finished the *Iliad* and could only say, "I am thinking about doing a sequel." Or, put it this way. The H. G. Wells of 1898, right after the publication of *The War of the Worlds*, would have very likely had a very different view of writing, science fiction, and the future of mankind than the Wells of 1940, who would have been a lot gloomier, political, and, very likely, out of touch with the field of literature he had helped to inspire. (But if Wells *had* held opinions about the John W. Campbell revolution and the work of the early Heinlein, don't you wish some interviewer had managed to get *that* on record?)

Certainly many aspects of interviewing today are themselves science fiction by the standards of 1973, when I started. I am writing this introduction on a computer, into a file which consists of the rest of the book, assembled from earlier files, which I have edited into a uniform format. There was a time when all this was done on a manual typewriter, with, at best a bit of literal cut-and-paste involving scissors, glue, and a photocopier.

Today, interviews can be done via e-mail. I have met Zoran Zivkovic since, but when I interviewed him I had not. He was in Belgrade and I was in Philadelphia. We communicated easily and instantaneously, with the result coming out in typesettable form. Now that's progress. I can barely imagine what it was like before the days of any recording equipment, when the interviewer's job was to engage his subject in conversation, then hurry to his desk and write down as much as he could remember as quickly as possible. In the old days, most interviewees tended to freeze up at the sight of someone taking their words down in shorthand. Fortunately today most people are used to microphones, and do not lose their spontaneity in front of them. I continue to prefer to interview people in-person, with a tape recorder, but I have learned to do interviews via e-mail instead. It's not the same as paper correspondence. It is a new skill, which nobody imagined a need for in 1973. If you're good at it, it can be nearly as spontaneous as speech.

But the principle is still the same. The idea is to get free-flowing conversation which illuminates the subject's thinking and his work, and which can go off in surprising tangents, quite aside from any pre-written questions. An interview is not a questionnaire, I hasten to add, and hopefully mine do not read like the results of one.

Who are my subjects? I gave some thought to including an extensive introduction to each interview, and maybe a bibliography, but decided against it. This isn't that kind of reference book. Let's devote all the space to the interviews themselves. Hopefully, in most cases, a science-fiction writer will know that Geoffrey Landis is a NASA scientist who doubles over as a Hugo-winning science fiction writer, or that Joe Haldeman wrote *The Forever War* and much else, or that D. G. Compton is the author of *Synthajoy* and many other celebrated works from around 1970 and who had not been heard from much of late (at least in the science fiction field) when I interviewed him. Robert Sawyer is one of the most successful SF writers of our time. George R. R. Martin has been a fan favorite since he was writing such stories as "A Song for Lya" in Ben Bova's *Analog* and has lately achieved bestseller status with an immense fantasy epic that began with *A Game of Thrones.* Zoran Zivkovic is a leading Serbian fantasist who came to the attention of Anglophone readers in the British magazine *Interzone* and who has had numerous books published in English since, mostly by small presses. He is a winner of the World Fantasy Award. And so on. If there really is somebody here you have not heard of, I hope it doesn't seem too haughty of me to say that's why God made Wikipedia. That is another sign of the modern age, right along with the fact that many of these interviews were first published on the Internet and have never actually been in physical print before. A book like this doesn't need quite as much introductory apparatus as it used to.

So let's get on with it. I always think of these collections as a compilation from my talk show. Here are some of my best recent episodes.

Darrell Schweitzer
January 19, 2011

GEORGE R. R. MARTIN

Q: You've made quite a transition from being an *Analog* writer to the writer of a multi-volume epic fantasy? Is this something you planned or even expected? I am sure there are some guys in the hard-science camp who are grumbling that George Martin is this traitor to the cause.... Have you given this much thought?

Martin: I've had an occasional review which says that I've changed from one thing to another, but it's really a misperception. Oddly enough, I've been through it before, because when I wrote *Fevre Dream* in 1982 I got a lot of stuff about how I'd changed from being a science fiction writer to a horror writer at that time. Now it's a high fantasy writer.

The truth is that if you go back and look at my career, you'll see that I have written in all these genres and sub-genres since the very beginning. My first story was a science fiction story in *Galaxy,* my first professional sale. But my second professional sale was a ghost story in *Fantastic*. I published a couple epic fantasy short stories in *Fantastic* during the 1970s as well, back when Ted White was the editor, as well as the stories in *Analog*. The stories in *Analog* got more attention, but the other stuff was there from the beginning.

I read all this stuff growing up and I read it pretty much interchangeably. I never made these distinctions between genre. I read H. P. Lovecraft. I read Robert E. Howard and I read Tolkien, and of course I read Robert A. Heinlein and Eric Frank Russell and Andre Norton; so I have always loved all three genres of science fiction and horror and fantasy, and have moved between them pretty freely. I don't think I've gone anywhere. I am in the middle of this very large project right now, which is epic fantasy, but when I am done with it, the next book, whenever that comes, could be science fiction or horror or even something else entirely. A mystery novel. Who knows? I just tell the stories that I want to tell.

Q: Do you find that the writing or the conception different if it's going to be science fiction, or not? Is the imaginative process any different?

Martin: No, it's not different at all for me. I think that for science fiction, fantasy, and even horror to some extent, the differences are skin-deep. I know there is an element of the field, particularly in science fiction, who feel that the differences are very profound, but I do not agree with that analysis. I think for me it is a matter of the furnishings. I have talked about that in some of my guest of honor speeches. An elf or an alien may in some ways fulfill the same function, as a literary trope. It's almost a matter of flavor. The ice cream can be chocolate or it can be strawberry, but it's still ice cream. The real differences, to my mind, is between romantic fiction, which all these genres are a part of, and mimetic fiction, or naturalistic fiction.

Q: There was a Heinlein argument that science fiction is a form of realism. Did he know what he was talking about?

Martin: I don't think so. [Laughs.] And Heinlein wrote fantasy himself, for that matter, from time to time, not very much of it; but he was perfectly capable of doing something like "Magic Incorporated," or even *Glory Road*, which has many of the trappings of a fantasy within a science fiction framework.

Q: This raises a point which others have raised before, that science fiction is a kind of language. You can have a fantasy novel within a science-fiction framework, as opposed to a fantasy novel *not* within a science-fiction framework. This implies a science-fiction discourse which can handle fantasy material. Wasn't that the whole point of the *Unknown Worlds* school, fantasy written as if it were science fiction?

Martin: Yes, and *Unknown Worlds* was a particular subset of fantasy, driven, I think, by Campbell's very deep rationalism, his desire to make magic obey the laws that engineering might obey. So you could discover the seven principles of magic and apply them. To my mind the ultimate *Unknown Worlds* stories were always the Incomplete Enchanter stories—the Harold Shea stories—by Pratt and de Camp. Harold Shea is always going into these worlds, and there is magic at work, but it's not mysterious. It is strange to him at first, but when he works out the underlying principles, he can easily become a magician, because he is basically an engineer. That was an amusing and, I think, an original take on it all at the time, in the '30s and '40s, but it's certainly not my take. I find myself more in sympathy with the way Tolkien handles magic. I think if you're going to do magic, it loses its magical qualities if it becomes nothing more than an alternate kind of science. It is more effective if it is something profoundly unknowable and wondrous, and something that can take your breath away.

Q: It's a matter of control. If you can retro-engineer Sauron's ring, it isn't as magical anymore. It's a matter of the characters getting control of the material, as opposed to being in a situation or universe where this is not really possible.

Martin: Yes. That's certainly part of it. Understanding is part of it. Of course you can go to the horror slant, too, with Lovecraft and his suggestion that if we understood some of these things, they would drive us mad, because the truths are too profoundly disturbing in what they tell us about the hostile or inimical nature of the universe or the strange and arcane forces that surround us.

Q: Do you find yourself more drawn to the magical approach, even with science fiction?

Martin: Yes. I think that if you look at my science fiction, even my so-called *Analog* stories, they were never comfortably *Analog* stories. I do think it's significant that my association with *Analog* that was very strong, and most of my early work that really established my career was published in *Analog*, all came during Ben Bova's editorship, which I think was *Analog*'s golden summer. If John W. Campbell had lived another decade, I don't know that I would ever have sold a story to *Analog*, or if when Campbell died, Stan Schmidt came in and became his immediate successor. Bova had a much more liberal approach as to what he would accept than either his predecessor or his successor.

Q: Let me guess that you are a writer who draws the story out of emotion and image rather than idea.

Martin: Yes, I think that's true. And if you believe in all this left-brain/right-brain stuff...but certainly the power of my fiction comes from the emotional side of things and not the rationalist side of things. I prefer, for example, not to outline. I did outline during my Hollywood decade, because it's required of you there, but on my own stories I have usually a general idea of where the story is going, but I do not break it all down and design it ahead of time. I just sort of fill in the blanks during the writing. The characters come alive and they take me to that destination, if the story is working.

Q: When you started *A Game of Thrones*, did you know you were going to write a multi-volume epic? I am thinking of Gene Wolfe's remark that *The Book of the New Sun*, which ultimately ran five volumes, began as a novella for *Orbit*. Did you have some broad plan of creating this whole epic, or did it just sort of grow?

Martin: A bit of both. To tell the truth, I read that novella. It was called "The Feast of St. Catherine." Gene presented it to the Windy City Writers Group when I was a member of it. In my case, when I wrote the first chapter of *A Game of Thrones*, I didn't really know what I had. In fact I was writing quite a different book, a science-fiction book, and this chapter just came to me so vividly that I put the science fiction aside and wrote it. At this point I didn't know if it was a short story or a piece of something bigger, but by the time I'd finished it, which only took two or three days, I was fairly certain that it was a piece of something bigger. It led to a second chapter and a third. I think that by the time I was four or five chapters in, I had some idea that, yes, I was working on a fantasy. I thought it was a trilogy. It was initially sold as a trilogy. Three books, three quite large books, mind you, but it grew even larger in the telling.

Q: How many books will the series be in all?

Martin: Seven is what I am looking at right now. I'm halfway through the fifth and hope to be able to complete that within the year, and hopefully on to the sixth and the seventh. But I am not writing that in blood. The goal is to tell the entire story as I visualize it, and that is more important than how many volumes it's divided up into. I do definitely see it as a finite series that has an end. I think a work of art needs an end, as well as a beginning and a middle. You do have to wrap it up. You can't drag it out forever. I think seven volumes will do it.

Q: At this point you must have a pretty clear idea of the overall structure.

Martin: Yes.

Q: How is the creation of an imaginary-world fantasy setting different from creating a planet in science fiction?

For example, in *Windhaven* you and Lisa Tuttle created a world, but it was a planet, not a fantasy setting. Is it a different kind of creation?

Martin: It's not terribly different in the way I do it. I was never a hard-science guy, despite the association with *Analog*. I know how people like Gordy Dickson and Hal Clement in his day would go about creating worlds by figuring out what type of star it was and how far the planet was from the sun and what its axial tilt was, its rate of rotation, its chemical composition. Then they would work things out from that. But I don't have that kind of background. Mine always came more from the effect. In the case of *Windhaven* we wanted flying human beings. We said, "How can we get people to fly and make it plausible to fly about on hang-gliders?" Well, a planet should have lighter gravity; that would help, and a lot of wind, etc. So we worked backwards. We didn't design the planet to see what it would be like. We looked at the effects we wanted and tried to retrofit a planet to that.

In the case of fantasy, of course, it's a little different. The most conspicuous aspect of the world of Westeros in *The Song of Ice and Fire* is the long and random nature of the seasons. I have gotten a number of fan letters over the years from readers who are trying to figure out the reason for why the seasons are the way they are. They develop lengthy theories: perhaps it's a multiple-star system, and what the axial tilt is, but I have to say, "Nice try, guys, but you're thinking in the wrong direction." This is a fantasy series. I am going to explain it all eventually, but it's going to be a fantasy explanation. It's not going to be a science-fiction explanation.

Q: In a fantasy you have to have a supernatural or mythic core to the story, rather than a scientific one.

Martin: Right. Yes. Exactly.

Q: Did you start *Fevre Dream* with just the image of a vampire on a steamboat?

Martin: Actually, I started *Fevre Dream* with the image of the steamboat. I was living in Dubuque Iowa for a number of years in the late '70s, teaching there. Dubuque is an old river town on the Mississippi. It's got a very strong sense of its own history, which included a period as a steamboat town. They manufactured some steamboats there. It was an important port on the upper Mississippi. I started reading about the history of that time and became fascinated with the steamboats and the river culture to the extent that I decided I wanted to write a novel about that. It seemed like a colorful sort of alien world.

Interestingly enough, John Brunner over in England was getting interested in steamboats at just the same time. But we went at it very different ways. Brunner decided to do a straight historical and he produced that, a novel called *The Great Steamboat Race,* which was, I think, quite a good novel, one of the better novels that Brunner wrote in the last period of his career. In my case, since I was a science fiction and fantasy writer, although I had the steamboat era, I never really considered doing just a straight historical. It had to have a fantastic element in there, and somehow vampires, which I had always been interested in independently, seemed to go with steamboats. The whole Dracula thing. There was a dark romanticism both to vampires and to steamboats. The two of them had to go together. Of course the fit wasn't precise, because there were certain elements of the vampire legend that are inimicable to the steamboat culture. The can't-cross-running-water thing was a big problem. So I decided very early on that I would do an almost science-fiction version of these vampires. I would try to justify them scientifically as best I could and figure out how vampires could actually live and work. I developed them not as your traditional mythic vampires, but more as a secondary race preying on us and living among us since the dawn of history. But the steamboats were the actual beginning of that book.

Q: I assume you could go back to writing more horror any time. You have at least one horror collection, *The Songs the Dead Men Sing*. Have you felt the inclination to go back and do more.

Martin: I never think in terms of genres like that. I never say, "I've got to do more horror." It's more, "Okay I have this story idea. I am enthused about this." Then I consider whether it's horror or science fiction, however it falls. If I have an idea that gets my juices flowing, I would love to do it. I do have ideas for various sequels to things that I have done in the past, including a sequel to *Fevre Dream*. But I've had that for years, and whether I will ever get around to writing it, I don't know. There are unfortunately a lot of ideas and things I would love to write, but only so many hours in the day and so many days in the year.

Q: It seems that what's hot right now is what might be described as vampire lifetstyle novels, a series of vampire lifestyle novels. I don't know if your sequel could fit in, a *floating* vampire lifestyle novel....

Martin: Vampires, unfortunately have been done.... At the time I did *Fevre Dream* in 1982, Anne Rice had done the first of her books. There were a few other vampire books out there, but there was not nearly the glut that there has been today. I am tempted to return to the world of *Fevre Dream*, but I have reservations about it too simply because I think that vampires are on the verge of being done to death, so to speak. It's hard to think of anything original to do. Maybe I should return to "The Skin Trade," my werewolves. They haven't been done quite as much.

Q: How about Lovecraft's themes, horror stories of the larger cosmos? Have you ever given that any thought?

Martin: I loved Lovecraft when I was younger. He was one of my favorite writers when I was high school. I read everything I could get by him. I've occasionally played with Lovecraftian things. There is a character in my *Wild Cards* novel who is haunted by Lovecraftian sorts of dreams at a certain point. I wrote up several of those, when the character was dreaming, in my best Lovecraft imitation. I am not sure how well I did. I certainly tried to do my best to capture it.

I don't think I could do a pure Lovecraftian story, because there is a certain passivity about his heroes that drives me crazy. Being driven mad by understanding the truth and giving in to it is not something I could do with my own characters. His view of the universe and the way he got horrific effects still could be effective, so maybe someday I'll do something with that. It was really Derleth who organized and codified his mythos, and I think that in some ways by doing that he did him a disservice.

Q: He basically wrecked it.

Martin: Yes.

Q: I wasn't talking about doing a pastiche, but extending Lovecraft's themes. I am not sure Derleth ever wrote a decent Lovecraftian story.

Martin: No. He certainly never captured the feeling. He could use the same names and books and dark gods and so forth, but never to anything close to the effect that Lovecraft achieved.

Q: We've been talking about novels here, but I can't help but wonder if, after having written seven long epic volumes, you will feel an urge for compression and write short fiction.

Martin: I think my work has gotten longer as I've gotten older and deeper into my career. I don't think, when I finish *Ice and Fire*, that I am ever going to do anything on that scale again. I'm not immediately going to start another seven-volume mega-opus. I can be pretty certain of that. But I am not sure I am going to go back to writing short stories either. The truth is, I haven't done a true short story in years. Even when I do write short fiction, it tends to come out at novella length. But I might very well, once *Ice and Fire* is done, do some novellas and maybe even a few novelets and certainly a stand-alone novel or two.

Q: Of course once *The Song of Ice and Fire* is done, the publisher could say, "This is so successful, here's five million dollars. Write me another one." What then?

Martin: I do wrestle with that. I figure it remains to be seen what will happen to me after *Ice and Fire,* the reception the next book will get. In some ways you never know. Is your audience going to follow you when you do something different? I now have hundreds of thousands, perhaps millions of readers, but are they *Ice and Fire* readers, or are they George R. R. Martin readers? Until I do my first new book after the series, I'm not going to know. You see examples on both sides in our field. You see someone like Strephen R. Donaldson, who can achieve huge sales with the Covenant series, but then when he moves to science fiction with the Gap series, it doesn't sell very well. On the other hand, you see someone like Stephen King. He can do stand-alone horror novels and the *Dark Tower* series and they all sell equally well. So King readers are really King readers, not readers of a particular book or a particular series. But Donaldson's readers were Covenant fans, not Donaldson fans. I don't know. But it is certainly something that concerns me. I am not going to say that I am going to be done with Westeros forever, this world I have created, but it is certainly not the only thing I want to write. So once it is done, I certainly will attempt to do other things in science fiction or horror or even in other genres that I haven't touched on yet, and the question remains, will my audience follow me there?

Q: Might you have to develop a series of pseudonyms and become several writers?

Martin: Hopefully not.

Q: Thanks George.

Recorded at Boskone, Boston, February 16, 2006.

JAMES MORROW

Q: So what's all this stuff about *reason?* Your latest novel, *The Last Witchfinder* is not so much about witches and devils but about rejecting the belief in them.

Morrow: *The Last Witchfinder* doesn't deal with what many people mean by witches, witches as a feminist cult of healing and cosmic consciousness, nor is it about the sort of witchcraft we associate with the Third World, having to do with, again, curing disease, or perhaps with raising the dead. I am addressing the *big problem* that emerged in early Renaissance Europe, and which quickly became a kind of holocaust: the problem of the specifically Christian heresy of Satanism.

If you told fortunes in those days or practiced some other esoteric pursuit—herbal healing, whatever—you were vulnerable to the charge of Devil worship. The problem was not the practices *per se,* but the redefinition of them as evidence of a Satanic compact. Today Catholic scholars would argue that this kind persecution was itself heretical, and should have been perceived as such. And, indeed, in the medieval era the Catholic Church held it to be anathema to go after witches.

But, for whatever reasons, theologians in the early Renaissance began noticing how damn much demonology there is in the New Testament. Jesus is forever casting out evil spirits and consigning demons to the bodies of pigs, wicked spirits that were once inside people. So you can't really argue that Christian demonology is an *aberration.* Sad to say, the persecutions trace to theologians paying attention to what's actually happening in the Gospels. It's not *all* that's happening, but there is an enormous amount of demonology in the New Testament, which seems to suggest a Satan, a Devil, a Dark One, who has dominion over this world, and once you've interpreted the Gospels in that way, you start looking around for the agents of that Devil.

Q: Do you think the witch-hunting came from the top down or the bottom up? That is, was it a means used by the authorities to control the masses, or was it a matter of popular hysteria over matters people could not control—the Black Death, Muslim pirates raiding the coasts of Europe, famines, etc.—demanding action from the government?

Morrow: I imagine both were going on at the same time. But what interests me—as a person who takes a very dim view of religious arguments about how the world works—is the top-down, institutionalized persecution of supposed witches. It was highly systematic, codified in the *Malleus Malificarum* of Kramer and Sprenger. There was a whole elaborate infrastructure of ecclesiastical and civil courts to prosecute the agents of Lucifer.

Of course, one can also psychologize about outbreaks of witch persecution. This is especially common in the case of Salem—there are scholars who say, "Well it wasn't really about theology, it was really all about neighbors settling scores with one another." Or they'll say, "The Puritans were obviously taking their fears of the Indians and projecting them onto their neighbors." Arthur Miller's play *The Crucible* seems to say the Salem tragedy was really about the frustrated libidos of the girls who brought the accusations. Some historians even insist it was really all about the girls going batty because they were eating bread contaminated with ergot, a fungal disease of rye plants.

These interpretations are all interesting—but, again, let's remember that the phenomenon of witch persecution went on for nearly three hundred years. That doesn't sound like hysteria to me. That sounds like something systematic and institutional. As I mentioned earlier—and this was a discovery that I made while researching the book—witch persecution is, alas, a logical implication of Christian theology. Yes, there is also some demonology in the Old Testament, but we find it largely in the famous translation authorized by James I, who fancied himself an expert demonologist and even wrote a book on the subject. The King James Bible was translated by witch believers, and this state of mind influenced many of their word choices. Think about that notorious line from Exodus, "Thou shalt not suffer a witch to live." Today a Hebrew scholar would translate it in much more innocuous terms. It would come out something like, "Thou shalt not provide a fortune-teller with his means of livelihood."

Q: Describe your book for our readers. It's about someone who wants to put an end to the witchcraft statues.

Morrow: A big influence on *The Last Witchfinder* is a book called *Masks of the Universe* by the physicist Edward Harrison—whom I must get in touch with: I don't think Harrison knows there's a novel floating around that traces directly to his notion of the witch-universe, the "psychic space" in which most people lived during the Renaissance. The big discovery I made, as I continued my research, was that a person born around 1678 would have lived in the transition from Harrison's witch-universe to what we now call the Enlightenment. So I said to myself, "Hey, that's pretty damn dramatic. I won't need a huge cast of characters to make this epic happen. It can be one woman's quest. It will be the story of Jennet Stearne and her obsession with bringing down the conjuring statues of her day."

Also, being a feminist—and knowing, as with *Only Begotten Daughter*, that for me it's always fruitful to put a strong woman at the center of a novel—I imagined Jennet as not only living through the great rotation, from the witch-universe to the scientific worldview, but actually helping to make it happen. She participates actively in the paradigm shift, by campaigning to destroy the 1604 Witchcraft Statute of James I, which gave an outward appearance of rationality to the witch courts.

Q: Curiously, you did this as a form of fantasy novel.

Morrow: I was just on a Readercon panel about the continuum that ranges from mimetic fiction to the fantastic, from characters who merely change internally versus those who come to a completely new understanding of how the world works. I think *The Last Witchfinder* ranges freely around among all these coordinates. Obviously it's not a fantasy in the wizards-and-elves sense, but rather a kind of postmodern experiment that maps pretty well onto strictly mimetic historical fiction—though, of course, it's all told by a very unusual narrator.

As you know, *The Last Witchfinder* is a book written by a book. It assumes a universe in which books are conscious and have agendas and write other books. So this free-floating spirit of Newton's *Principia Mathematica* is able to move effortlessly through time and space and therefore comment on the philosophy of science and Jennet's efforts to bring the new universe into being.

Up to a point, my *Principia* narrator is even willing to talk about the downside of science and technology. Near the end of the book, he-she-it visits the Place de la Révolution in Paris at the height of the Terror and possesses a priest who is subsequently marched to the guillotine—the French Revolution, of course, being Exhibit A in any indictment of the Enlightenment. The *Principia* is willing to acknowledge that, while the Enlightenment came along just when it was needed, it was by no means an unalloyed blessing.

At the same time, *The Last Witchfinder* is obviously a defense of the Enlightenment. I take Exhibit A seriously—but it's hard to find Exhibits B, C, D, and E after that. The Marxist totalitarian states are "atheist" or "neo-Enlightenment" in name only. Operationally, they function exactly like theocracies. No doubters allowed.

Q: At one of the funnier moments, the Principia does a critique of the Universal horror films of the 1940s, *House of Dracula* and so on. What does this do to the drama of the story to have this clearly artificial framework, which makes you stand outside of the story? It constantly reminds us that this is a story.

Morrow: I was certainly taking a risk. I tried to keep these interruptions by the *Principia Mathematica* to a minimum, so the "color commentary" occurs only once per chapter, and with clearly marked transitions: I use a typographical trick whereby the last sentence of a *Principia* interlude blends into the first sentence of the next scene in the main story. The preponderance of the scenes belong to a more-or-less realistic drama set in the past. I tried to establish that when Jennet and the other main characters are on stage, we are really in their heads, not the *Principia*'s head. We're not getting the book's subjective account of the action. The events are supposed to be happening before our own eyes.

I did have a lot of trouble selling this book, and one of the agents I approached suggested removing the *Principia* narrator. He said, "I don't know if I can make things happen with this book, boosting you to a new level in your career. But if you'd take out the framing device, we would clearly have a flat-out historical novel, and that might go over better with editors."

Well, I just wasn't prepared to do that. Sure, I suppose that if that same agent had said, "If you kill the ghostly narrator, I can get Knopf to give you a hundred thousand dollar advance, and they will promote it as a breakthrough in historical fiction," then, yeah, I might have bitten that apple. But he was merely saying, "Consider taking out that clever postmodern gimmick, but even then I'm not sure that I could sell it."

Q: It would have changed the tone of the book profoundly. It seems to me that a straight, realistic treatment of this story wouldn't be as funny. It would be full of pain and loss and rage. It would be all about this woman avenging her beloved aunt who was burned at the stake in an act of gross injustice. But as the book exists, it has an arch tone which steps aside from the material.

Morrow: In retrospect, I see you're right. I don't think I consciously added the humor to leaven the horror. But maybe intuitively, as I was writing, I thought, "Well, I'd better make the *Principia* interludes funny, and that will serve as a corrective to the distressing subject matter."

But even with the satiric tone, I know the book makes people squirm. I didn't hold back when describing the ordeal of being tested for the Satanic compact: for example, the way a suspect was pricked with a needle to see if one of her blemishes bled, because if it didn't bleed, that proved that the protuberance was really a teat for suckling an animal familiar, or else it was a mark indicating that the woman was bonded to Satan. I also dramatize the other main ordeal—the cold-water test—pretty vividly. You tied a rope around the witch's waist and threw her into a river. If she floated, she was guilty, because water is the medium of baptism. Pure, running water is offended by a Satanist's flesh and wants to eject it. If the suspect sank and was thus vindicated, the witchfinder would try pulling her out in time, although I am sure there was more than one case of the accused witch drowning while being proved innocent.

One editor who almost bought the book felt that, even with all the funny observations by the *Principia,* the book was too morbid in tone. But I didn't want to compromise the torture and testing scenes, because the witch persecutions were really a kind of holocaust, as I said earlier. And yet, for whatever reasons, I still added a lot of satiric distancing. I guess that's the sort of writer I am.

Q: I think a lot of satire works this way. If you had written the novel absolutely straight, it might have been too shrill. Often the grimmest and blackest and most terrible things have to be treated in a funny manner, even if they build up to tragedy. You can name any number of writers who do this, T. H. White most especially. What I am suggesting is that the distancing is necessary because of the nature of the material. Otherwise you wouldn't be able to make it bearable.

Morrow: Novels that seem shrill, to use your word, preachy, novels that somberly tell the reader how he or she is supposed to be feeling about the material—such books don't enjoy the same affection in our hearts as the more playful and satiric works. I think of Upton Sinclair's *The Jungle*, which is unrelievedly grim, totally without humor. Yes, it did galvanize people to reform some of the practices of the meat-packing houses, but that wasn't an *artistic* accomplishment. One critic made a remark to the effect that Sinclair "aimed to touch people's hearts and ended up hitting them in the stomach." Readers were repulsed to learn that the meat that ended up on their dinner table very likely contained bits of rat meat.

I've started an historical novel that will be in some ways analogous to *The Last Witchfinder*. I want to dramatize the story of Charles Darwin and the arrival of *that* universe, today's universe, in which we perceive ourselves as animals and understand they we're evidently connected to all the other species on the planet, and they're connected to each other as well. It won't be a biographical novel about Darwin, but rather an epic about the exploits of a character who's living during Darwin's life and times.

The whole story will elapse between the voyage of the *Beagle,* which ended in 1834, and Darwin's publication of his theory in 1859. Many years went by during which Darwin temporized and procrastinated and anguished over going public with his big idea. I have what I think is a pretty neat plot device whereby a clever woman, scheming but sympathetic—I think her name will be Chlöe—she has occasion to recapitulate Darwin's travels, collecting the very same specimens. Chlöe is hoping to claim a huge cash prize being offered by a Percy Bysshe Shelley cult. They'll award it to anyone who can prove or disprove the existence of God. Chlöe herself doesn't care about the God question one way or the other, but she plans to argue the case for atheism because she needs the money. Her nautical adventures will be as mimetic and dramatic as I can make them.

At the same time, I'm once again going to use a postmodern, playful element, whereby an insane bishop locked up in an asylum will be visited by homing pigeons, which are reporting in to him from a second expedition—one that's out to find Noah's ark on Mount Ararat in Turkey. The Noah's ark team also hopes to claim the big prize, by proving God's existence. It will soon become clear to the reader that, as a function of the bishop's insanity, the pigeon messages are actually from the future: accounts of evolutionary thinking post-Darwin, such as Mendelian genetics and the deciphering of the DNA molecule. And, of course—because the Bishop is crazy—these messages also contain far more information than you could squeeze onto a piece of paper wrapped around a pigeon's leg.

Q: This is pretty much what you've always done with fantastic elements from the beginning of your career, use them satirically. I observe the paradox that most fantasy is about things we don't believe in and don't want to believe in. It is much easier to write a story in which witches or demons are real than one in which they are not. Do you have a sense of this?

Morrow: I think the reason that William Morrow ultimately published *The Last Witchfinder* as mainstream historical fiction—and I'd have to say that, because of that decision, the book got a lot more critical attention than normal—is that my witches do not have supernatural powers. My demons and devils are purely human inventions. The world of the novel is non-supernatural—anti-supernatural, really, as we've been saying—even though at the same time there's this crazy central conceit of a conscious book.

I guess my fantasy novels are ultimately pretty paradoxical. They use the supernatural to argue against the supernatural. In the case of *Only Begotten Daughter* I took the Christian argument at face-value. There is a creator God, and this deity has a particular interest in our species and this particular planet. But after taking that claim at face-value, I began exploring the possible psychology of a supernatural being, so that my heroine Julie Katz, who happens to be the daughter of God and the half-sister of Jesus Christ, decides she doesn't really want to be divine. She ends up hating supernaturalism. She becomes an advocate of evolution and subscribes to the scientific understanding of reality. I guess the book is questioning the assumption that embracing the Christian worldview—or any other variety of supernaturalism—is some sort of accomplishment or end state. Something like the opposite, I'd say. There are always more questions to ask.

You mentioned the Universal horror movies that are satirized at one point in *The Last Witchfinder*. I always find it strange how in, say, the Mummy series—most of which starred Lon Chaney, Jr.—when we get to the end of the picture, the characters don't seem to have noticed that the entire fabric of consensus reality has evidently changed *completely*. Everything that modern humans assume about Nature being driven by rational laws, without a supernatural substratum, has just been proven utterly wrong—and yet the characters go right back to living their mundane little lives, as if the paradigm shift hadn't occurred. It's a very bizarre convention. Because if you really had a mummy running around in Louisiana or New England that would throw the entire Enlightenment argument about how the world works out the window. The Universal monster movies always beg the question of why the heroes and heroines don't have nervous breakdowns at the end.

True, in the universe of these movies, the vampires and werewolves and mummies operate by laws, too, and so you have Edward Van Sloan knowing exactly what it takes to vaporize a vampire, or Turhan Bey knowing exactly how many tana leaves it takes to get Kharis's heart beating, and how many it takes to get him shuffling around and abducting people. But these aren't remotely scientific principles. There's no explanatory mechanism involved. They're magic. Maybe someday I'll write a mummy novel in which the characters think through the full epistemological implications of their adventures, and end up going insane.

Q: I suspect that the serious answer to this is that most Americans today still live in the witch-universe. The Enlightenment has not penetrated below the level of the intellectuals. Even to this day most people believe in psychics, UFOs, astrology, ghosts, and such. They probably do believe in forms of magic. Certainly a lot of them do. Then there is the Christian Fundamentalist side of the population, which is enormous, who would probably be afraid to read your book because it would evoke the Devil. So I think the real answer is they're still in the witch-universe.

Morrow: Good point. I suppose *The Last Witchfinder* is not about the death of the witch-universe *per se*. It's about the death of the witch-universe as a political force that made courts and magistrates behave in abominable ways toward people we would now regard as innocent of any demonic compact. Of course, these victims weren't necessarily people of tremendous virtue. They weren't John Proctor in *The Crucible*. They weren't pure of heart. They were the outcasts. They were the people upon whom this sort of persecution could be performed with impunity.

I guess I'm saying that, yes, as individual private selves, we all want to live in a supernatural universe. It's instinctive, and we all have a right to our private fantasies. Nevertheless, the reining intellectual consensus, thank God, is that promiscuous supernaturalism is not the case, and we have no business putting gods and demons at the center of our political institutions. It's been remarked that the most important word in the United States Constitution is the one that isn't there—the word

"God." I think that's genuine progress.

Now, I know that our postmodern brethren have problematized, I think legitimately, the notion of progress. You always have to ask, "Progress for whom?" But I think even the Bush Administration recognizes that fundamentalism is a terrible idea. I am continually struck by the irony of Bush and his henchmen being perfectly happy to allow a low-grade, smiley-face, feel-good theocracy emerge on these shores, even as they pursue the opposite agenda in Iraq. I think of the recent Supreme Court decision that taxpayers cannot sue the government for having recently broken down the wall between church and state through so-called faith-based grants. I think of Bush going on record as saying he thinks Intelligent Design is commensurate with Darwinism and should also be taught in public school classroom. I think of his canceling stem-cell research for reasons that ultimately trace to his supposed personal relationship with Jesus.

At the same time, we have the Bushies realizing that what they want in the Middle East is a process we would have to call secular and rational. Saddam Hussein constantly used religion to manipulate his bleeding country, even though it was technically not a theocracy, and now the great fear—great and also justified—is that this same theocratic impulse will reemerge in Iraq in a different form, and that society will become every bit as much of a nightmare as it was before we invaded. Certainly for women Iraq threatens to become a nightmare. The *Koran* has very little in it that's good news for women.

The Bushies would never admit this paradox. They would never come out and say they're contradicting themselves. But what they're hoping for is some kind of neo-Enlightenment, secular democracy in Iraq—a regime that religious skeptics like Ben Franklin and Thomas Jefferson would recognize and salute for its lack of a supernatural argument at its center.

Q: Despite which, in the United States, there was just a few years ago an episode of witchcraft hysteria in a day-school, in which they managed to get all the children to testify about Satanic ritual abuse. Remember that? It *was* Salem all over again, with neighbor suspecting neighbor, and people being assumed guilty until proven innocent and guilty by association. It was exactly the same phenomenon.

Morrow: That sort of hysteria, when it crops us, is always very disturbing. But at least today—here in the post-Enlightenment West—today we pretty much accept the idea that our courts and other legal institutions have an essentially secular mission. The Devil doesn't routinely appear before judges and juries anymore. Our justice system is not shot through with supernatural assumptions about the world, or even shot through with theism, and so the fantasies of children as no longer admissible, as they were in Salem. Yes, you do have to put your hand on the Bible when you testify in court, but after that something resembling reason kicks in.

So while that Satanic ritual abuse phenomenon was horrible, it was also short-lived, because at a certain point it became clear that the accusers didn't have cases, that they had run out of evidence, and that the children themselves were being manipulated. Anyone who knows even a little bit of child psychology would recognize that these kids were telling their supposed deliverers what they wanted to hear. The motto of the people who thought they were acting in the alleged victims' interest was "Believe the children." Well, it turns out that what they really meant was "Believe the children unless the children say they haven't been abused."

It was a terrible abuse of the trust that a child naturally has in adults, ironically in the name of protecting children. I think virtually no evidence emerged that ritual Satanic abuse was actually occurring. But, yes, it was hysteria, and one can certainly psychologize about it, as one can do about Salem. My novel is about the fact that at least we've gotten rid of fantasy, private delusion, and religious mania as admissible evidence. It suggests that, in certain public contexts, theism is a luxury we simply can't afford.

Q: Then again, you've written about God being dead and found floating in the Atlantic. I can't imagine this has been published in, say, an Arabic translation.

Morrow: [Laughs] Not likely. But I have to say I get quite a bit of fan e-mail from believers, and that's very gratifying to me. I think I value those letters even more than the ones I get from militant atheists, who cheer me on and say, "Go for it, Jim. Give the carcass of organized religion another kick in the groin."

I'm pleased to find there are a lot of readers out there, people of faith, who enjoy my novels as theological speculation, as thought experiments that satirize the misuses of religion. You can be part of an institution and still perceive its dark side. You don't have to resign from an institution to critique it. You might actually be doing the world more good by staying within your church and trying to reform it. In that regard, I may be in a worse position to do good than believers. I'm not actively trying to change the homophobia that seems rampant in so many evangelical churches, but there are people inside those evangelical churches, I am sure, who are making arguments against that kind of bigotry.

Q: At what point in your life did you abandon God and discover his corpse was floating in the Atlantic?

Morrow: It's true that I was once a believer, as a kid. My parents were not aggressively religious, but I think they did have an inoculation theory of church-going. You should give your son a small and harmless dose of religion, lest he discover one day that he had no natural defenses against it. I imagine they were afraid that otherwise I would show up and say I'd decided to become a monk or something.

So they gave me a generic, white-bread religious education, dragging me to a Presbyterian Sunday-school in Willow Grove,

Pennsylvania. Naturally I ended up believing. How could I not? This was suburban Philadelphia in the 1950s. God was the default assumption. God in the air. God was in the water. I never thought of God as a thesis, a hypothesis about how the world works. I thought of God as a fact. Adults seemed to agree on this fact, and adults don't lie, so they?

Luckily, back then suburban Presbyterianism was a pretty tepid thing. It was not salvationistic. It did not threaten us kids with images of eternal damnation and fears that our sins would catapult us into the fiery abyss. But I do remember assuming that God was behind it all, and I know I prayed for good fortune in my own life.

My inverse road to Damascus was the World Literature course I took as a tenth-grader. Those of us in the honors English class at Abington Senior High School found ourselves suddenly confronted with the miracles and splendors of Western literature: plays and poems—and especially novels—that were alive with ideas, usually subversive and skeptical ideas. We learned that novelists were often people at odds with the received wisdom of their day. They were contrarians. These voices stood outside of their cultures and critiqued them—and, above all, they were *honest* voices: at least, that's what I found in Voltaire's *Candide* and Camus's *The Stranger* and Kafka's *The Trial* and Flaubert's *Madame Bovary*. Even a believer like Dostoyevsky—we *did Crime and Punishment*—even Dostoyevsky dramatized belief as something that is troubling and paradoxical and terribly complex.

The honesty of these writers—the voice of an anguished atheist like Camus—that struck a chord with me. It really was a kind of revelation. It garnered my respect in a way that my Sunday-school teachers never did. The Presbyterians seemed to dodge all the hard questions. They weren't liars, exactly, but intellectually, for me, they left much to be desired. Gradually my faith evaporated.

Of course, it also helped that I'd never had an experience with the supernatural. I'd never encountered an angel or witnessed a miracle.

Q: How do you think you'd respond if you did?

Morrow: [Laughs] That's a really good question. I'd like to think that, if I really believe my own worldview, my first question would be, "Might I account for this angel, or this out-of-body experience, or this miracle, or whatever, in strictly material terms?" But, sure, okay, if my supernatural experience was something utterly unequivocal, fine, I guess I'd try to swallow it.

But let's remember that most religious arguments about the world are far more optimistic and soothing than the secular-humanist view. We'd all like to believe our deaths aren't synonymous with oblivion. We've all got a built-in—and highly suspect—motivation to believe in the miraculous. We're predisposed to embrace supposed evidence for the supernatural simply on the grounds of our mortality. Religion solves the death problem, so of course it's always going to win the battle for the private human psyche.

So I like to think it would take more than one angelic visitation to convince me that angels are factual. It's often said that extraordinary claims require extraordinary evidence. I hope I would spend a lot of time worrying about whether I was deluded, whether my angel was entirely subjective, whether he was just wishful thinking, whether this was incipient schizophrenia.

I am continually struck by the fact that, whether the argument is coming from the New Age camp—"crystals heal," "astrology works," that sort of claim—or by those with conventional religious views—I am struck by that fact that the *main* thing that's going on in every such instance is a person, a mere human being, standing in front of you insisting that the supernatural is the case. That's it. Period. A person. Nothing more, nothing less.

At the last Conference on the Fantastic in Fort Lauderdale, I noticed that our pathetic little convention was happening alongside a presentation attended by thousands of people who all wanted to hear this guy talk about life after death. He had lots of messages from beyond the veil that he wanted to share. The crowd lapped it up. Nobody seemed to notice that all they were actually getting was a person very much like themselves, and in many cases probably *better* than themselves—more honest, less egomaniacal, less publicity hungry—doling out the inside dope on the afterlife.

There is nothing you can go out and do yourself to corroborate the worldviews of charlatans. In those few cases where those of New Age or supernatural persuasion have allowed a test, some tentative attempt at falsification, their claims and beliefs have always come a cropper. Every systematic investigation of astrology or ESP or prayer suggests that there's absolutely nothing happening there. This malarkey is *not* a new understanding of reality. It's wish-fulfillment at best. It's stuff that we'd prefer to be the case. But it doesn't seem to be the case—not in this life, and not in this universe.

[conducted at Readercon, 2007]

JACK DANN

Q: Let's start with what you're doing now. The last book of yours I am aware of is the one about Leonardo da Vinci. I am sure I missed something. There was a book about the Civil War I saw you showing around earlier this afternoon.

Dann: The da Vinci book was *The Memory Cathedral*, which I've had really good luck with. It was about the time that the book came out in the States that I moved to Australia. HarperCollins Australia also bought the book, and it was a bestseller there. It topped the bestseller list on *The Age* magazine. The other big surprise was Germany, where it sold heavy-duty numbers—for me anyway. The cover price was 49.5 deutchmarks, which is about $50 Australian. When I heard what the price was going to be, I asked, "Are people going to pay $50 for a hardcover book?" I guess they did. So that book went into about ten languages. The next book was a Civil War novel called *The Silent*. It isn't a genre novel. It was published here, and it was also published in Australia and Germany. While I was writing *The Silent*, I was also editing *Dreaming Down-Under* with Janeen Webb. That's the Australian anthology. Again we were lucky. It won a Ditmar Award in Australia and the World Fantasy Award here. One of our purposes in doing the anthology was to try to get Australian genre writing noticed in the States and Great Britain. I think we succeeded in our small way. I'm still doing the *Magic Tales* anthologies with Gardner Dozois. Those are still coming out at the rate of about two a year. And I'm working on a big James

Dean/Hollywood novel that I sold to HarperCollins US. It's basically the story of James Dean *after* his accident. So I am doing this as a mainstream, alternate-time novel.

Q: You seem to be moving very much to the fringes of traditional science fiction, or beyond it completely. Is this an intentional career strategy, or are things just working out that way?

Dann: I think it's just things working that way. When I'm told I'm this kind of a writer or that kind of a writer, my response—like Harlan Ellison's—is that "I'm a writer." I guess a politically correct way of saying it is that I write "across the genres". That will probably translate into "out of genre." This Quixotic course is a marketing nightmare. I've actually been very lucky in Australia, because HarperCollins has been publishing me there as a Flamingo author—that's their literary line—and they have also been pulling in my science fiction readers. My early science fiction novels such as *Starhiker* and *Junction* and *The Man Who Melted* were on the far-out edges of the genre. *Junction* was a weird, fringe, where-do-you-put-it novel, although *The Man Who Melted* was a straight science-fiction novel. (I thought so, anyway!) As for *The Memory Cathedral*, some people are calling it fantasy, some are calling it SF, and some are saying that it isn't genre at all. So I just don't worry about it. I think of my novel-in-progress about James Dean as mainstream in intent, but it really is an extrapolation of what could have happened if James Dean had lived. He goes into politics. He hangs around with the Kennedys. He beats Reagan in California.. I wanted to play around with the idea of cultural icons and myths. If Dean had lived, would he have the same iconic stature that he does now? I don't think so. Look at Brando. If he had died young, he, too, would have become a cultural icon. So I am dealing with stuff like that, with Marilyn Monroe, with Elvis Presley and Bobby and Jack Kennedy—they're all major characters.

Am I intentionally moving my career into the mainstream? I think I am intentionally trying not to be categorized, but that's just because of the kind of writer I am: I get interested in something and want to write it, and it may be genre, or, as is usually the case, it may not be.

Q: I guess you could say the James Dean book is a non-category fantasy, which means it's a fantasy but you don't tell anyone it's a fantasy. I understand that Mark Helprin, for example, is very defensive about not being labeled a fantasy writer, because everybody assumes fantasy means elves and unicorns. Of course fantastic literature is much broader. But as we well know from all those books that you haven't heard of before they win World Fantasy Awards, there is a great deal of interesting fantasy being published outside of the fantasy category. So I guess you're very lucky to be able to publish fantasy as mainstream. Great work if you can get it.

Dann: Certainly with *The Memory Cathedral* I am doing the same sort of thing that John Crowley is doing. And there is the same sort of problem of where to categorize it. But, you see, I love the genre, so it's not as if I don't want to be associated with it. I just want to have any given book reach its audience. I'll give you an example. When *The Memory Cathedral* won the Aurealis Award in Australia, it was selling very well there, and it was selling as a mainstream, historical novel. I was very lucky. It got full-page photo reviews. When it won the Aurealis Award, my publisher decided to do a sticker, which I thought was a great idea. It read, "Winner of the Aurealis Award for Best Fantasy." Within two weeks, the books disappeared from the center shelves, where they had been selling very well. I asked bookstore clerks and managers what had happened, and they told me, "People who read historical novels want everything to be real. Of course we know that this is a historical novel about Leonardo da Vinci. But the sticker says 'fantasy', so historical-novel readers won't buy it." I had effectively lost the mainstream audience. So when my novella "Da Vinci Rising", which was adapted from the novel, won the Nebula Award, Harper made a bigger sticker, which read "Winner of the Aurealis/Nebula Award." It had "Aurealis" on top, "Nebula" on the bottom, but it said nothing about fantasy. Two weeks later, the books were right back in the center and they were reaching that audience again. True story. Now you and I both know that this is insanity, but it's the way that stuff gets categorized. So when I say I don't want to be categorized, I try to make sure that when one of my non-genre or cross-genre books comes out, it's going to be able to reach that mainstream audience.

Q: There are others who luck out like this. James Morrow, for example, is reviewed as mainstream but also sells as fantasy. Harlan Ellison has certainly made a very vocal point throughout his career of not being categorized as one type of writer. But there are many others who may strive their whole careers and never be discovered outside of the SF/fantasy field, no matter what they write.

Dann: Again, I've been lucky. I've had publishers who were willing to work with me, and so far I have been able to walk the tightrope.

Q: Did it make any difference because you moved to Australia? Norman Spinrad refers to the "prince from another land" strategy. Were you able to do some of that?

Dann: I wouldn't call it a strategy, because for me it wasn't a strategy. I have always been very lucky in that here in the States, and also in Australia, I have had editors and publishers who really believed in the work. This has been a huge help and has made me feel very secure, shall we say, as I am not one of those writers who can knock out a novel or two a year.

The irony is that since I've been living in Australia—it's been about seven years—I have more of a presence in the United States. I was at a convention and Bob Silverberg said, "You're 50...and you're hot." [Laughs.] When I lived in Binghamton, in upstate New York, George R. R. Martin referred to me, correctly, as the hermit of Binghamton, because you couldn't get me out of upstate New York. I am more present now in terms of a public person, and in terms of just being around in the country, here in the States, than when I lived here. When I travel now, I make a point to be "out there." I'm in New York and I'm in LA, and I'm at this convention.

Since I've been living in Australia, my career has been doing well. In the "bad old days" I would spin off other jobs to stay afloat. I'd say, "I'll try marketing," and before I knew it I'd have a viable company that was demanding time. Would you believe it? I took a job in insurance because the hours were good, and after I left, I was asked to be on the board of directors. Crazy stuff. In Australia, I just write and pay attention to the writing. That made a big difference. I was able to make enough money by focusing on the writing.

Q: How has moving to Australia affected your writing? I notice that the first book you wrote after going there was about the American Civil War. Do you have a different perspective, viewing the United States from the outside now?

Dann: I had sold that novel before I moved, but I found myself commuting, living in Melbourne, but commuting back and forth to Virginia. I am one of those writers who tries to get as much information as possible. So I walked all the places depicted in the novel. I was there. But people kept laughing and chuckling and saying, "You're living in Australia and you're writing a novel about the American Civil War," and I noticed that in the reviews, especially the ones in Australia, there was much talk about the idea of distance and perspective. I suppose I am obsessed with my own culture. I think that being out of one's culture changes the way you see everything.

I did an article for the *SFWA Bulletin* called "Double Vision." I see things as an American, enmeshed in my culture, basically, as a New Yorker, but I also see things now from an expatriate perspective, and *everything* looks different because of that distance. When you travel as a tourist, you take your own atmosphere with you. It's different when you find yourself living in a place. After I was living in Australia for about eight months, I realized that Australian culture and American culture *look* very similar, but are really profoundly different. Even the language is different. So, although I'm here [in the USA] and I am comfortable and this is my culture, I *feel* like an outsider because I can never stop seeing with this double vision. I'm comfortable everywhere, but always an outsider. So I think it has given me this strange kind of perspective, and I am very interested in trying to figure out my home culture.

Q: I am sure a lot of writers have done that—

Dann: Of course, Hemingway living in Paris—

Q: With any number of expatriate Russians.

Dann: But I didn't do it for that. I met Janeen, and I never believed in this, but it was basically love at first sight. And three months later the Hermit of Binghamton was living in the center of Melbourne and trying to navigate the infrastructure. I would try to dial "operator" on the telephone. I would dial zero and nothing would happen. I would get into a car to drive and then I would have to remember that the steering wheel was on the other side. In other words, I wasn't saying, "I'm going to go and immerse myself in another culture to have stuff to write about." I found myself there, and then all that stuff started happening. So it was all unplanned.

Q: Most writers lives are, I suspect, unplanned. Real deliberation doesn't work.

Dann: For me, life and writing are like gambling. You can *feel* when you're on a roll. Salesmen know about this. You can knock on doors and keep knocking on doors and nothing happens, and then suddenly you get on a roll and you could sell ice to Eskimos. So I've been on a roll. Every once in a while it stops, and nothing you do will work. You just keep walking and walking until something else happens. So I guess in a way I am not a tremendous planner.

Q: Are you ready to write about Australia?

Dann: I'm getting ready. I think there can be a rather long period of gestation between experiencing traumatic, life-changing experiences and writing about them. I wrote a story called "Jubilee," which was one of the first on-line stories. That was when *Omni* was testing the, er, aether with *Neon Visions*. That story is in my new collection called....*Jubilee*. Part of that story takes place in the States and in Greece, because I had been in Greece just before I wrote it, and part takes place in Melbourne. I think I am beginning to see the Australian culture now and what aspects I'm interested in writing about. So it may happen in the next couple of years.

Q: Getting back to science fiction, wouldn't this kind of perspective better equip you to write about another planet?

Dann: [Laughs.] When I was working on *The Memory Cathedral*, the idea came to me of history being a different place, a dislocation....I was on a number of panels here [at the World Fantasy Con in Corpus Christi] and I was listening to a number of people asking questions about myth and about how stories worked in the past, and we were all assuming that the mindset in the past was the same as the mindset now. I feel that people in the Renaissance had a completely different mindset, a different sensorium. They perceived things differently.

Most novels about space-travel don't talk about the tremendous, hollow alienation that is a consequence of being away from everything familiar. You feel this distance toward everything. When I moved to Australia, when I started living in a different culture, even though it's an English-speaking culture, I viscerally felt that dislocation. So, yes, I expect I'll try to write about that in the future. I want to write about never being able to go home again in ways that maybe haven't been done a lot in the genre. Fool that I am, I suppose I want to write the great American novel. [Laughs.]

Q: You could take your experiences and then make up another planet, and deal with the sense of dislocation far more convincingly than could a writer who has never been out of New Jersey.

Dann: Being a science fiction writer gave me a leg up when I tried to write about the past. It was a question of extrapolating backwards! The alieness of the past fascinates me, and I tried to recreate that alien world called the Renaissance in *The Memory Cathedral*, just as I tried to recreate another alien world, that of the American Civil War with *The Silent*.

But, to answer your question, which I keep dancing around, yes, it would be interesting to write about science fictional alien cultures as I did with, say, a novel like *Starhiker,* but with my own experience behind it.

Q: I would also imagine, by way of perspective, that your view on science fiction now is very different from what it was when you started out. Surely you are now writing things which you would never have imagined yourself writing, back at the beginning of your career in the early '70s.

Dann: I have become a completely different writer, but part of that is just growing as a writer and, dare I say it, as a person.

When I was flying over here, we stopped in Sydney, because I had to give a lecture about Leonardo da Vinci at the Powerhouse Museum—they had the Gates Codex on exhibition. Later on, I bumped into a friend at the Sydney airport whom I hadn't seen in twenty years. She used to have a bookstore in my hometown, and she was visiting Australia. She had known me from the time I was fifteen and was one of the people who had guided me toward books and educated me. To paraphrase what Gene Wolfe once said about Damon Knight, she grew me from a bean. So there I was chatting about my career and talking about Hong Kong being one of my favorite places, and how I wouldn't be making it back this year...blah-blah-blah.... And she said, "Listen to yourself. Did you ever think way back then that you would be living as you're living now?"

No, I could never have called it....

One of the things that I think has happened since I have been in Australia, which I am proud of, is the effect that *Dreaming Down-Under*, the anthology I edited with Janeen Webb, has had on genre publishing in Australia. When Harlan Ellison visited Sydney a few years ago for a conference, he said, "You know, you guys are having your golden age right *now*." He'd touched a nerve. There was a real zeitgeist going on. Writers were starting to talk to one another, and there was a lot of excitement. Our *Dreaming* anthology became a sort of focus, a showcase for that excitement.

It has been wonderful to see these writers starting to publish in the United States and in Europe. I acted as a facilitator for a lot of people in the early days. They didn't have a sense of how American publishing worked, so I was acting as a *de facto* agent. It was a real kick because I could see the effect on the industry, and it was lovely, positive stuff.

Q: Are you going to do another *Dreaming Down-Under*?

Dann: I wasn't going to do another anthology like *Dreaming* unless something really big came along. People kept asking, "Why don't you do another volume?" I kept saying, "No, another volume in maybe five years." But *Dreaming* was like *Dangerous Visions*. It had that same effect in Australia. Janeen and I wanted to wait until new people came up before editing another *Dreaming Down-Under*. We didn't want to edit another volume prematurely just because the first anthology worked commercially. Then Ramsey Campbell and Dennis Etchison approached me with an idea for an international horror anthology, using really powerful writers, putting the bar very high. Dennis would edit the American portion. Ramsey would edit the British portion, and I would do the Australian. So we would cover a good portion of the English-speaking horror genre. The idea was that it had to come out simultaneously in the US, Great Britain, and Australia. Tor is doing it in the US, and HarperCollins will publish it in the Australia and Great Britain. The anthology will be called *Gathering the Bones*, or maybe just *Bones*; we're not sure yet. It's another one of those big projects editor/writers do out of love.

Q: You must have a better sense of this than most editors. What differences in approach do the Australians have toward fantasy or horror?

Dann: That's a difficult question. It was interesting to see the American reviews of *Dreaming,* which were very good. Again we were lucky. But reviewers seemed to think that Australian fiction would be about *place.* In other words, Australian geography would be the great influence. There are stories in which geography *is* very important, but I don't think that is at base where the difference lies. I think it's in the language and culture. You could almost say that Australian English is built on irony. I often tell tourists that all Australians know about ten thousand jokes and anecdotes. When they're chatting with you, they'll use these anecdotes and bits of wonderful irony, but they'll only tell you the punch line. You're supposed to *know* the rest to 'get it'.

Australian English *sounds* like the same language we use in America, but I often find that when I'm just having conversations with my wife, who is Australian, that we can *think* that we're saying the same thing, yet we're misunderstanding each other because the words don't mean the same thing.

I think, however, that in the genres there is a commonality that runs among English-speaking writers. In, say, science fiction, in the States, in England, and in Australia it's not the place that makes the profound difference, because I think we're all dipping into the same wells. We're all cross-fertilizing each other. There *is* that difference of perspective and geography which every once in a while makes you say, "Ah...." But I think it's the quality of the work that is important, and the fact that a given location has a number of writers who are doing really interesting work. If you look at the stories in *Dreaming,* you wouldn't necessarily look at them and say, "These are Australian." You might look at them and say that this or that story is wonderful.

Q: I'd think that the one thing the Australians would have in common with the Americans is a sense of frontier or at least a memory of a frontier. You go to Britain and you get the sense that every clump of trees has a name that's probably recorded, with the name of a forester, in the *Domesday Book*. But in Australia and in the United States there is empty land. In that geographical sense, I would think that the U.S. would have a lot more in common with Australia than with Britain.

Dann: I think one of the differences between Australia and the United States is that in Australia there is *still* the sense of frontier. It's very strong. You can move. You don't have to be near people—your closest neighbor can be a hundred miles away. Yet you've also got this wonderful *frisson,* if you want to use the word, of world-class cosmopolitan cities such as Melbourne and Sydney.

I think that in the States we are starting to feel a limitation on Manifest Destiny, an end to the frontier. I don't know that this is necessarily real, but I think this sense of limit is becoming part of the emotional consciousness. I think Americans perceive Australia to be what America once was. Again, it's the idea of the frontier. When I first got to Australia, for the first number of months, I felt a crazy sense of freedom, that I could just go out on the road and never stop.

Q: Is that any different from, say, Arizona or other parts of the U.S.?

Dann: Probably not. The Outback can be like the Gobi Desert; so if you're going to go from X to Y, you've got to know that you have enough water and such, because if you get stuck, you could be dead. The U.S. is almost completely habitable. It's a big country with a lot of people. Australia is a big country that is *not* completely habitable. You can basically only live around the edges. The interior is like the Red Planet. The Outback...where the myths reside.

One of the things that I've noticed as an ex-pat is that Americans look inward. It's the idea that everything is right here and available in the United States, and to a certain extent everything *is* here. We produce what has become world culture. We radiate our culture out. Also, in terms of military might, we are very secure. The major superpower.

By contrast, Australia is a country that looks outward. Australia is always looking out at what is going on in the world. That is why you see Australians everywhere—they are always traveling. That's a big difference, culturally, in the way people perceive themselves and perceive the rest of the world. Americans take it for granted that they're from a place that is powerful, central. We assume that as Americans we're in control, that most countries can't screw around with the U.S. and, indeed, must make accommodations. In many ways, we Americans really are insular...insulated. You can get an idea of this by comparing news in the States with news media in Europe or Australia. Again, it's a question of how we sense ourselves and our place in the world.

Q: The perspective I had going to Europe for the first time was an appreciation of how much older European cities are than

American cities. In Rome you can see what New York will be like in two thousand years. I coined the term "the layercake of history" because you see layers upon layers from different eras. Australia is even younger than the U.S. and has even less of this. My favorite symbol of it all is in Rome: a seventeenth-century marble elephant by Bernini, with an ancient Egyptian obelisk on its back, and a papal cross on top of that. It's as if time-travelling aliens had just grabbed all this stuff and assembled it at random.

Dann: Well, cultures subsume each other. If you conquer a country, you tear down its places of worship and build your own mosques or churches over the sites. I think you're spot on about the U.S. and Australia being new countries. I have a friend who is a Brit, one of my dearest friends in Australia; he moved there about fifteen years ago. He tells me that when he was living in England, he could feel the accretion of history, almost like weight. There, you could be walking along the street and come across a thousand year old cairn. When you're living in all that antiquity, the past can seem more important than the present. One of the reasons that my British friend feels such a sense of freedom in living in Australia is because everything isn't mired in the centuries past. There is a different energy. The U.S. and Australia are similar in that respect. I think one difference between the US and Australia is that Australians still perceive England as the mother country. There is still a sense of deference here toward Great Britain, even though the majority of the people want a republic. Americans don't feel that kind of deference, perhaps because we shrugged Great Britain off during the Revolutionary War. Australia simply wasn't in a position to do that, primarily because communications technology had changed, allowing easier and faster communication between the colonies and the mother country. The advent of telegraphy, perhaps more than anything else, allowed England to maintain a firm hold on Australia. Before that, it could take months for messages from England to reach Australia. They left quite a bit of leeway for independence and self-government. There was a small rebellion in Ballarat, which is not far from Melbourne, after the United States declared independence, but it failed. So although the idea of a republic is very much in the public mind in Australia and it is debated constantly, the relationship between Australians and the Brits still feels to me to be somewhat colonial.

Q: This is the sort of thing you can write straight mainstream fiction about, or historical fiction, or we get back to the idea of transmogrifying the experience and writing about another planet. You'd have even greater freedom on another planet, where everything would be absolutely fresh, particularly if it was far enough away that you couldn't get back to Earth.

Dann: [Laughs.] In a sense I'm sort of living in one of Harry Harrison's worlds. Most unfriendlies in Australia can kill you. Spiders are deadly. Almost all the snakes are poisonous. There is one particularly nasty spider whose bite causes something like gangrene to set in the wound. There's no antidote for it; the area just rots away. In America and Europe, most of the wildlife is benign. Not so in Australia. That puts a different perspective on things. For instance, in Queensland, you "watch out for redbacks" (spiders) before you plant your bum (ass) on the toilet.

Q: Have you met any Aborigines?

Dann: My novel *Bad Medicine*, which will be published as *Counting Coup* in the US, has just been published in Australia. One of the protagonists is a Native American medicine man. While researching this novel, I spent about a year ceremonying with Sioux people. But that's another story for another interview. I was very interested in meeting Aboriginal people when I first got to Australia. I could see that there were certain similarities with native Americans. They're what I think of as the similarities of natural people, that sense that they have taken on the moral and ethical roles of caretakers of the land and its deep history. But I didn't have any real interaction until last year when my partner Janeen Webb and I were invited to be guests of the Perth Writers' Festival. I met a guy there by the name of Boori Pryor, an Aboriginal writer. We just hit it off. As a result, I became an honorary "Blackfella", and he became an honorary Jew. I taught him how to do Jewish schtick; he taught me Blackfella stuff.

One of the really interesting things that happened was this. We were talking when we first met, and he told me that he takes everything he writes back to his people in Queensland, and the tribal elders look at it before it's published. The elders have the final say. We were discussing reconciliation between the government of Australia and aboriginal peoples, which is a major issue. We currently have a rather right-wing, conservative "Liberal" government. About forty years ago, Aboriginal children were taken from their parents by the State to be re-educated and re-acculturated. That generation of Aboriginals has come to be known as the Stolen Generation. As aboriginals were considered to be primitive, the government policy was to "save" the children by forcing white culture on them. Now there is a reconciliation process going on at all levels in the country. Whites from all walks of life are saying..."We're sorry." But John Howard, the Prime Minister, doesn't believe that the present government should take responsibility for what happened in the past. When I first met Boori, we talked about his books and about reconciliation; and I said, "Look, if people won't accept you, screw them. You don't have to take this shit from white people." His response surprised me. He said, "No, we're all involved. We've got to reach out to each other. It's not about anger. The idea is that we're all in the world together." This from a guy who has been beaten senseless by the police... who has lost family members and other people he loves. But he had no anger toward whites. *I* was the one feeling angry. And I had gotten it completely wrong. Boori and I will hang out in the future, and eventually I hope to learn something about his culture...and maybe about myself.

Q: You're looking at this material with what is presumably a science-fictional method. That is to say, if Ernest Hemingway went to Australia and saw the things that you saw, he would write a reportorial book. You might turn it into something else.

Dann: I've mentioned this before. I think that working in the genre for a lifetime as I have gives you certain tools. Pam Sargent, Kim Stanley Robinson, and I have talked about using the tools of science fiction to write historical fiction. When I write historical fiction, I "extrapolate" the past, which is as alien as the future. As a science fiction writer, I look for the alien... and the past is an alien country with mindsets that our not ours. And naturally I am always looking for the alien in the familiar, for that strange kind of magical sense of wonder, that *frisson* that makes me want to write. That's why all of my work, even the mainstream work, has an underlay of magical realism. I think that magical realism describes something vital and evocative about our lives. It's that numinal, luminous, vital stuff that interests and excites me. That's what I want to write about. In science fiction that's the sense of wonder. Even with *The Silent,* which is a Civil War novel, I was using techniques gained by writing science fiction to create my young character Mundy McDowell. He is dislocated and alienated. He has witnessed the rape and murder of his mother, heard the screams of his father, who was trapped in his burning house. So Mundy makes himself...invisible and follows ghosts and spirits, who teach him how to survive. That's the kind of stuff that interests me. That's the underlay of this "mainstream" novel. I used genre techniques to extend the layering of consciousness of my young protagonist.

Q: Does he literally become invisible?

Dann: *He* thinks he's becoming invisible. *The Silent* is narrated in first person point of view. Mundy is a darker version of Huck Finn. As a reader you see how Mundy reconstructs reality; you see the world through his sensorium...through his eyes, the eyes of a child, and if I've done my job properly, you'll also see with a sort of double vision—you'll see the past through the lens of the present, and through the eyes of a child of the nineteenth century. You'll see Mundy's world and the objective world superimposed. The fabulous inheres in the mundane. Our mundane, go-to-the-office-and-come-home lives are limned with the mysterious, shot through with the laser light of the numin. As a writer, I try to capture those magical and often terrible superimpositions. And I like to think that science fiction gives me an edge....

(Recorded at the World Fantasy Convention, Corpus Christi Texas, Oct 26-28, 2000)

An Afterword from the Present

Dann: Reading this interview conducted in October 2000 gave me a strange sense of *déjà-vu*. Much of it can stand, and I found myself...agreeing with myself. A lot of the politics have remained the same: John Howard's conservative government is still in power here in Australia; and I'm still the proverbial stranger in a strange land, although the strange land has become home in some ineffable, profound way. But home is also Los Angeles and Binghamton and New York. Where else (but New York) can you get an egg cream, I ask you?

But in some ways this interview feels like it was written long, long ago in some sense because it was pre-9/11. A time when Americans were unbeaten, when we were the iconic leaders of the pack. We are still all of that...yet we aren't. We've become something different. The world has shifted.

America has become darker, less secure, and the sinister shadows of fear are growing ever longer. Our culture is fracturing at the edges while its center is becoming more homogenous. Our President is acting out a religious morality play. And we are experiencing political and cognitive dissonance.

Australia, which prided itself on being "the Great Experiment," has been flatlined by conservative politics. It has become an integral part of the Coalition of the Willing... America's "Sheriff in Asia." Education, which was free when I arrived here, is free no longer. The majority of citizens have done quite well economically—Australia is a Standard & Poor's dream—but Australians have become politically passive and unaware, while a pro-business, anti-union government has profoundly changed the nature of workplace relations. We're reliving the greedy eighties here in Australia, and arbitrage and Reagan's trickle-down theories reign supreme.

Yet the culture remains vibrant, and Janeen and I spend most of our time writing at our farm by the sea, and making forays to our apartment in Melbourne.

A good life between the lengthening shadows.

And the Dean book was published in 2004, titled *The Rebel: An Imagined Life of James Dean*. The U.S. paperback edition should be in bookstores by the time this goes to press. Although I would guess that a lot of my genre readers didn't see the book, which was packaged as mainstream, the genre reviews were terrific. (*Locus*: "Jimmy's personal discussions and confrontations, often by phone, possess a crackling laconic energy worthy of a powerful film script. In this Dann has embraced a technique perfect for a Hollywood psychological novel, and it is by his words, tender or frenzied, that the phantom of James Dean acquires full, extraordinary life. No superficial Tinseltown gossip here, no languorous intrigues on the film set: instead, private torment, public rage.")

Some of the mainstream reviewers loved the book, others couldn't understand the idea of writing alternate history as literary mainstream (*But James Dean died! How can you write a book about his life after the accident?*), and a few became really upset with my literary icon-smashing. *Kirkus Reviews*, for instance, called *The Rebel* "Relentlessly trashy and profane, name-dropping and scandal-mongering"..."a Harold Robbins-style tale of gratuitous sex, ambition, and famous people behaving badly." (I really did try to explain to my film agent that this was a negative review, but she just wouldn't believe me.)

I still haven't written my "Australian" novel. I'm working on a novel based on my novella "The Diamond Pit." I'm still fascinated with America and the American Dream, and the novel will be a sort of family saga that begins in the 1800's, works its way through the 1920's and into the present. Well, I *think* it will end in the present. For me, stories are live things that constantly surprise and confound all my preconceived plots. Oh, yes, I've done a collection of my collaborative short stories called *The Fiction Factory*, which will be published in October; and I'm working on a number of anthologies. I'm also working on a psychological novel about nasty politics tentatively titled *Extra Duty*.

After all, I have to keep up my reputation as the new Harold Robbins.

19 June 2005
Windhover Farm
Australia

GEOFFREY A. LANDIS

Q: Would you describe your background, how you got started, and what you were doing before you wrote SF?

Landis: I started writing when I was in graduate school. I was a physics graduate student, and I guess I just decided to start writing for no real reason, except that I had read science fiction since I was a little kid. I read every kind of science fiction, just everything I could get my hands. I had always loved science fiction, and I eventually got to the part where I said, "Gee, I'm going to start writing." I was very young and naive at the time and thought I was going to just write a story and send it in and get it published. Actually, it turned out that was pretty much the way it happened; I wrote a story and sent it in and it got published.

Q: But something a little more extraordinary happened. Is it not true that while you were a student at Clarion, you had a story on the Hugo ballot? This must have been a first.

Landis: In fact my very first story ended up being a cover story for *Analog,* and it made the Hugo ballot. So when it made the Hugo ballot I looked at it and said, "Gee, this writing business is kinda cool. Maybe I should do more of it. And maybe I should learn how to write." So I decided to go to Clarion, the well-known science-fiction writers' workshop, and while I was at Clarion I had a story on the Hugo ballot. That was fortunate for me because I knew it wasn't going to win. I was up against a really good John Varley story. So I had all the advantages of being on the Hugo ballot, but I didn't have to be nervous.

Q: It still must have been an extraordinary situation, because most students at Clarion have not published anything and are at least secretly afraid that they may never. But you had achieved something that many of your *teachers* had never achieved. This is the *only* time it had ever been done. How did people react to that?

Landis: I think that once my classmates actually realized it, they were a little bit disconcerted by the fact that I had already published and most of the rest of them hadn't, although a good percentage of our Clarion class went on to publish professionally. But I think that after a while they got used to it and said, "Oh, yeah, there's this guy Geoff and he's already had a couple of stories published." The one nice thing about it is that it gives you a lot more confidence in listening to people critique your stories if you know, well, I am capable of being published and achieving a little bit of notoriety for my stories.

Q: In the eyes of many people you must have seemed to have started at the top. There was probably someone there who wanted to quietly drown you, because they were jealous.

Landis: Now that I look back on it, it must have looked pretty daunting to the others. But if they were jealous, they were nice enough not to say so.

Q: How then did you avoid a sense of anti-climax? What followed next?

Landis: One thing I will give Clarion credit for is that it did give me a little more literary ambition. I wasn't just trying to write for a very narrow audience of very technical, hard-science readers, but I started to think, well, I want to write stuff that is really good and that a wide audience can enjoy.

But at the same time, of course, I was finishing off my Ph.D. in physics and getting ready for a real job, a job actually in science. So writing was not my main preoccupation at the time, so I didn't worry to much about whether my writing career was going up or down or sideways. I was mostly focussing on finishing off my research and then writing my dissertation and then going on to take a job at NASA-Lewis Research Center.

Q: Now you have the advantage of being one of the few science-fiction writers who is actually a working scientist, who knows what the other side of things is about. So, how do you balance or blend the two, being a science-fiction writer and being a scientist at the same time?

Landis: I've discovered that my science colleagues are remarkably tolerant of the fact that I am a science-fiction writer. Of course every now and then they give me a little bit of ribbing and say, "When you write a paper, how do we know if that's science or science fiction?" But in general they're very supportive. They think it's cool. A lot of the people at NASA and the people I work with are in fact science fiction readers. They think it's great. A lot of them, I think, secretly wish that they weren't scientists but could be a famous science-fiction writer instead.

Q: At the same time you get to do things that science-fiction writers only dream of. You got to name rocks on Mars.

Landis: That's one of the great things about working at NASA. I was very lucky to come in at the right time. One of the projects that I was working on at NASA-Lewis, which is now named NASA-Glenn Research Center, is to look at the question of solar energy on Mars. The question we're asking is: Does enough sunlight get through the dusty atmosphere to power a solar-powered spacecraft on the surface of Mars?

That work led directly into an involvement with the Pathfinder project. That was a lot of fun. I had a little experiment on the corner of the Sojourner rover, an experiment about the size of an Elvis postage stamp, but we were in there getting our data from Mars all during the Pathfinder mission. We learned a lot of important information about dust on Mars, the process that raises and deposits dust in the Martian atmosphere. It's a blast to work on a mission like that.

Now the geologists talk about rocks all the time. That's what they do. And so that the know what they're talking about, they name all the rocks that they talk about. The way they name rocks is that they have the panorama of the view from Pathfinder, and anybody who wanted to give a name to a rock would just write the name to a little yellow sticky-note and stick it on the panorama, which was on the wall of the science conference room. So I named quite a number of rocks on Mars. I named, for example, a rock called Yogi, which turned out to be a pretty well-known rock; and a number of the other rocks are ones that I named.

Q: Do you get flashbacks of Arthur Clarke's *The Sands of Mars* and the like? You read about Mars as a kid, and now, in a sense, you're there.

Landis: I guess I have to say that I always did want to do this, just because of my reading of science fiction. Arthur C. Clarke and all the great writers who wrote about Mars have really been an inspiration to me.

Q: I imagine that the type of satisfaction must be different, between something that is very concrete and real, and something that is artistic and speculative. How does doing science feel different from doing science fiction?

Landis: The experiences of doing science and science fiction are in many ways similar, because you have to come up with interesting ideas; and in some ways they're different. When you're doing science fiction you have to come up with an idea, and the first thing you have to say is, well, "What kind of plot and what kind of characters go with this idea. Who are the best people to explore this concept?" Whereas when you're doing science, you're asking "What kind of experimental evidence could prove or disprove this idea?" and "What kind of theoretical analysis can be the background for the idea?" So, for science fiction you move from the idea to the people, and for science you go from the idea to the mathematics and the experimental hardware.

Q: I am sure that when you read other science fiction, you can sometimes tell that the author doesn't know any scientists. What are some of the things writers get wrong about depicting the way scientists work and the experience of doing science?

Landis: I guess the one thing that is disappointing about doing science is that in science fiction one guy comes up with a great idea on Monday afternoon, and by two paragraphs later they're building the apparatus. Probably two or three pages later in the book they're testing the apparatus. Then maybe they have to take out their soldering iron and fix it a little bit, but things work pretty much the first time. That would be nice if science works that way, but it doesn't. There are hardly any lone inventors sitting in the lab with crackpot theories that really turn out to be correct. Mostly the theorists aren't the experimenters, so the theorists work on the theory and somebody else is doing the experiment, and things never work the first time and hardly ever work the second time or the third time. Most ideas turn out to be dead ends. So science in its way is slower and more frustrating than science fiction. In a science fiction story, you know that if somebody comes out with an idea, their theory is going to be the right one. In science that is rarely the case. There's a lot more of purely doing the brickwork of step by step by step that just gets glossed over in science fiction.

Q: Is it possible that science fiction can be a wish-fulfillment for scientists? I remember a letter to *Analog* once that said, "What I like about science fiction is that all the experiments in the stories *work.*"

Landis: Absolutely. Science fiction is my wish-fulfillment. It's where you describe things the way you wish that they would happen, not the way that they do happen.

Q: But in order to make the plot work, something has to go wrong.

Landis: That's true. Preferably in science you don't have the life-threatening emergencies and the things that blow up and the devices that have to be fixed with the contents of your pocket and a couple of paperclips. That's not something we see a whole lot in science.

Q: As someone pointed out, if you'd written the story of Apollo 13 in the 1940s, it would be science fiction, but it probably wouldn't have met the expectations of science fiction at that time. It would have been difficult to sell to *Thrilling Wonder Stories.*

Landis: Yes, that's true. The one thing you notice when you consider the true story of Apollo 13 is how many people were involved. In a science fiction story it would be the three people in the capsule. Maybe they talk to Earth, but they solve their problems with the paperclips and bubblegum that they have on the spacecraft. In the real world of Apollo 13 there was a team of hundreds of people on the ground working frantically to try to come up with the sequences and the work-arounds to make the vehicle come back and have all the people survive. That's the way science really is and the way spacecraft work. There's a big team of people. You can hardly ever say that one person is responsible. It's everybody. There are teams of hundreds that work on a mission.

Q: I wonder if, then, science fiction isn't *behind* reality rather than in front of it, because science fiction is following a model that is more based on Thomas Edison, that of the lone inventor or the lone explorer. In the early part of this century that was a valid model, although of course Edison was one of the first people to make inventions a team and assembly-line affair. So maybe the way science fiction depicts these things is behind the times.

Landis: One thing that I've noticed, since I am also a space enthusiast, that a lot of people think that science must be really easy. It comes from too much science fiction, where people build spacecraft in their back yards, that people wonder why NASA is spending these hundreds of millions of dollars. They ask, "Can't we make it cheaper and just throw something together?"

In fiction if you do something really cheap and just throw something together, it works, and people build spacecraft in their back yards and go off to have wonderful adventures. But in the real world, it's hard. Building a spacecraft and getting to work and getting all the pieces to go together is not easy. There is a lot of engineering to be done that's just glossed over in science fiction. So I think science fiction has just given people the wrong view of the world. On the other hand, science fiction has inspired a lot of people to go into science and make it happen. So it's good and bad.

Q: Can you see science fiction having a real didactic purpose in that sense, that you can write SF in order to inspire people to make science happen? This is what we used to call the Gernsback Delusion. Is there any truth to it?

Landis: I talk to a lot of scientists and engineers. Not all, but quite a lot of them were inspired by science fiction. So I think there's some truth in that. Science fiction gets people interested in science. But at the same time it tends to give them wrong views about science. People probably still believe that Mercury keeps one side to the Sun and the other side is eternally cold, because that's the way they read about it in old science fiction stories, so that's the way it must be.

Q: I wonder if what doesn't really give the public the wrong idea is the imagery of science fiction filtering into the popular culture, so that by the time it gets to the supermarket tabloids it's very distorted indeed. I am sure you must get people all the time asking you about the face on Mars and the subsequent coverup. Has that ever happened to you?

Landis: Occasionally people have asked me about the face on Mars I try to be polite. I guess they have a legitimate question to ask: "Can't we take a closer look at this formation and see what it really is?" It seems pretty unlikely to me that it is anything other than an unusual rock formation, but, hey, the public should get a chance to say which way to point the cameras, too.

Q: I'm thinking more in terms of UFOlogy. A portion of the public will assume what they want to believe, and then when you fail to produce the supporting evidence, they conclude you're part of the conspiracy to cover it all up. Maybe it's Elvis on Mars.

Landis: That's the problem. Once you start assuming there is a conspiracy to cover up the evidence, the frightening thing about that is that you can explain *everything,* because any time there is something that doesn't fit your worldview, the explanation is, "Oh, that's part of the conspiracy." Once you start really believing there is a conspiracy, there is no possible way to be dissuaded, because any piece of evidence can be explained as part of the conspiracy.

Q: It assumes a naive faith in the ability of the illuminati or whoever to make all of this *work*. You being a part of a large team doubtless know that the larger the team gets the more likely someone is going to screw up. The CIA who are covering up the presence of aliens on Mars must consist of supermen, because they are awesomely competent and never break ranks.

Landis: I wrote a science fiction story about that once. It was called "What We *Really* Do At NASA." It's a spoof about how we go into work and play cards with the space aliens from the crashed saucers and have perpetual-motion machines in our basements. But that's not really the way it happens, although I did get a rather strange call from my boss when he heard that I wrote this story. Then a little while later he said, "Okay, somebody gave me a copy of this story and I can see that it's a humor piece." But for a while it looked like my boss was a little disturbed that I was writing about flying saucers and the face on Mars.

Q: He thought you'd done an exposé?

Landis: Maybe when he heard that I was writing about this he thought I had gone off the deep end.

Q: Of course the true believer in such things will say that anyone who has a sufficiently unorthodox idea will be dismissed as being off the deep end. So it all becomes part of the larger conspiracy. Which brings us to a more serious question: science fiction as a method of perceiving reality. Robert Heinlein used to insist that science fiction is a form of realism. Do you find that, indeed, science fiction helps you perceive and deal with reality differently than other literature does?

Landis: Science fiction has the ability to make you speculate and stretch your mind and, of course, think about the future. It's a cliché, but it's been said that the future is very important because we're going to live the rest of our lives there. That's really very true, and science fiction is the only literature than asks, "Is the future going to be different from how it is today? And how is it going to be different? How is that going to change the way that we live?" That is important. Science fiction is dealing with our true reality. That reality is that we're living in the future and it ain't going to be like today. So maybe we should think about that a little bit.

Q: I understand that your first novel just appeared.

Landis: Yes, *Mars Crossing*. It came out in December 2000. I guess it is inevitable that eventually I would write a Mars novel. Of course this is by no means the first or the second or even the tenth science-fiction novel about Mars. I like to think that mine is more realistic than some of the novels about Mars and certainly more realistic than some of the recent movies about Mars. So I certainly would invite you to find a copy and read it and see what you think.

Q: Why did it take you so long to write a novel, when you'd been writing short fiction for ten years?

Landis: I mostly write short fiction because I have a short attention span. I just like the idea of a short story, that you can write it and finish it off and get to the end pretty quickly. Writing a novel is really a very different experience, where you sit down every day to write and you know that it's not going to reach the end this week or this month or probably next month either, that you're just writing to continue on the journey, and not to press on to the end. It gives you a chance to be closer to your characters and to explore them a little bit more. Now I find that after I've finally done it, it was fun.

Q: Are you sufficiently obsessive about the details that you'll want to keep making changes in future editions when the next mission to Mars finds something wrong in your book? You're writing about something right on the edge of discovery. Aren't you afraid that it might even be dated even before the paperback comes out?

Landis: That's always a problem when you write about real space missions. New things that come out are likely to make what you said obsolete, but by the time the real missions to Mars tell us that everything I thought I knew about Mars was wrong, I suspect that I'll be well on to writing about new planets and new adventures, so I don't think that I'll go back and try to rewrite the old stories.

Q: You could make a running gag out of it the way Larry Niven has. Every time there is a "new" Mars, Larry Niven sets a story there. They're now mutually exclusive. But for the longer term, I suppose the best prospects for reality-based SF would be to set stories in the newly discovered solar systems around the nearer stars. They'll probably hold their own for a while, before we are sure which ones have small, rocky planets and which ones don't. Have you already been thinking in that direction?

Landis: I have been fascinated by following the results of planet-hunters who have been finding planets around other stars. They have completely changed the way that we view the universe. In the old days of science fiction, everybody just assumed, for no good reason, that other solar systems would be a lot like ours, with terrestrial planets on the inside, maybe some gas giants further out, maybe an asteroid belt, and nobody ever possibly guess that there would be these giant planets, bigger than Jupiter, but closer in to the star than Mercury. Nobody guessed that there'd be solar systems with these wildly eccentric orbits that have planets that go way in close to the sun, past the orbit of Mercury, and then way out on the other part of their orbit, as if there were one planet that was simultaneously moving between the orbits of Venus, Earth, and Mars. Things are a lot more different than we'd ever guessed that they might be. It has just been amazing results.

Q: Do you see science fiction as something which then follows new scientific data and expands down the new avenues opened by it?

Landis: Well, there are many different types of science fiction. There are certainly some science fiction writers who closely follow the newest results and are trying to write stories based on the latest, most up-to-the-minute findings. Then of course there are other science fiction writers who are more interested in exploring other parts of the future, and are interested in society or economics or the relations between the sexes, or any of thousands of different themes that are common in science fiction.

Q: So I guess the one thing we can reliably say is that science fiction isn't going to run out of material any time soon, because science continues to generate more of it.

Landis: There is always something new. Science fiction moves to keep looking at the new things. Twenty years ago science fiction didn't realize how much computers were going to change out lives, and now it seems that every other science-fiction story that you see is talking about cyberspace and virtual realities and downloading humans into computer worlds. So I think it's safe to say that there's a lot of life left in science fiction.

Q: Where do you see your own fiction going?

Landis: I see my own science fiction just exploring new ideas, and what are the consequences of some of the things that we're going to see in the future for our own lives, and the way that society and people interact with each other.

Q: Thanks Geoff.

(recorded at Chicon, 2000)

JOE W. HALDEMAN

Q: I don't know if this has occurred to you, but you're now an elder statesman of science fiction. It has been something like forty years since your first sale.

Haldeman: Not quite forty....

Q: 1969, wasn't it? It will be forty years by the time this interview comes out. It must have been a long, strange trip for you. How has science fiction changed your life?

Haldeman: It has been my life. Science fiction has changed a lot, so my life has changed with science fiction. I wish it were the way it used to be. I liked it when there were lots of magazines and no so many writers, and when you could write a book in 65,000 words and it would be unremarkable. Today they say, "It's a stand-alone novel!" as if that were some sort of remarkable feat." [Laughs.]

Q: I once organized a panel at a convention called "Your Book Is Short, You Must Have Clout."

Haldeman: Maybe so.

Q: Well, you probably do have clout by now. Do you find that publishers want you to write multi-volume big-crushers, or that they just want a Haldeman book?

Haldeman: I never read them, so I wouldn't write one. I have written *a* trilogy, which was three related books, and each book was approximately 75,000 words. I am doing one now, which is the same thing. It's about the same people.

Q: I wonder if this insistence on long series is less of a problem in science fiction than in fantasy, where they want a McTolkien. A *big* McTolkien. You've never been moved to write in that direction.

Haldeman: I just write what I would like to read, and I would never pick up one of those. It just looks like too much work.

Q: Your career must have given you the perspective that we're now living in "the future." You can remember, as I can, when the near future in SF was about 1970, and the far future was 2000. Think of Heinlein's *The Door into Summer*. Well, now that we're living in the future, it's not the way science fiction depicted it, is it?

Haldeman: No, in fact science fiction missed some of the most important factors of the future. The internet sucks up one or two hours of my day. That was only hinted at in very few stories.

Q: I confess that as late as 1976 I wrote a story in which someone a hundred years in the future is using a typewriter.

Haldeman: [Laughs.] *Mindbridge* has a guy trying out one of these new voice-operated typewriters and talks about the trouble he is having with it. I didn't get that right at all.

Q: But then, in a sense science fiction isn't predictive, is it?

Haldeman: No, it's not. It's about the present. It's not about the future.

Q: Who was it—was it John Clute?—who observed that every science fiction novel has a real date, in the sense that *The Space Merchants* is really about 1952? Isn't science fiction also about the *process* of the future? That is, what change feels like, rather than the specific details. I am sure you could write a story about someone like yourself, a hundred years hence, wishing for the good old days of 2050.

Haldeman: Yes, you can. But it seems to me it's all about creative refraction, or whatever you want to call it. We write about our own lives and our own perceptions. We warp them around to make them interesting. Nobody would write science fiction if it wasn't more interesting than just plain fiction to them.

Q: You have written two mainstream, realistic novels, which were both about vital things in your life. But I take it you don't feel a general urge to write realistic, non-speculative fiction.

Haldeman: I wouldn't mind. If there was a market that is a solid as the market for my science fiction, I would probably write a lot of mainstream novels. Not all of them. I think a lot of what I would write would still be science fiction, but I've got one I am working on now, sort of in my spare time, that's only borderline SF. It's set a little in the future, but it's mostly about being a writer and slowly recovering from wartime experience.

Q: Is this because you got established as a science fiction writer, that you don't have a steady market for mainstream books? I am thinking of that paperback of *War Year* which was made to look like science fiction.

Haldeman: [Laughs.] Yeah, that was interesting. You rarely saw it in the mainstream section of the bookstore. It was always in science fiction. But they admitted to me when *1968* came out that they didn't have any idea what to do with a mainstream novel by a science fiction writer. It's not a problem in Britain where this happens all the time. I said, "Why don't I make up a new name? That will be my mainstream name." They said, "No, we want to get your regular readers," which would evidently make the book profitable even if it didn't sell an awful lot of copies. So I don't know even now if it was a good decision. I'd sort of like to have a mainstream persona, so I could write plain novels.

Q: You could possibly do what Iain Banks did. Fool around with initials. He has a code. If the byline is Iain M. Banks, it is science fiction; if it's Iain Banks, it is mainstream—sort of.

Haldeman: That's a good idea. My first mainstream novel appeared as by Joe W. Haldeman. When my brother was writing, he asked me to change my name to Joe Haldeman, because he was Jack C. Haldeman II, and so he didn't want my middle initial to confuse people. That's why I became Joe Haldeman.

Q: Don't you think that out of natural inclination, most of your books would have been science fiction anyway? You mentioned once that you initially wanted to be an astronaut.

Haldeman: Yes. Probably they would be science fiction because that's what I grew up reading.

Q: Have you ever speculated on how your life would have worked out if you'd been an astronaut?

Haldeman: [Laughs.] No, I just wonder. The people who were astronauts seem to live in this strange, public-relations universe. They were astronauts for a few years, and then they were sort of spokesmen for technology, for government, for democracy. That's not what they signed up for. They wanted to keep being astronauts and go to Mars. It wasn't in the cards. So I don't know. I probably would have gotten out of it soon enough. I would have had a Ph.D in astronomy. I probably would have gone and become an astronomer.

Q: Or like Fred Hoyle, you could be a Ph.D. astronomer and write science fiction.

Haldeman: Right. It could have happened.

Q: The real science fiction writer will come out.

Haldeman: Also if I'd been an astronaut I'd also be a celebrity, so I would have had best-sellers all the way.

Q: How does *The Forever War* look to you after all this time?

Haldeman: Well, I just reread it last week, because I got the page-proofs for the new edition. It holds up okay. I would write it much differently now. But I think anybody who is sixty-five would say that of a novel he wrote thirty years ago.

Q: I am reminded of something Jack Williamson said. I asked him how it felt to have written the books for which he is most famous some decades ago. He replied that it was great to have written a classic at any time.

Haldeman: That's true. I'd go along with him on that. It's nice to have a book or two that stays in print, no matter what. That's real security.

Q: Has *The Forever War* been solidly in print all this time?

Haldeman: It's been out of print for about three months, and it will be out of print until January [2009—so it is back in print as you read this. –DS] while the new publisher takes over. The paperback had been a five-year license thing for the past twenty-five years, and the hardback publisher, St. Martin's decided that this time they would keep the rights to publish an edition themselves. In the interim the old license to Ace ran out, which caused me a certain amount of trouble because I'm a college professor and a lot of other professors teach that book. So they're saying. "Where is the book?" I say, "You have to go to a used book store."

Q: Do you ever wonder why that one of all your works has endured so well, or isn't it actually pretty obvious?

Haldeman: I think that it was a book whose time had come right when it came out. It impressed a lot of people who became teachers, and right away they started teaching it to their students. That's a way to, not immortality, but longevity.

Q: It's also a book which is very viscerally about things that had happened to you not all that long before you wrote it. It wasn't a book you had to make up.

Haldeman: Right. I was lucky about that. But you know, in generations preceding mine, almost every male writer wrote a war novel among his early works because he was a soldier. Everybody was a soldier back then. Nowadays it's a more rare thing.

Q: Other than *Starship Troopers,* I can't think of very many other great science fiction war novels. And of course Robert Heinlein was never in combat.

Haldeman: No, that's true. Neither was Stephen Crane. In fact, there are so many bad books written by combat veterans that you could almost say that the best preparation for writing a war novel is not to become a soldier.

Q: I should think that the problem of writing a science fiction war novel would be how to make it genuinely speculative, rather than making it a costumed account of what you experienced.

Haldeman: And to be truly inventive rather than just doing war tropes over and over.

Q: It might be that because you wrote a straight war novel too, that you could stand aside from the material and write a science fiction one.

Haldeman: Yeah. That's quite possible.

Q: Do you think that there is an actual science fiction method, in the sense that science fiction is almost a specialized language for dealing with fictional materials? Whose idea am I stealing here? Probably Clute.

Haldeman: I think it probably is Clute. I agree completely. Teaching gives you some perspective on this. You tell the people, "A book can be a good science fiction book without being a good book." We all have read these things, books which have neat ideas or characters, but which you would be embarrassed to hand to someone who is not a science fiction reader, because science fiction is a way of thinking as well as a way of writing. If you look at science fiction novels written by people who have not read a lot of science fiction, you get this kind of hollow feeling. They don't have that way of thinking. They just have spaceships and robots. It's a very strange world we inhabit, but it's our own world.

Q: Sometimes I wonder if we are living in Philip K. Dick's future.

Haldeman: [Laughs.] I don't take that many drugs. I don't know.

Q: I remember something Alfred Bester said in an interview I did with him, that the limitation of science fiction was that it is inherently made up. Is it, or is it really transmogrified life?

Haldeman: Well, I can see what Bester was talking about. But Bester had such a low opinion of science fiction in the first place. I don't know. I think good novels are all made up anyway. If you don't want to make stuff up, you ought to write non-fiction. Yeah, science fiction is made up in a special way. It is reality re-invented.

Q: So why don't you tell me something about the novel you are writing now?

Haldeman: I wrote a book called *Marsbound,* which is just out in paperback now, and when I came to the end of it I realized, "Oh, you know there is a sequel here." I really was about twenty pages from the end when I realized that my next book would be a sequel to it. Then when I wrote up the proposal for it, I realized there had to be a third book. It became a trilogy in the space of a few months. I have just signed the contract for the next two, so that's what I will be doing for the next three years or so. I am trying a fairly obvious experiment, that is to say, the three books have the same characters, but they are each different kinds of books. The first one is pretty much a Heinlein type science fiction novel. The second one is more Twenty-First Century space opera. It obeys all the physical laws that apply, etc. but the characters go out to another star, and they have good reasons for doing it. The third one is a kind of post-modern look at the limits of civilization. It takes place back on Earth, and it's a different look at the Singularity. I have issues with it. Although I enjoy the books, I am going to do my own take on it. So the three books, although they're a single plotline and they have the same characters, they are three different kinds of novels.

Q: Would you care to describe some of your issues with the

Singularity? Terry Bisson has suggested that it already happened and we missed it.

Haldeman: [Laughs.] That's part of my thing. I think that it is a spread-out phenomenon, and yes, it started quite a while ago. I don't have any problem the way Vernor Vinge does it. I think his initial essay was brilliant, defining it. I just think the time-scale is wrong. I think it started about the time the Internet started. I don't think it will be completely in place until after about a generation. Then, yes, human nature will have changed profoundly, but people won't be able to point to a year or a month in which it happened.

Q: It seems to me that maybe human nature will have changed profoundly in some parts of the world, but in other parts there will still be subsistence farmers who have never heard of any of this because they haven't learned to read.

Haldeman: As Heinlein said, "When men first walk on the Moon, there will still be outhouses in upstate New York." He was right about that. I think that principle is certainly going to be true whenever the Singularity happens, or whatever its name is.

Q: I might suggest that by the time some of us have bioengineered and enhanced ourselves into something that is post-human, there will also still be hunter-gatherers.

Haldeman: Yes, that's true. And probably people who have had the choice between being post-human and hunter-gatherers and would rather be hunter-gatherers.

Q: There may be some people who just haven't heard of it either. Recall that Isaac Asimov wrote a series of stories—this is the background if *The Caves of Steel*—in which he suggested that the human race would divide into two species, one technically and medically enhanced, and one not.

Haldeman: I think there are any number of ways to divide the human race into two groups, including the ones who are sensitive to science fiction and the ones who are "straight."

Q: I am sure that in a university setting you must have encountered professors who can't understand what this science fiction "nonsense" is about. Thackeray didn't write it so it can't be any good. You know.

Haldeman: That doesn't happen at M.I.T., fortunately. I meet people like that in academia outside of my own institution, but people at M.I.T. are pretty hep to science fiction. Whenever a Neal Stephenson novel comes out, they have to close down the school while people go out and buy it and read it.

Q: I can certainly remember having professors say, "This isn't literature" in tones of stern disapproval.

Haldeman: I got that when I was getting my Master's degree. In fact I had one professor who absolutely forbade me to write science fiction, Stanley Elkin, who's quite a good writer, and he writes fantastic fiction himself. But he couldn't see any connection between his literary fantasies and the type of fantasy that I call science fiction. So I went along with him. In fact that was when I wrote the first part of *1968*, which I called *Spider's Web* at that time. He liked that. He said, "Yeah, get out of this science fiction crap."

Q: I've always suspected there is a double-standard in academia, which is that fantastic literature us okay up to about 1900, as long as it has some moralistic or satirical edge. So perhaps the last respectable fantasy writer would be Mark Twain. After that, Realism equals Literature. It's kind of a Protestant work-ethic.

Haldeman: I think it is a misconstruing of the uses of realism. Science fiction loves realism, but it's a different kind. Heinlein is a great realistic writer, even within his strangely romantic view of the world.

Q: Heinlein may transcend all of this. There could come a time when he is seen as the leading twentieth-century American writer. In your work, you are still talking to Heinlein.

Haldeman: True. I think Heinlein will be forgiven his literary sins in another thirty, forty, fifty years. He will be seen as a very important twentieth-century writer. People will say, "Isn't that cute what he did with dialogue?" and "His characterizations are so *amusingly* sexist," and so on but he will be acceptable again.

Q: Maybe he will have an up-and-down career like Kipling.... It's interesting to speculate if the people fifty years from now will still be reading you. I am sure every writer speculates about this.

Haldeman: I assume they will be, and I am trying to affect that outcome. I am giving my papers to a university, and I am leaving behind all kinds of things that will let people do cheap master's degrees and have all the source material. I write my books in longhand for the first draft, so there is no question of it actually being a first draft, which gives me a couple of points over all my contemporaries who just write on a computer, because the provenance of something on a computer disk is just your word against someone else's.

Q: But a writer has to write for the present, not for the hoped-for future.

Haldeman: It's a thing I became aware of, actually, mostly when I wrote *The Hemingway Hoax* and had to go sorting through all those attics of literature and finding writers who leave a big paper trail.

Q: I am reminded of a story called "The Best-Known Man in the World" by Daniel Pearlman, which is about a would-be poet so obsessed with future scholarship of himself that he leaves this amazing paper trail carefully files and catalogues his every draft, laundry lists, diaries, and notes, keeping careful records of what he wrote when, and when he had this or that thought for the first time. In time he actually does publish some poetry and become somewhat well-known, but his poetry is seen as only a minor sideline of the man who created this amazing archive. It becomes like the Winchester Mystery House of literature.

Haldeman: I haven't read that. It sounds interesting.

Q: Any last thoughts? Anything beyond the trilogy?

Haldeman: I have a couple books on the back-burner. I always have. That is never a problem.

Q: Thanks, Joe.

ZORAN ZIVKOVIC

Q: Your work first came to my attention with the splendid "The Astronomer" in *Interzone*, which is not only a story about a powerful moral dilemma, but one of the best uses of the "Lady or the Tiger?" ending I've ever seen. Was that your first publication in English? How long had you been writing in Serbian before that? What had you published?

Zivkovic: Yes, "The Astronomer" was my very first publication in English. It appeared in the July 1999 issue of *Interzone*. In 2000 it was published in the USA, as the introductory part of my mosaic-novel *Time Gifts*. Eventually, "The Astronomer" was reprinted in the UK in 2006 in the *Impossible Stories* omnibus.

I started to write fiction only in 1993, when I was forty-five. By the time "The Astronomer" was first published, I had only four prose books: *The Fourth Circle* (1993), *Time Gifts* (1997), *The Writer* (1998) and *The Book* (1999). The beginning of the new millennium was my most prolific period so far. I am currently finishing my seventeenth book of fiction. *Escher's Loops* is due to appear in May.

Q: Related to this, were you actually familiar with the famous Frank R. Stockton story "The Lady or the Tiger?" or am I being too provincial about this? (It is probably the most famous American story with an indeterminate ending which forces the reader to guess on the basis of clues laid down. Published about 1900.)

Zivkovic: I wasn't aware of Frank R. Stockton's story at the time I wrote "The Astronomer", in early 1997. I read it only years later. But I have read many other "open-ended" fictional works. It is an ancient narrative strategy. As I teach my students attending the creative writing course at Belgrade University, the purpose of prose isn't so much to provide definite answers, as to ask the right questions. Readers of "The Astronomer" shouldn't be too much concerned about what monosyllabic answer the protagonist gives at the end, since, as is shown in the conclusive part of *Time* Gifts, it is basically irrelevant...

Q: What is your background in fantastic literature? Did you grow up reading American and British science fiction (possibly in translation?) or eastern European fantastic literature?

Zivkovic: I read both. My formal education is in literature. I first graduated in the comparative literature department and subsequently I received my master's degree and my doctorate in the same discipline. A substantial part of world literature belongs to one or another form of fantastical fiction. Modern day "science fiction" and "fantasy" (I am not entirely happy with either of these terms) are part of a very long and very fruitful tradition. On the same tradition, twentieth century European fantastic literature is based. Instead of "eastern", I would rather call it "middle" European.

I was reading American and British science fiction and fantasy first in translation and then, as I became able to read in English, in the original. For years I was an ardent promoter in my country of English language SF & F in the capacity of both a translator and a publisher. I translated more than fifty books, mostly from English, and published nearly two hundred and fifty. The vast majority of these books appeared at a period when it took courage, both academic and political, to be a supporter of these genres.

I definitely abandoned any academic, translating or publishing involvement with science fiction after my two volume set of the

The Encyclopedia of Science Fiction was brought out in 1990. It was the fourth book of that kind in the world by the time it appeared. Why did I take that decision? Because I finally wanted to accept the ultimate challenge: to start writing prose myself. That happened three years later, in 1993, when my first novel, *The Fourth Circle*, was published. It was a very fortunate realization that I wasn't in the prime of my youth any more to drive the parallel slalom: being an author and a publisher or translator at the same time. To be a writer is a full time job. I made my choice and I haven't regretted it. So far.

Q: You say you cut loose from academe, although you still teach a writing course. Is it actually possible to make a living as a writer of fantastic fiction in contemporary Serbia?

Zivkovic: I started teaching a university creative writing course only a semester ago. No, it isn't possible to make a living as a writer of any kind, not only of fantastic faction, in contemporary Serbia. There isn't a single full-time, professional prose writer nowadays in my country. Not even Milorad Pavic, whose novel *Dictionary of the Khazars* was a world best-seller in the late eighties. No wonder, since Serbia is such a tiny market. An average print-run is only 500 copies. Three thousand sold copies is already considered a best-seller. It wasn't like that in the country where I was born. Former Yugoslavia was a huge market. Alas, it disintegrated in a civil war in the 1990s, leaving former Yugoslavs in a number of small countries. Serbia is one of them. I can only hope we unite again, if not politically then at least as a market.

Q: How is fantastic literature regarded where you are? In the US, as you may know, it is still somewhat associated with cheap pulp fiction and not regarded as real literature by many establishment critics. Do you ever encounter that kind of division?

Zivkovic: Such prejudices aren't very widespread in Europe, where fantastic literature has a long and outstanding tradition and is generally considered by the literary establishment not only as a legitimate part of the mainstream but often as its peak. Bulgakov and Kafka, two among the most prominent European authors of the twentieth century, are primarily masters of the noble art of the fantastic. I guess we are rather fortunate still not to be so much dominated by the publishing industry. I believe it is this industry, with its paraliterary standards and obsession with profit before all else, that is mostly to blame for the way your fantastic literature is treated within your academic literary establishment.

Q: And if I may venture an overtly political question, well, political conditions were surely very different in Yugoslavia in 1993 when you started writing. Did you have problems with censorship? How did you cope?

Zivkovic: I never experienced any censorship problems in Yugoslavia. It's just one of many stereotypes introduced by decades of Cold War political propaganda. We never belonged to the Soviet bloc and were an open and free country as much as any other in the West. Let me give you an example. With my red Socialist passport I could travel to all but two countries in the world without a visa. Now, with my blue passport, the very symbol of freedom and democracy, there are only two countries left in the world for which I don't need a visa...

Q: Robert Heinlein once famously described science fiction as a form of realism, that is, serious speculation about things that might be, told in a realistic manner. That doesn't fit your work at all, which seems closer to Borges or Kafka than to Heinlein. So how would you describe your approach? What is the use of unreality in describing thematic truth?

Zivkovic: First of all, I don't write science fiction. Nor fantasy for that matter. I feel rather uncomfortable whenever labeled in any way as an author. I consider myself a writer without any prefixes. I am just a humble practitioner of the ancient and noble art of prose. No more, no less. Any prefix would be either misleading or limiting. Labels are invented by the publishing industry which doesn't see any art in prose. For them it is just another product whose sole purpose is to be sold. My writing belongs to the middle European fantastic tradition. I feel strong literary kinship with such masters as Bulgakov, Kafka and Lem. I write fantastic fiction because its non-mimetic nature enables me to tell something that couldn't be expressed in any other way.

Q: No writer likes to be corralled by definitions, but let me argue for a moment. If "fantasy" is defined as something broader than "books which imitate Tolkien," but is taken more to mean any story which contains non-real elements, which the author and the reader both acknowledge are impossible—I am thinking of that statement at the front of Lucian of Samosata's "True History" in which he says "I have not seen these things, nor have I heard them from another, nor do I expect to be believed"—then surely you, Kafka, and Bulgakov are all authors of fantasy. Much of what goes on in your work is impossible by most people's standards, and people do not really turn into enormous insects, nor did the Devil go touring around the Soviet Union in person, as in *The Master and Margarita*. So is this fantasy? Don't we mean by "fantasy" the broader tradition of the fantastic, rather than the narrower, commercial genre?

Zivkovic: In this part of the world we use "fantastika" as the generic term for all non-mimetic prose works. It is the opposite of "realism" which is, by definition, mimetic. "Fantastika" is non-mimetic in the sense that it doesn't imitate the real world, but tries to invent a new kind of reality. There is a multitude of forms of "fantastika": folklore, oneiric, surreal, supernatural, to name just a few. Each of these forms has its immanent type of "reality." Science fiction is also one of the forms of "fantastika," probably the closest to mimetic/realistic fiction. The English language equivalent of "fantastika" is "fantasy," but the term has been used in a narrower sense in recent times. It comprises predominantly the "Tolkienesque" or "sword and sorcery" type of "fantastika." Time and again, the publishing industry is to blame for this limitation.

Q: As for science fiction, well, when Lem is voyaging to other planets by scientific, rather than supernatural means, even if the book is about the limitations of human knowledge (as in *Solaris*), that would seem to be science fiction. Your "The Astronomer" could well be read as being about time-travelers from the future informing the prisoner what will happen.

Zivkovic: It could be, yes, if you read it out of the context of the mosaic-novel *Time Gifts* to which it organically belongs as the first of four constituent parts. Within the context of *Time Gifts*, however, there are no time-travelers from the future. The denouement is, as you know, of an entirely different nature...

Q: Is there any real distinction between "the middle European fantastic tradition" and what an American would call "fantasy"? If so, is it a matter of theme, approach, underlying philosophy, or what?

Zivkovic: I would consider one of the greatest American masters of the art of "fantastika," Edgar Allan Poe, much closer to the middle European fantastic tradition than to modern-day American fantasy. H. P. Lovecraft also. There were no fundamental distinctions between middle European and English language "fantastika" until approximately the mid-twentieth century. Both had the same roots, emerged from the same cultural tradition. But then the publishing industry took over in your part of the world. I am very much afraid it is soon to dominate globally. (We live in an era of globalization, don't we?) "Fantastika" will be reduced then to a literarily worthless, but otherwise more or less commercial genre.....

Q: Well it seems to me that Lovecraft is very much part of the Gothic tradition and also the ghost-story tradition—he has much in common with Poe, Arthur Machen, and Algernon Blackwood—and his rationalism leads him to approach science fiction. What makes him more "fantastika" than some of his contemporaries and colleagues, such as, say, Robert E. Howard or Clark Ashton Smith?

Zivkovic: One can identify in Lovecraft's works a variety of influences besides the Gothic tradition. But I am not an expert in Lovecraft. I just mentioned him as an example of an outstanding writer whose literary roots are much deeper than it might seem, particularly if his opus is seen through the lens of only one language.

Q: In any case, wouldn't you agree that labels are most useful in retrospect? As the author of an encyclopedia of SF, you must have had to categorize and label quite a bit. But I don't see how labels like "science fiction" or "fantasy" or "fantastika" are of much use to the writer when actually writing the story.

Zivkovic: This is going to be somewhat simplified, but it is how I basically see it. "Categories" are for sciences. "Labels" are for supermarkets. I am very much afraid we have already entered an era in which books are being sold predominately in supermarkets. Labels are required in such surroundings to distinguish books from other goods. Macaroni, for example.

As for a writer starting a story, she/he always faces a simple dilemma. An author can write for the sake of art, in which case she/he isn't restricted by any other limitations but her/his literary abilities. On the other hand, she/he can decide to write for the market, in which case it has to be taken into account what's currently marketable, what would please their omnipotent majesties: the sales and marketing directors. And these people—sales and marketing directors—couldn't possibly care less about such a triviality as art.

I have written a story about it, "The Telephone." It is included in my omnibus, *Impossible Stories* (PS Publishing, UK, 2006). The Devil telephones an author suffering from writer's block and offers him a choice: to be rich and famous in his lifetime, but forgotten afterwards, or to remain poor and unrecognized, but to acquire a prominent place in literary history. What would you choose? If you decided to take both fame in your lifetime and literary immortality, I must warn you that this option isn't within the Devil's jurisdiction. You should apply for it from a higher authority....

Q: Well if everything gets completely globalized and Wal-Mart takes over the world—which sounds like a scenario for a Pohl/Kornbluth novel of the 1950s—then presumably "fantasika" would become one more marketing label to put on the spines of books.

Zivkovic: I don't think so. Supermarkets need more specific labels than "fantastika." One doesn't expect every article in the food department to be labeled just "food." By the way, in my humble view, *The Space Merchants* is one of the greatest American novels of the twentieth century....

Q: Let's talk for a minute about "mosaic novels." An interesting term. I've been reacquainting myself with your work by reading *Four Stories Till the End*, which is a mosaic novel, though even the episodes have episodes within them. Many of your books fall into this pattern, a cycle of four or five stories, each complete in itself, but forming a larger structure which (as in the case of "The Astronomer" as it appears in the context of *Time Gifts*) can change the way we read a story. I see that there IS a difference here between a "mosaic novel" and a collection of linked stories, and I will even candidly admit that I was overtly imitating your structures when I wrote *Living with the*

Dead. (You may have seen three parts of that in *Interzone* right before David Pringle left.) Is this a distinctly European form? Why write these, rather than more seamless novels, or just collections of short stories?

Zivkovic: *Living with the Dead* is one of the best things I've read of yours. Not because you also used the "mosaic-novel" structure, but because it is a genuine piece of the noble art of "fantastika". You were not imitating, you were legitimately relying on what's a part of our common literary heritage. The term "mosaic-novel" isn't a European invention. It was coined by the great Ursula Le Guin. I found it in an interview of hers and it seemed to suit perfectly the narrative form I was mostly using. I am not aware of any other European authors writing "mosaic-novels". There isn't a simple answer why I prefer this form over others. I don't decide consciously about it. Once a new work is ready to be delivered from the place where all my fiction originates, my subconscious, it takes whatever form is the most convenient. It so happens that my subconscious seems to be rather fond of "mosaic-novels"....

Q: You mention that the market in Serbia is so very small that 500 is the normal print-run and 3,000 is a bestseller. But I wonder: is there still a flourishing community of Serbian authors of "fantastika" that English readers have never seen? I have to confess that the only two Serbians I can name, much less have read, are you and Milorad Pavic. Which other such writers among your countrymen do you think deserve wider attention?

Zivkovic: A number of contemporary Serbian writers have received international recognition recently. David Albahari, for example. Goran Petrovic also, although he isn't yet translated into English. You see, this is one of the main problems an author writing in a small language is faced with. As I once remarked, if you write in Serbian, you don't write at all. If you, however, wish your books to be available in English translation and thus accessible to the whole world, not only the English-speaking regions, you have to invest a small fortune. Many good Serbian writers can't afford such a luxury and therefore remain "invisible" internationally. I am currently working with our Ministry of Culture to arrange a program that would provide assistance to the most prominent Serbian writers to get their books translated into English.

Q: To back up just a little bit, your comment on Lovecraft is intriguing, that the depth of his literary roots show when he is filtered through more than one language. I assume you're talking about reading him in translation. The only language other than English that Lovecraft was at all fluent in was Latin. But are you saying that by reading him in translation you see an affinity to other parts of world literature that might not be so evident to a native English-speaker reading him in English?

Zivkovic: What I meant regarding the depths of Lovecraft's literary roots was that they become more evident if one takes into account what has been written in other languages. Although Lovecraft probably wasn't aware of any prose works that weren't available in English (or Latin) translation, there are still similarities between them and his opus. There is no mystery in it. This is how the art of literature has worked ever since it was invented. Various authors, who are in no way aware of each other, make similar literary "discoveries." If I were much younger, I might be tempted to write my doctoral thesis about certain parallels between Lovecraft's "fantastika" and the Serbian folklore "fantastika" (in which, by the way, the term "vampire" was originally coined). But, alas, at this advanced age, I am just a humble writer and a creative-writing university professor. Fortunately, young scholars are coming and, who knows, some day, such a thesis could be written. We can only hope it won't remain imprisoned forever in the small Serbian language...

Q: How does being multilingual affect your understanding of a piece of literature?

Zivkovic: It's a privilege to be able to read in as many languages as possible. The more languages one speaks, the more windows are open for one....

Q: What are you working on these days? What is coming up soon? I am sure your faithful readers—and you DO have an English language audience—will want to know.

Zivkovic: I am deeply honored to have my faithful English language audience. This is something a writer of the art of "fantastika" originating outside the English-speaking world can only dream of. I do hope my readers in the US and UK enjoy my new novel, *Escher's Loops*. It is about to be finished and the English translation is already well under way. In the meantime, before *Escher's Loops* is published, as many as six other books of mine will appear this year in English translation: *The Last Book, The Writer, The Reader,* and *The Bridge* in the UK (PS Publishing) and *Impossible Encounters* (Aio Publishing) in the US.

Q: Thank you, Zoran Zivkovic.

(Conducted via e-mail in 2008)

ESTHER M. FRIESNER

Q: The earliest things of yours I can remember are a couple stories in *Amazing* in the early '80s. One was called "A Game of Crola," and was eerie and serious—was that your first sale?

Friesner: No.

Q:—and then there was "Dragonet," which was more the work of the Esther Friesner we all know. So, where does it all begin?

Friesner: As far as selling stuff, the first thing I got published was in *Asimov's SF*, when George Scithers was the editor. He had this wonderful, wonderful, kind thing he did, which was to send you back checklists with "This is what you did wrong" for very common mistakes. Then you would start getting letters, which would say, "Okay, you have learned from the checklist and you are making *un*common mistakes," and then finally you would stop getting letters and you would get a check and a contract with no letter whatsoever, and that was great.

I believe my first sale through that route was called "The Stuff of Heroes." It was about a romance writer who had no talent for writing, but she was scientifically gifted, so she had created the first reading system where you got a palpable hologram of the hero. You started the book, the hero appeared, and you were cast in the role of the romance heroine. And of course he was extremely dishy, and well, hijinks ensued.

That was obvious "go for the comedy" gold. The second one

was more ironic comedy. It was called "Write When You Get Work," also sold to *Asimov's*, about a solution to overcrowded prisons, and what happens when you are dealing with the results of that solution.

And from there, on we went. I've done funny stuff; I've done serious stuff; I've done horrifying stuff. It's always a lot of fun for me, because, well, if it isn't fun, why am I doing this? The glamour, the respect, the huge piles of rubies.... [Laughs.] Yeah, I would, but nobody has been offering me huge piles of rubies. What's the matter with this system?

But that is where my first sales of science fiction and fantasy started.

Q: You have to admit there are certain perks. There may not be piles of rubies, but I doubt that many mainstream literary writers were ever carried into a convention room on a palanquin borne by scantily-clad, muscular slave-boys.

Friesner: Well, you know, that's because they never *asked*. That's the problem. Usually I ask for something—see rubies, above—and I *get* it. Plus, we live in a frighteningly creative community and there is always someone who thinks, Gee, that would be fun. Let's see if we can get together and do that.

So I was in a discussion, and we were talking about what's your fantasy, and I mentioned being borne in triumph on a sedan chair by very nice looking young gentlemen. Some friends of mine said, "Okay, we can do that for you at Balticon," and they did, but you know what the problem is? More people found out about it and I couldn't turn around without someone saying, "Hi, we've got a sedan chair. We've got a bunch of scantily-clad young men. Would you like us to do that again?" I've had that done now three times. I think it's enough and it's time to move on to the rubies.

Are you paying attention? That's *rubies*.

Q: I saw it done at a Phrolicon.

Friesner: Yes, that was the second time.

Q: I have always appreciated your ability to move on before the gag goes stale. For example, we are beyond Cyberprep now. But it was great while it lasted, a response to Cyberpunk, and a way to promote good manners and niceness in science fiction in the 1980s.

Friesner: I am, I confess it, sometimes a curmudgeon. I now hear people laughing and going, "Sometimes? *Sometimes?* she says. The sun sometimes rises in the east."

But, long, long ago, when Cyberpunk first started, there were a number of its advocates who being very vehement about the fact this was *it*. This *was* what science fiction was going to be. This was the one, true science fiction. There could be no other. Anyone who thinks there can be any other kind of science fiction—insert rant here.

And I was just listening to this, and my curmudgeonly nature took over, which is basically expressed in the mantra, "Well says *you.*" I thought about it, and having observed the way the world works, I concluded that things get accomplished—whether it's the exploration of space or whatever—when there is money to be made for someone. So probably the conquest and exploration of space isn't going to be accomplished so much by the people with the chips in their heads as by the people who have the money to start with and want more of it. At the time, "Preppie" was a kind of icon. It was the days of *The Preppie Handbook.* So, instead of Cyberpunk, all this nitty-gritty, I thought we should start Cyber*prep,* because if space will be conquered, it will be conquered by the trust fundees who are terribly polite about it. But you don't want to get in their way. They can be ruthless.

So, it was a very nice joke. I was in this with Susan Shwartz and Judith Tarr as well. Once we had the core idea, we started riffing on it. I wrote the Cyberprep manifesto—

Q: It wasn't—

Friesner: It wasn't a manifesto. *Pronunciamento* because a manifesto is *ever* so Red and well, Communism is just *so* inconvenient to our interests. I went and around a convention getting people to sign it. I got Isaac Asimov's signature. I still have that document, so it is probably now worth, oh, many rubies.

And we had a party to launch Cyberprep. From then on we started having other parties to continue it. Pink and green were the Cyberprep colors. The alligator was our symbol. We had very lovely tea parties. We had a butler at one. It was just a good joke, and then after a while, as with after a good joke, we decided it was funny enough and we stopped it. But it was *fun* while it lasted.

Q: I was one of the signers. My Cyberprep name was "DC." John Betancourt was "Biff."

Friesner: Yes.

Q: Do you remember the Cyberprep blazer? There was going to be a final Cyberprep blowout at, I think, the Atlanta Worldcon in 1986, or it might have been New Orleans two years later. There was a power failure and the party was not held.

Friesner: I wasn't even there.

Q: Then I can tell you a story. I had worked out the proper male Cyberpreppie attire for this. I was wearing a green blazer with a pink alligator on the pocket, which I had made by drawing it on an piece of pink cloth and cutting it out, because I couldn't find a pink Izod alligator. The party was cancelled but I decided to wear this getup anyway. I was wearing a pink shirt, green slacks, a green tie, and penny-loafers, along with my Cyberprep button, and I got into an elevator with Susan Shwartz, who just lost it...and missed her floor.

Friesner: [Laughs.] Oh...my...goodness.... Now I do remember that when we had a Cyberprep party at a World Fantasy Convention, Susan brought a bread in the shape of an alligator, and we gave Jane Yolen the first Lizzie Award. It's a big lizard like the one on all those preppie shirts. But just before we served the alligator-shaped bread, Susan raised a knife and yelled, "Think of the New Sun, Alligator!" and chopped its head right off. It was *grand*.

Q: We almost reach a serious point here. The essence of comedy is timing, and the essence of timing is knowing when to stop. This must be the essence of comedy writing too.

Friesner: It depends on the type of comedy. But sometimes people get tired of a joke. You can't tell the same joke over and over unless you're making that movie, *The Aristocats*, I suppose. But there is always something new to write comedy about, because there is always something new that annoys me. Good comedy, as many people have said, makes you think about things. I always wind up citing Terry Pratchett, because he writes wonderful comedy, and it does make you think about certain things you've just kind of sailed through unconsciously in your day-to-day life. He actually makes you pay attention, and say, "Wait a minute. Is that right? Is that good? Why are we doing this again?"

But before Terry Pratchett, what my father used to read to me for bedtime stories was Walt Kelly's *Pogo*. And *Pogo*, some of it sailed right over my head, all of the stuff he wrote during the McCarthy Era. He had a character, a wildcat who was a caricature of Joseph McCarthy, known as Simple J. Malarkey who started a witch-hunt in the swamp. It was a blood-curdling thing if you knew what was going on in politics. But I was six years old or something, and I just thought it was funny. And then they had the Jack-Assed Society. I didn't know about the John Birch Society. I didn't know why my father was laughing hysterically reading about that. But there was enough for him to think about and appreciate, and for me to appreciate as a kid.

That's another thing about good comedy. Some things are "in" jokes. You can't do something solely based on an "in" joke unless you know that your entire audience is going to get the "in" joke. For instance, if you say "Red Shirts," from *Star Trek,* more and more people know the joke about the red shirts. Whoever wears the red shirt in classic *Star Trek* on an away mission, if he's not one of the main characters, that guy's not coming back. If you wear the red shirt, you're gonna die. Ensign Expendable.

This joke has gotten so accessible that on an episode of the cartoon show *Kim Possible*—it's always fun, though it is a repetitive gimmick where the characters get sucked into a television and go through all the shows. She winds up in a *Star Trek* type universe. She contacts the kid who is her anchorman. He is a prodigy at the computer. His name is Wade. She says, "I'm in some kind of sci-fi show and I am stuck in this shirt," and he says, "What color is it?" "Red." "Oh my God! I've got to get you out of there in a hurry!" And, apparently enough people know the red shirt joke. Years ago, there wouldn't have been enough people who did for it to work.

So you have to have something to make everyone laugh, those who know the "in" jokes, and those who don't know the "in" jokes.

Q: As we edge into satire, it would seem that a lot of successful comedy is complaint. Comedy is in effect the use of laughter to prevent things from becoming too bitter. You're talking about your curmudgeonly side. So, have you written a lot of comedy as a form of complaint?

Friesner: Oh, you bet. I am not particularly meek, but I am small and slow, so my ability to effect any sort of change could result in my getting hurt by the people I am complaining about. So, if I can't do anything else, I can at least point out some of the things I find to be ridiculous and hurtful.

One of the stories I wrote was called "'White,' Said Fred." I was driving home, listening to public radio, and they had a story about how in England skinheads were now not merely targeting Pakistani immigrants; they were targeting the children. These full grown men were harassing Pakistani schoolchildren.

I was livid. Now, obviously, even if I were in England, what could I do about it? I am not exactly the sort to go over to a skinhead and say, "And you must stop that now." So I just had to get rid of all the anger I felt about this, and I wrote "'White,' Said Fred," in which three skinheads, who are definitely "We are the master race" supremacists, find a genie in a bottle who turns out to be a skinhead as well, and he gives them the requisite three wishes. Of course they try to change the world to fit their prejudices, and hijinks ensue. I got to do dreadful things to them and that is the closest I'll ever come, but gosh, it was fun.

Q: Lately you're been writing lots of fiction based on Greek mythology. Would you say something about that?

Friesner: I don't know why, but I have lately been on quite the Helen of Troy kick, and other Greek mythology aside from Helen too. I don't know why. I think it might be, "Oh, I've got a new toy," or it might be that there is so little told about her. In the stories of the Trojan War she is portrayed as not much more than "This is the woman who started it all. She is so beautiful." Even at the end of the war her husband doesn't kill her when he gets her back, because she exposes her breasts to him, and he drops his sword. "Oh, ten years of war. You ran off with that guy. All these other guys are dead, but—wow!" He takes her back.

I wondered, first of all, is that all there is to her, just a pretty face and a pretty...what she exposed? I wanted to explore the character in both historical directions. I wrote a story called "Helen Remembers the Stork Club." I took Helen of Troy because she's half divine. Well, she probably wouldn't have died so young. So I said, "What happens to a woman whose whole identity is that of the most beautiful woman in the world, but she continues to age?" She doesn't age at the normal rate, but she does age. Now here she is in New York City where, if you are a woman of a certain age, people tend to turn you invisible on the street. They bump into you. What if you are that woman of a certain age, and you have been so beautiful that no one would dare overlook you? How does she cope with this new identity? It's almost like Gloria Swanson's role [Norma Desmond]in *Sunset Boulevard*. She used to be this gorgeous movie-star, glamorous, and now all she's got are her memories and her delusions. I did not turn Helen of Troy into Norma Desmond, but I had fun exploring how the character would deal with being there and being who she was and who she had been.

I am also doing the backstory of Helen of Troy, which hasn't been told. What we have of Helen's story, Troy aside, is her conception—Leda and the swan—her birth, coming out of an egg, and her twin, Clytemnestra, who was the only half divine. There were four children born of the union of Leda, Zeus, and Tyndareos of Sparta. Two of the children were Tyndareos's children. Two were Zeus's. So two of the twins were mortal: Helen's sister Clytemnestra, and I forget whether Castor of Polydeuces was the mortal of those two. But the other boy was, like Helen, half-divine.

Helen in the myths is abducted at a very young age by Theseus. She is about twelve years old, and in studying this I learned some kind of creepy (to modern sensibilities) facts. In one of the stories, by the time Helen has been rescued by her brothers from Theseus, she has borne Theseus a child, and that child is Iphigenia, who was sacrificed on the altar by Agamemnon, because Clytemnestra, Agamemnon's wife, adopted Iphigenia and raised her as her own daughter.

So I am sitting there saying, "Twelve years old. May have been all right then. Creepy now."

Q: A little early even then. They could have waited a couple more years.

Friesner: Yeah, still pretty creepy. So I wrote a story about Helen of Troy as a girl being abducted to Athens. I thought, well, you know, she's not a classical Spartan. She's not of the era of the Three Hundred. She is pre-classical. She is a Minoan-Mycenaean era Spartan. But I thought that maybe the whole thing of educating the daughters in throwing the javelin, the whole physical fitness thing, training them almost as much as they trained the boys—almost; the boys had it much harder. Maybe that didn't come out of nowhere. Maybe there was a tradition of giving the girls some kind of physical training. So I had Helen be beautiful, but why can you not be beautiful and smart? She's smart. She's got some idea of how to take care of herself physically. So instead of waiting for her brothers to rescue her from Theseus, she rescues herself.

This story was in the *Young Warriors* anthology from Random House, and I got a letter back saying, "We really liked the story. We'd love to see a novel." And now I have two novels about young Helen of Troy's backstory. One is called *Nobody's Princess* and the other is called *Nobody's Prize*. That's coming out this April. [2008—DS] And I've just had so much fun playing in the field of Greek mythology with Helen, giving her something more to do than just sitting around being beautiful and a pawn. She is an intelligent young girl and she has adventures.

Q: Are you going to take her into adulthood and retell the classical story?

Friesner: These are YA books, so nope, we stop it before she becomes an adult, before she gets married to Menelaus. But we did have Clytemnestra's first marriage, because I found, reading deeper into mythology, that Agamemnon was not Clytemnestra's first husband. She was first married...this gets into a very complicated thing. Let's just leave it at that before I tell the whole darn myth about the House of Atreus, which is definitely not YA material, a lot of that. It's bloody, scary stuff.

Q: There's the spike through the head—

Friesner: Not even that. There is the killing, cooking, and serving the sons of one of the two brothers [Thyestes and Atreus, who was the father of Menelaus and Agamenon] to their father. Thyestes is fed his own children and he doesn't know it until his brother tells him, "Oh, guess what you just ate." Not exactly your functional family. I think even Jerry Springer would be hard-pressed to deal with the House of Atreus.

Q: You could do another series, unless you're becoming typecast. I could see it happening that, from another publisher, you did an adult, bloody account of the House of Atreus, but there might be concern that the readers of the YA books or the librarians of the YA books might find the adult version and put it on the same shelf. Is this an actual concern when you become a YA author? You are known as "the Queen of Silly," I'll have you know. [Friesner laughs.] So, if you made such a departure, would you have to use another byline?

Friesner: My reputation seems to still be very much about the comedy. And yet I have almost a shadow-reputation of being able to write very dark things, or certainly serious, if not dark things. Both of my Nebula Award stories were dark stories, especially "A Birthday." That was super-dark. It was also about dealing with a social issue. I think that the whole worry about librarians putting a dark, scary, inappropriate book next to the rest comes down to the individual librarian. If the librarian is paying attention—I know they don't have time to read every single book that comes in—but if they just take the time to look at the precis of the plot that comes with the material, they'll make the right decision. I know they can do that. I trust the librarians.

Also, I don't think I'm getting typecast because I am doing another YA series about Nefertiti. Helen of Troy, I have written a story for YA. I have written a story for the general populace. I have written two YA novels. Now I want to do something else. I am moving on. No one can typecast me but me.

Q: All writers should agonize over the terrible nightmare that begins when somebody says, "Here's a half a million bucks. I want another one just like the last one, and another, and another." [Friesner laughs.] And it keeps going on. It is possible to be trapped by success. Perhaps both Edgar Rice Burroughs and Frank Herbert were.

Friesner: True, but you mention the nightmare of being trapped in the millions of dollars...well, look at J. K. Rowling. She said, "I'm going to be done at number 7." Now, granted, we don't know what will happen within the next ten years, but, so far, she seems to be sticking to her guns.

Q: She can't be tempted by a mere half million the way many of us could be.

Friesner: It really comes down to the personality and also the financial necessity of the author. One of my favorite things about D. H. Lawrence, and perhaps my only favorite thing about D. H. Lawrence was a little poem he wrote:

> He found the formula for drawing comic rabbits.
> The formula for drawing comic rabbits paid.
> So in the end he could not shake the tragic habits
> the formula for drawing comic rabbits made.

I think I'd get bored if I had to do the same thing. Yes, I'd like to have a half a million dollars. I'd like to have a million dollars. I could have an awful lot of fun with that kind of money. But if I am not enjoying what I am doing, it will show in what I am writing. If I am not having a good time, the reader will not have a good time. The reader will not buy the book and the next time they come around they're not going to say, "Here's a half a million dollars, or a million dollars. Do it again." Readers should be given credit for being smart. They know what's good. They know what's bad. People do not really want junk food. Sometimes they want a little candy, just a totally relaxing thing to read, no need to put in any critical input, but they don't want to be talked down to. They can *tell* when the author is just phoning it in, like "Here's the slop, give me my check." I don't want that done to me and I don't want it done to the readers. I'm a reader too.

Q: I am sure you would never never allow your books to be franchised out. That's when the tired hacks show up.

Friesner: Oh my gosh, I never even *thought* of that.

Q: In the World of Esther Friesner...

Friesner: Or even worse, can you imagine I'm dead and I'm V.C. Andrews. I'm dead and still the books come out. When you said being franchised, I was sitting there thinking, "Oh I'd love to have McDonald's toys and happy meals from one of my books," which probably wouldn't happen if I wrote the Dark House of Atreus. You wouldn't want to be eating any hamburger that came with the House of Atreus.

Q: I think a certain number of twelve or thirteen year old boys might go for that.

Friesner: And you're going to be wanting to watch those boys. Really watch them. But I think it would be great fun to see what they would do with a book of mine if they translated it to the screen. When *Who Framed Roger Rabbit?* came out, I went to see it. I bought the book. The book was quite different from the movie, and the author said he was really pleased with how they changed it. It was a good movie, different from the book but still good. I like happy surprises. I realize I might sit there and see one of my books up on the screen and it's just "What did they do to that?" or it could be, "Wow, that's pretty cool. I didn't know Johnny Depp could do that."

Q: Have you ever had any Hollywood interest, with or without Johnny Depp?

Friesner: I have had a couple of books optioned, but so far nothing has happened. But that's how it works. You get someone who says, "Hey, let's put on a show. My uncle has a barn," and then the uncle doesn't let them have the barn. I don't know all about how it works, but it's nice to think somebody thinks one of my books might make a good movie sometime.

Q: If you were to radically change direction again, have you any guesses as to where you might go? I can just imagine you as a hard-science writer. It would be interesting. [Friesner laughs.] How do you think Esther Friesner the *Analog* writer would be?

Friesner: Pretty much impossible. I'm not saying this because I'm a girl and I'm a blonde and as blonde Barbie girl says, "Math is *hard*," but I have so many things in my background that I already know about, and I never did very well in school in the hard sciences. I could see myself writing an *Analog* story in one of the so-called "soft" sciences, and I have done books using biology. But chemistry and physics.... I never took physics and in chemistry I managed blow up the impossible-to-explode oxygen-making setup experiment.

Q: I saw somebody do that when I was in high school.

Friesner: Oh *really?* This was great....

Q: The guy I saw do it brought down the overhead lights with the force of the blast and hurt himself.

Friesner: Wow. I didn't do that, but we did have flames shooting out of the mouth of the test tube and the teacher came over and said, "It appears you've had an accident here." That was when I thought, you know, I don't think I'm going to like chemistry very much. And I never took physics. My husband has despaired of me. He is very much into the hard sciences. "But...physics is *fun! Physics is so cool!"* You know, he said the same thing about calculus. I don't believe him very much.

Q: Maybe the approach to writing about science, and the way into *Analog,* would be satire.

Friesner: Really.

Q: *Analog* has always run funny stories, particularly in the Probability Zero department.

Friesner: I have found funny stuff in science before. Some of it is pseudo-science. When I get my hands on it I can get that science to pseudo up so fast it would make your head spin, as in the first thing I ever sold. Well, there's a device here. That's the core of the story. Granted, someone will never be able to come up with this technology, but you can't say we *never* will, can you? And it was a funny story.

I never know where I am going to go next, so maybe I would do a science story, although right now my latest reading for pleasure project, which is usually where I wind up getting my ideas from, is alternating between reading Marcel Proust's *Remembrance of Things Past* in English translation—my French is good but not that good—and finally reading through the entire Bible. I have decided to read a chapter a day and really pay attention to some of the things that are said. Since I've never done it. I've read spottily through the Old Testament and *very* spottily through the New Testament. Now I am going to read the whole thing, including all of those "And so-and-so begat so-and-so..."

So far I have actually come up with the idea that if they can calculate the date of creation, as Bishop Usher did, then they can certainly calculate the date on which the Ark finally landed. Why don't celebrate Ark Landing Day? And somebody said, "Yes, that would be May 5th." So happy Ark Landing Day, everybody. It's just full of ideas. It's wonderful. So, I'm not reading anything in science that is inspiring me at the moment. Marcel Proust and the Bible.

Q: Which is funnier?

Friesner: I'm the girl who found a comedy moment in *Moby Dick*. And it was supposed to be a comedy moment too. I wasn't just pulling it out of thin air. The chowder scene. It's pretty funny. In *Moby Dick* it is all by itself and very sad and lonesome, but it is a comedy moment. So I really don't know. I am going through them both very, very slowly. But it's rich reading. I'm enjoying it. I think that's the key to what I do. I enjoy what I do. I like writing even when it's hard. It's like solving a puzzle. I don't consider it to be a chore. I don't consider it to be a stern duty. It's fun.

Q: What are your actual writing methods like. [Friesner laughs.] I collect them as a hobby...

Friesner: Not particularly anything fancy. I will sometimes get an idea out of a weird title. A title will pop into my head or present itself to me by the strangest means. The first time I won a Nebula Award it was for "Death and the Librarian." I got the idea for the title because Terry Pratchett gave me two little pewter figurines. They were about an inch and a half high, from Diskworld. One was of Death and one was of the orangutan who is the Librarian. And I go, "Ooh! Death and the Librarian! Thank you!" And then I sat there and the words just echoed. I thought, that's a good title, "Death and the Librarian."

The story that I wrote couldn't have anything to do with

Diskworld; but it was not dark, but an emotional piece. It was the sort of story where when I stop reading it in public and look up, there are people weeping. So it does what it is intended to do. But my method is that sometimes I start with a title, and decide, "Well, what can I hang off this title?"

Sometimes I start with an idea and I flesh the idea out, and if it doesn't work, you can throw it out. I bless the day they made word-processors, because in the old days I would write something on a typewriter and being pretty lazy I'd say, "Yeah, that'll do," even though it could have stood a rewrite. I think I am writing much better now that I can rewrite easily.

Q: That may depend on how you do your rewrites. I actually had to learn to rewrite on a computer.

Friesner: Oh....

Q: My method involved typing one draft, and then marking it up and the retyping the entire thing, to gain a certain creative momentum. It is the difference between saying, "Remember that joke I told last night? The punchline should have been this ___" and telling the joke again, with all the timing and gestures in place. I went through a transitional stage where I would write the first draft on a typewriter, and then do this creative rewrite on the computer. So did you find that your actual methods changed when you switched to computer?

Friesner: I don't think so. I always was a child of the keyboard. I never wrote in longhand. My parents always let me near the family typewriter and didn't care what I did. So my handwriting stinks and it is slow, so I don't think writing has changed that much, except that it's so much easier to move the block of text here where it should be, or take things out. But sometimes I'll miss something when I am rereading on the screen. You can't do the riffle through the pages. But if that were really to adversely affect the writing, I will just have a printout and riffle through the pages and say, "Okay, this should have gone there." I've just gotten used to it. I haven't noticed a change. I haven't had a problem. The only change I have noticed is that it is so much easier.

Q: I always tell new writers that if you can't write a novel with a pencil, you can't write one with a computer, but if you can the computer's output will be a whole lot neater. What would be your sage advice for beginners?

Friesner: Okay...there is a lot of sage advice, but it is not the advice of absolutes. When you are a writer you have to be very sensitive and observant, because if you are not you won't be able to create characters except for walking yourself through things. You will not be able to think, how would someone who is not at all like me act? I have had some characters in my stories who are just monstrous beings doing things I would never do in my life, but I can imagine how they would do it. But you also have to have something of a tough skin, because writing, especially if you want to have it published professionally, brings rejection. I have been writing since I was about three years old, telling stories, having my mom write them down. But when I started sending stories out, I'd get a rejection and I'd stop writing for months, because I thought "They hate me." No they didn't. They just didn't like the story. So you have to get over that. You have to be persistent, but you shouldn't be pig-headed. You can stand there and say, "Oh, they don't like me because they're stupid and horrible and evil," or you can sit there and reread what you have written and say, "You know, this could have been better. Let me try a different way."

So it's a balancing act. You have to know yourself, and you have to be willing to face truths about yourself. You also have to pay attention to the fact that writing is an art, but it's also a craft. You may have written the most beautiful thing, but if you are sending it out to an editor, well, do you know who many manuscripts most editors have to go through? You had better know how to make a professional-looking manuscript. You have to be able to know that your writing may be special and you may be a special human being, but there is no special treatment for you when it comes to submitting. If they say "No e-mail submissions," yes, they mean you. No e-mail submissions. They're not going to make an exception. They're very, very busy. Writing is an art, writing is a craft, and writing is a *business*. Sometimes very fine writing does not get published because the people who are in charge of publication don't consider it to be commercially viable. How are you going to get paid if they're not earning money selling stuff people want to buy?

I always used to love the idea of being just the writer as artist, but the reality is that you have to be artist, craftsman, and business person. You have to be able to hear no, and you have to be able to say, "No this time, but maybe next time yes. What can I do to get to that yes?" I think you have to like what you are doing, because if you are only writing so you will be rich and famous, and you don't like writing, if you don't enjoy it, it's going to show. People have their own troubles. They are not going to want to be *not* entertained by what you have set in front of them.

Q: Thank you, Esther.

(Recorded at Lunacon, March 16, 2008.)

KRISTINE KATHRYN RUSCH

[Note: This interview was done for the DNA Publications website, just as Rusch's "Flower Fairies" appeared in the October 2009 issue of *Realms of Fantasy*.]

Q: Would you tell the readers what is the background of "Flower Fairies"? How did it come to be written?

Rusch: I dreamed the opening. That almost never happens any more, but this one did, and the story happened very fast after that.

Q: When your subconscious just heaves up an opening like that—*i.e.*, in a dream—what then? How deliberate is the construction of a story for you?

Rusch: Not deliberate at all. I just followed the image where it took me. I generally do that. I get an opening and I continue to write.

Q: Now, you say you start with the image (that in this case came in a dream) and just follow it where it goes. I, as a writer, have some sense of what this process is like, but I am not sure that our readers do. Is this free-form association? Like dreaming on paper? How practiced (or deliberate) is the technique?

Rusch: Well, writing a story itself is a learned technique, but the hardest part of the technique is to then forget everything you learned and trust the process. If you think too hard about it, you'll screw it up. So basically, I tell myself a story. In this case, I wanted to know why that little girl fairy was in a flower arrangement in a funeral home. As I kept answering the questions, more arose, until I had answers—and a story.

Q: Do you have time to write many stories between your numerous novels? Do you have to deliberately schedule short-story writing time?

Rusch: Sometimes I do have to schedule short-story writing time. I write stories between novels. I also write stories to deadline—which I find fun. I often write for anthologies to have the deadline and the challenge of writing about a particular topic. I feel that it stretches me.

Q: What sort of fiction would you *prefer* to be writing, all other things (like the money) being equal?

Rusch: I write what I feel like writing that day. I never write for money (not anymore). I already write what I prefer to write. What I would prefer is to hit the *New York Times* list with a novel or two, but that hasn't happened yet and is wildly out of my control.

Q: You're a writer who has written in a broad range of genres, so you may have a good sense of what the market wants today. Do you have any sense that, as some people argue, fantasy is beginning to displace science fiction in the marketplace? I note that just this year, for the second time, a YA fantasy novel won a Hugo. Some of the hard-science types are beginning to circle the wagons. What is your opinion of all this?

Rusch: I just wrote a column on that in IROSF. It's easier to point it out than it is to reiterate. http://www.irosf.com/q/zine/article/10569.

Q Your article on the *Internet Review of SF* raises a further question. Do you make a distinction between actual *forms* of writing—in the sense that an epic is not a ballad—and marketing categories? Is there actually a distinct form called science fiction and another one called fantasy, which exist regardless of how they are packaged?

Rusch: Hmmm. Not sure I entirely understand your question, which is probably an answer in and of itself. But I'll give it a whirl. I think all fiction—even mimetic fiction as John Gardner and the mainstreamers like to call it—is fantasy. After all, it's made up. So it's not real. Which makes it, by definition, fantasy.

The categories differ if you're talking to professors or you're talking to marketing. Professors also use the old-fashioned tragedy and comedy definitions—comedy not being something that's funny, but something with a happy ending. So it can get confusing.

As for marketing categories, they're always shifting too. I recently talked to the head of a fantasy book line and she told me that they can't take any stories set in the country or rural areas. Nor do they take alternate world fantasy (what we used to call traditional/high fantasy). In other words, they only take fantasy set in cities in modern times, probably with a kick-ass heroine. To me, that's a subset of fantasy. Call it urban fantasy or contemporary fantasy (the 1990s term), but it's a subset. For this publisher, it's their entire "fantasy" book line.

As you can tell, I'm not a big fan of categorizing fiction. I don't write only in one category and I don't read in one. I actually feel sad for folks who only read one genre. They're missing so much good stuff! Of course, the other side of this is that I get overwhelmed whenever I go into a bookstore. So many books, so little time. I envy my sister, who recently retired. When asked how she's spending her retirement, she answers, "I'm reading."

All day. Every day. If only.

Q: As to form, I am making a distinction between literary form and a marketing category. It seems to me that there are distinct forms. When Shakespeare was writing *Hamlet* he knew he was writing not just a verse play but a revenge tragedy (a genre form) which imposed certain requirements on him, particularly as to the development of the plot. When Virgil was writing the *Aeneid* he knew he was writing an epic, which observed specific conventions. A sonnet is a distinct form, in a very technical sense. fifteen lines and it is not a sonnet. It may be a good poem, but it is not a sonnet. A detective story observes certain conventions. If there is no crime and no detection, then it is not a detective story. In each case the writer is conscious of the form before starting to write.

So, is there a form that can be called "science fiction," possibly a subset of fantasy, quite irrespective of marketing strategies? When you suggest that science fiction may come to an end soon, do you mean that the literary form itself has exhausted itself in the same sense that, say, the lost race novel has, or that the marketing strategy of putting a rocketship on the cover and the words "science fiction" on the spine no longer sells books?

Rusch: I think science fiction will always be a literary form and is more viable now than ever in that capacity. The mainstream market uses SF a lot, witness Cormac McCarthy and Audrey Niffenegger. Not to mention Jasper Fforde and others. Science fiction is everywhere, but the marketing category is in trouble, and I think we did it to ourselves, unfortunately.

Q: As for that editor who only wants fantasy set in urban settings with a kick-ass heroine, this seems awfully narrow-minded, don't you think? Would this editor have rejected *The Lord of the Rings*? After all, it's mostly rural in its settings and features a kick-ass heroine (Eowyn) only incidentally. This sounds like the very worst sort of bottom-line editing.

Rusch: Well, yes, and no. Right now, urban fantasy with kick-butt heroines is hot, and that's what this particular line is chasing. And yes, if they'd gotten *The Lord of the Rings*, they would have rejected it in a heartbeat. But fortunately, other publishers have a fuller-fledged fantasy line, and would still buy *The Lord of the Rings*. I think it has always been thus, and always will be. Some publishers will embrace narrow marketing structures (the easier for the sales force) and others will have a broader view.

Q: If all New York publishing becomes like this—prose television, chasing the latest trend—doesn't this leave a huge opening for independent publishers like Small Beer, Night Shade, or Tachyon? Where does the genuinely innovative or even just sincere writer turn? You might have some insight on this, as you were deeply involved in independent publishing at one point through Pulphouse.

Rusch: I think the innovative writer must always look outside one particular genre and try to find the innovative publishing houses. Those houses aren't always small, btw. I'm seeing a lot of creativity in some bigger houses on the mainstream level right now, a willingness to incorporate genre trends from all the genres, so long as the writing is good and the characterization stellar. YA in particular seems to embrace everything.

I often think specialty publishers point the way. What they do is prove audience. Once an audience is established, the writer can sell the book to the bigger presses. Websites will do that now as well and so, oddly enough, can self-publishing. It couldn't in the past, but with the internet, people from all over the world can find a self-published book. So access is changing, and that's a good thing, I think.

Q: So, tell me something about the beginnings of your career. How long have you been writing?

Rusch: Oh, sadly, I've been writing since I was seven years old. When I turned twelve, my wonderful brother gave me a subscription to *Writer's Digest*. I've been paid for my writing since I was sixteen and started writing the high school news column for the local paper. I'm an early bloomer as a writer, selling my first major short story at twenty-five (I sold others to small presses in college) and my first novel at twenty-nine.

The upshot of all of that is that the field has known me for more than twenty years now, and everyone thinks I'm an old fart. I'm only a middle-aged fart, with at least another thirty years ahead of me. Bob Silverberg and I have discussed this, since he's gone through the same thing, and he finds it as amusing and frustrating as I do.

I feel like a Monty Python character—"Not dead yet!" she writes, shaking her pen at people. "Not dead yet!"

Q: If the category is in trouble because of what "we" did, what do you think we did? Pursued short-term profits at the expense of long-term growth?

Rusch: A lot has changed in the past ten years, Darrell. A lot has changed in the world. Science fiction is everywhere—in commercials, in romance novels, in movies (all the biggest movies are SF), in television. *The Big Bang Theory* makes SF references all the time and expects the audience to understand them.

So why isn't SF the marketing category selling well? Because the SF community made SF a closed system. We made people think it's hard. My professor sister, who gave me *Flowers for Algernon* and several other SF books because she liked them, was asked to teach an SF course at her college when her colleagues found out I was an SF writer. She called me in a panic, telling me she never read SF. It was too hard, too hard to understand, too boring. And yet, she had read a lot more SF than I had. She had just discovered it outside the category.

Her reaction is pretty typical. A lot of people think SF the genre category is a tough read. We did that. By saying that no one can use the old tropes, that books must build on previously published things (out of print for fifty years!) and by using jargon instead of clear language.

Q: Sure Cormac McCarthy's *The Road* is SF, but has much changed then? SF, at least by approved writers, has always been able to sneak into the mainstream, as long as you don't call it SF. Thus critics have go to great lengths to explain why *Brave New World* or *A Clockwork Orange* or *Riddley Walker* not SF. This is a combination of snobbery and a marketing strategy, but do you think it still works? Would the same science fiction novel, published as mainstream, sell more copies than if it were published in category? Do you think that would work with one of your books?

Rusch: Wow. Lots of questions here, Darrell, many of which I've covered in columns, articles, and essays, including "Barbarian Confessions" in Asimov's http://www.asimovs.com/_issue_0612/thoughtexperiments.shtml, and more recently in an internet review of science fiction column http://www.irosf.com/q/zine/article/10569. I've written about this a lot, and would rather have people look at the entire arguments than distill them too much in an interview.

So...could one of my SF books sell well in the mainstream? Now, yes. The Retrieval Artist series has a lot of mainstream/mystery readers. It would have more, but it was marketed into SF ten years ago. I suspect some mystery editors would take a plunge with the series now.

And—my alternate history story, "G-Men," published in *Sideways in Crime*, is in the prestigious mainstreamy *Best American Mystery Stories 2009*. The mainstream/mystery/other marketing categories have accepted SF if it's understandable and readable to people who weren't raised in the genre.

Would McCarthy's book sell to an SF audience? That's a "Huh?" question as far as I'm concerned. Why would he want to? Let's see—sell one million plus copies all over the world or

10,000 copies in the U.S. Which audience would anyone want?

Q: Or does "mainstream SF" have different requirements and actually constitute a different genre?

Rusch: No.

Q: Do you think it possible that in the near future Science Fiction will be subsumed into Fantasy, the way that, forty years or so ago, Fantasy was a small subset of the Science Fiction category? (This sure sounds like Gregory Benford's worst nightmare, doesn't it?)

Rusch: Possible. I doubt it though. I think the SF category will go the way of the western, which means it'll be hard to find, read by die-hards, and SF itself will be scattered throughout the bookstore in other genres—unless the gatekeepers, the editors and publishers, start making SF accessible again and somehow convince readers to go back to the SF aisle in the bookstore.

YA may prove me wrong here. SF growth in YA is astounding, and those editors aren't in the mainstream of SF. They understand that sometimes the old tropes are the best tropes. Plus the stories are accessible and they have voice, something SF lost in the past thirty years (or maybe never really had, except for folks like Douglas Adams).

Q: Tell me a little bit about your days as editor of *F&SF*. What impact do you think you had on the field? How did the experience impact you as a writer?

Rusch: I don't know about the impact I had on the field. That's for others to decide. Maybe it came in all the new writers whose first stories I bought at *F&SF* and *Pulphouse*. Many of those writers are still working in the genre.

As for me, I learned all kinds of business things—the economics of publishing, how editors/publishers think, why rejection isn't personal. I also realized that writers can be real dumb, and the ones who had no idea of business were the worst. I have a mountain of bad-behaving writer stories, many from some well-known names, stories I'll never share outside of a private conversation.

I also have a lot of respect for the editors and publishers toiling in the field. Even though I say that the gatekeepers need to open the gates and I criticize the way the SF category has been going, I still know how hard it is every single day for editors to get the work done, for publishers to sell books and still make a profit. I know these folks are in the business for the love of it, just like writers are.

Q: But surely there IS some difference in the requirements between SF for a mainstream audience and that for the (possibly shrinking) core audience. You've said as much yourself, where you observe that much SF has made itself closed-off and boring to outsiders. For example, an opening line like "The jumpship dropped out of null-space three parsecs from Rigel IV" isn't going to work in a story aimed at a mainstream audience, particularly in the story itself is an answer to something H. Beam Piper wrote in *Analog* in 1962. So how do you solve the accessibility problem? "Good writing" would not seem to be enough.

Rusch: My bad. I didn't define good writing. To me, "good writing" is clear and understandable. That sentence you quoted is only understandable to a small subset of the SF audience, therefore it fails the good writing test. If you're going to introduce words like "jumpship" and "null-space," don't do it all in one sentence. Do it in a page or so, and explain a little.

The only folks who can get away with something like that are people who write thirty-five-book series, and they think their readers know all this stuff already. (That's why the later books in a fantasy series are often inaccessible to new readers.)

SF has done this for far too long, and it should really stop. Have some respect for your audience. Not everyone has combed used bookstores for iconic novels before they approached yours.

Q: As for mainstream audiences vs. SF audiences and their relative sizes, it can work in reverse. James Morrow described to me in an early interview how he was published as mainstream, reviewed in *Newsweek* and in other places that would never review SF, but he didn't actually sell very many books until *This Is the Way the World Ends* reprinted by the SF Book Club and the science fiction audience discovered him. And any SF fan has whole shelves of rare and half-forgotten and often brilliant SF or fantasy novels which cannot be reprinted these days because the author is forgotten in the mainstream and lacks sufficient genre recognition. Examples that come to mind include *Limbo* by Bernard Wolfe and *The Unfortunate Fursey* by Mervyn Wall. I have a lot more. Mary Doria Russell's *The Sparrow* may fall into this category within twenty years. David Hartwell pointed out in a recent issue of *The New York Review of Science Fiction* [Aug. 2009] that even so famous a "mainstream" work as T. H. White's *The Once and Future King* crossed over into the fantasy genre sometime in the 1970s and is now found in the fantasy section of the bookstore. The implication is that if this had not happened, it might be out of print. So aren't there times when being recognized as part of the SF genre club is actually to the writer's advantage?

Rusch: There's an assumption to your question, Darrell, that these genres are static. Jim Morrow's experience from twenty-five years ago is irrelevant today. If he had published that book now, he'd probably do a lot better in the mainstream than in SF. In fact, it seems to me, his latest books have more mainstreamy covers than SF covers.

Why is T. H. White mainstream? I found his book in the fantasy section as a kid. My copy of that book looks like Tolkien, and I have had it since the early 1970s. Marketing is marketing is marketing—which I need to remind our readers is what we're talking about. We need to get folks into our section of the bookstore or, failing that, we need to position our books in other parts of the store. I'm making the assumption that the books we all like are high quality. Just not easy to find.

Q: T. H. White is or was mainstream because he was originally published that way. The paperbacks from the '60s often mention the musical *Camelot* in their blurbs, but never Tolkien. The hardcovers to this day—since Putnam never changed the jacket—are decidedly mainstream. There was no fantasy category in the '50s. The edition you're describing is clearly a post-crossover, "fantasy" one. The current Ace edition describes the book as the "gold standard" by which all fantasy novels are measured. When the first edition came out, the concept of a "fantasy novel" would not have been understood. Indeed, in the early '70s Lin Carter told me that he had a great deal of trouble getting the concept of "adult fantasy" across, even to many of the writers who submitted manuscripts to him.

Rusch: That's because in the 1920s, fantasy/fairy tales became relegated to children's literature. Of course, in the 1920s, the concept of children's literature was born as a marketing concept.

If what you say about T. H. White is true, then entire generations of SF/F readers probably never read him. The lines between marketing genres were a lot more solid in those days. So no wonder he had a revival in the 1990s, when the fantasy audience discovered him.

That's the key: getting discovered by your audience, whatever it is.

Q: Maybe you're not quite old enough to remember what it was like to be a fantasy reader before there was a genre. I barely am. A science fiction reader before about 1970 had a clearly labeled product. A fantasy reader did not. One of the key skills for any fantasy reader was finding the fantastic in books not ostensibly labeled. A few were disguised as science fiction, such as de Camp's *The Incomplete Enchanter*, a few were published as children's books, like *A Wizard of Earthsea*, but most fantasy was to be found, unlabelled, in the mainstream. You had to *know* that T. H. White or James Branch Cabell or Lord Dunsany were fantasy writers. This was precisely the skill Lin Carter utilized to create the Ballantine Adult Fantasy Series, and from that, the fantasy category. Before that, there were few guidelines. The Anthony Boucher's book reviews in *F&SF* in the '50s made a point of mentioning fantasy published in the mainstream, including first-publication reviews of some obscure, non-genre trilogy by a certain Professor Tolkien, which didn't become a fantasy category item until a decade later.

Rusch: You're right, Darrell. I don't think I bought my own books before 1970. I was ten in 1970 and read everything in the house. (Imagine my mother's dismay when she caught me reading Harold Robbins at nine.) My parents were not SF/F readers. My sister was, but didn't know it. She sent me books all the time. In fact, she's the one who gave me *The Once and Future King*, as well as C. S. Lewis, *The Wind in the Willows*, and *The Lord of the Rings* (although she gave me that when I was in high school—winter of 1977, to be exact, because I had mono and read the entire thing with a 103 temperature).

I did read a lot of gothics and ghost stories and books like *The Witch of Blackbird Pond* [by Elizabeth George Speare], but I can't remember buying a fantasy novel until I was in high school at least. Which corresponds to what you're saying here. I do remember the scandal when Terry Brooks hit the *Times* list, so I was in the genre at that point—or I was at least dabbling in it.?

Q: So, what are you working on now? What can readers expect from you in the near future?

Rusch: I'm doing a lot of short fiction right now. So go to the magazines, folks! Look at my website for current news.

My next novel is SF, however. It's called *Diving into the*

Wreck, and it has one of the greatest covers I've seen. I'd buy this book based on the cover, even if I didn't know the author. (I'm thrilled. It's a modern Andre Norton cover—and representative of the book.) [To be published by Pyr, November 2009.]

Readers can expect the unexpected from me, as usual. Different genres. Different lengths. Different styles. Impossible to pin down. That's me.

Q: Thanks Kris.

HARRY TURTLEDOVE

Q: How did you turn out to be a fiction writer and not a historian? Which came first, the desire to write fiction or the degree in Byzantine history?

Turtledove: The desire to write fiction came first. I have the degree because I was an sf reader. I found a copy of Sprague de Camp's *Lest Darkness Fall* in a secondhand bookstore when I was fourteen or fifteen, and got hooked trying to find out how much of the story was real (most of it) and how much he was making up (very little, it turned out). After flunking out of Caltech at the end of my freshman year, I ended up earning the Byzantine history degree at UCLA...and my dissertation ran a year later than it might have, because I was working on the first novel that sold at the same time, and also on the piece that became my first short-fiction sale (to David Hartwell's *Cosmos*, which expired before the story saw print, though I did get a check).

Q: So, did your fellow graduates regard you as the guy who broke free and got to do something more fun? Or did they figure you had made a frivolous use of your education?

Turtledove: I'm still friends with a couple of the people with whom I went to grad school. Another guy bailed out of the program after getting his master's to try to make it as an opera singer. He didn't, but he met his wife while performing in a musical, so he figures it was worthwhile—he ended up in the computer world. My buddies are bemused, but they're pleased I found a way to make a living at least partly related to what I studied.

And what goes around comes around. I was speaking about how I researched my straight historical novel, *Justinian* (with the H. N. Turteltaub byline—old H. N. looks a lot like me, poor sap), at a Byzantine studies conference at UCLA around the turn of the century, and after I got done this grad student came up to me. He said he got interested in Byzantine history through my alternate history, *Agent of Byzantium*. So, just as de Camp warped my life all those years before, I messed up this fellow's. Writers can be dangerous people.

Q: How do professional historians regard alternate history fiction?

Turtledove: Well, what historians call "counterfactuals" are popular these days. The real historians have realized that looking at what might have been can help illuminate what really happened and why it happened. I don't mean to sound disrespectful—mmm, maybe I do, a little—but to me "counterfactuals" are like alternate history without characterization.

Q: You wrote as Eric Iverson for a while. Why was that?

Turtledove: Back at the end of the 1970s, I sold my first sword-and-sorcery novel to Belmont-Tower Books, and the editor there renamed me: she said no one would believe Turtledove, which is my real name. I kept the pen name for a while, as I was also publishing some academic nonfiction, and I thought having one name for each might be useful. Then I sold the four books of *The Videssos Cycle* to Lester del Rey. He said that if I wanted to be Iverson, he wouldn't buy them—he claimed people would remember Turtledove much better. Since I had exactly no leverage, I yielded. It's worked out all right, but I may be the only writer in captivity to have his pen name and his own name imposed on him.

Q: Did you always assume that you'd write fiction based on history, or did That just work out that way? For example, I thought as a teenager that I would be a proper science fiction writer and write about spaceships and time-travel and the like, and that is not what has happened at all. The desire to write was there before I really found my subject matter. Was it that way with you?

Turtledove: When I was fourteen or fifteen, my sf was full of spaceships and post-atomic-war futures. I've done regular sf professionally, too, in a couple of novels and quite a bit of short fiction (I've got a twenty-second-century novelette under submission right now). But the first novel I finished—I must've been sixteen—was an (unpublishable) alternate history, and the larger part of what I've done since has dealt with history one way or another ever since.

Q: A friend of mine stubbornly refuses to read alternate histories at all. His objection is that the change made by the author (so-and-so didn't win the battle, somebody died prematurely, or whatever) is arbitrary, and this leads to a whole series of equally arbitrary changes, particularly involving famous people. He then cannot escape the sense of the story being transparently made up, and cannot get involved in it emotionally. How would you answer this?

Turtledove: Fiction is not about the created world. Let me say that again: no fiction is about the created world. Fiction is about the world the author lives in, and reflects the concerns of the author and his or her culture. What's fun and interesting about alternate history is that it lets us look at our world in a funhouse mirror we can't get any other way. And I'm sorry for your friend, because she or he is missing some marvelous books, from *The*

Man in the High Castle to the recent and splendid *The Yiddish Policeman's Union*. If your friend can look at this world the same way after reading those, I'd be very surprised.

Q: By "created world" I assume you mean the objectively real world. You're saying that all fiction is a matter of an author's individual perspective then? I wonder about some pulp super-hacks who did their best to suppress all individuality and write absolutely what the market wanted. (H. Bedford Jones or Arthur J. Burks, for example.) Of course they didn't write about the objectively real world either, but instead used agreed-upon formulas to pretend to describe it. It is a fine philosophical point. If no fiction actually describes the objective world, but instead it is a matter of the author's personal "headspace" (to use an archaic, '60s term), then possibly the difference between compelling fiction and dull, routine fiction is only a matter of the author's passion and sincerity. Yes? No? Have I gone off the deep end here?

Turtledove: By "real world" I mean the objectively real world. By "created world" I mean the one the author writes about. To my way of thinking, all fiction-writing is in created worlds, but all writing is about the real world. The difference between dull fiction and interesting fiction is a matter of how well it's done. One can certainly be passionate and inept at the same time; indeed, that's depressingly common. Anna Russell's comment regarding opera was, "You can do *anything*—as long as you sing it." Same goes with fiction—you've gotta sing it, or all you have is a boat that won't float.

Q: I think my difficult friend IS missing some great fiction, but I can see part of his point. I have certainly read alternate histories which lost my interest quickly because they seemed to be about a clever schematic diagram and forgot the human drama. So, how do you get an alternate history story to work? Or, I suppose, what are the unique qualities which made it a different kind of drama? You could write a straight war story about courage, heroism, loss, treachery, political stupidity etc. etc. and just use a real, historical war as the background. The emotions and the personal experiences of most of the characters will be all there. So, when does the story demand that you depart from the consensus historical background and take an alternative course?

Turtledove: Most of the tricks that apply to a-h stories apply to any stories. You've got to have reasonably good writing, characters the reader can care about, and an interesting plot. The particular attraction of a-h, as I've said before, is that it lets you look at real-world people and events and their consequences and influences in a way you can't do with other kinds of fiction. You can either make the world that you want, and then reason backwards to see how it might have arisen or change something and see what might have come from that. (Notice I say "might," not "would": the most you can aspire to is plausibility, not certainty. People have been known to miss this point.) I usually prefer the second method, but the first can also work—see Steve Barnes' *Zulu Blood* and sequels.

Q: I suppose the distinction is between story and idea. How do you develop a counterfactual idea (which could be expressed in an essay) into a counterfactual *story*?

Turtledove: The same way you turn any idea into a story. You find characters and plot to make the reader care about what's happening. If you can't find those, the idea sits in your file for years and doesn't become anything. I had a Post-It with a note about a world where Ptolemaic astronomy and Aristotelean physics were true. It never became more than a note, because I couldn't see how to flesh it out. And I sure won't now, because Richard Garfinkle wrote *Celestial Matters* and did it for me. He found a way to make the idea work, and more power to him.

Q: You've also, intriguingly, done a series of what might be called alternate natural history stories. I am thinking of *A World of Difference* with its depiction of an early America in habited by homo erectus or the one in the recent *Space & Time* ["Moso," in issue 104], which seems to be set in a more or less contemporary (or recent) Africa, save that there are sabertooth tigers. I'm not quite sure what one can call these. Are you inventing a new genre?

Turtledove: I've done more of that kind of story than the ones you name. I also wrote "Down in the Bottomlands," the novella about the world where the Mediterranean never refilled after drying up 5,000,000 years ago; *A World of Difference*, about a different planet in the fourth orbit; and the current Atlantis books, where much of eastern North America rifted away from the rest of the continent 85,000,000 years ago, producing an enormous island in the Atlantic uninhabited by man till Europeans found it in the mid-fifteenth century. The novellas "Audubon in Atlantis" and "The Scarlet Band" are set in that world, as are *Opening Atlantis* (out last year), *The United States of Atlantis* (due out in December) and *Liberating Atlantis* (almost done).

Did I invent this kind of world? Nah. Harry Harrison's *Eden* books and the Garfinkle I mentioned above use the trope, and they're far from the only ones. Physical changes can be as interesting as political ones.

Q: Nevertheless, you seem to be drawn to a different form of SF than most writers: not "what might be" but "what might have been." You've made yourself the master of this in the same way Asimov made himself master of the robot story, but we inevitably wonder: does the possible future not hold equal charms for you?

Turtledove: I dunno; if I get a future idea that seems interesting, I'll write it. But since I'm a trained historian who wants to write sf, what I'm doing now seems the way to go as often as not. There's only so much any one person can do in his or her lifetime. Right this minute, I'm having fun doing what I'm doing.

Q: I note you've written about what I'd call the Big Three in American alternate history subjects: the Civil War, World War II, and the Roman/Byzantine Empire. (For British writers, the preoccupation seems to be the *Pavane* or *The Alteration* scenario: a Catholic Britain.) Do you do this with a sense that you're going to have to top all previous writings on the subject?

Turtledove: I hope I'm not that immodest. You do the best you can; that's all you can do. (By the way, in *Ruled Britannia*, I've had a whack at the Brits' obsession, too.)

Q: So what gave you the impulse to toss an alien invasion into World War II, which created the WORLDWAR series?

Turtledove: I got the idea for that one back in the 1970s. Didn't write it then because I was convinced—accurately, I think—I didn't know enough and wasn't anywhere nearly good enough to bring it off. The thinking was something along these lines.... An industrialized planet probably isn't as easy to conquer from space as most people make it out to be. What's the most interesting industrialized planet? Why, Earth. When? How about when World War II was at its most even point in late spring 1942, before the Japanese wreck themselves at Midway and the Germans at Stalingrad? That seemed to work, even though it was in a horribly challenging period: within living memory but not within mine. So, after I finished *Guns of the South*, I thought, if I can't bring it off now, I'll probably never be able to. I gave it my best shot, and most people seem to enjoy the story.

Q: A lot of alternate history seems to be about war, doesn't it? I suppose this is a natural tendency because most of the dramatic hinge-points in history seem to have a war involved. But of course there are other possibilities too. If you were asked to write a story for an anthology *Alternate History Not About War*, what would you write about?

Turtledove: I have no idea what I'd write about. I'd probably change either geography or religion. War is a good subject for a-h, though, partly because it offers plausible scenarios for how things might have gone differently, and partly because the two things that best illuminate character under stress are love and the threat of getting killed in the next few seconds.

Q: I note your most latest book, *The Man with the Iron Heart,* is based on the premise the Heinrich Heydrich, the infamous Nazi "Hangman," was not assassinated, but lived to lead Nazi terrorst resistance after the defeat of Germany. This leads to a matter I am sure you have pondered at considerable length, both as a historian and as a writer of alternate history. What do you think of the "Great Man" theory of history? How much of history turns on the presence or absence of a single person motivated and talented enough to bring about change, and how much is a confluence of circumstances? Heydrich would be a particularly sinister example. You posit that his individual survival would have made a huge difference.

Turtledove: Depending on story purposes, I can be persuaded to stand almost anywhere on the line between the overwhelming influence of the one Great Man and his impotence struggling against vast socioeconomic forces. In the real world, I think the latter tend to win more often than not...but this would be a different-looking place if, say, the assassination attempt on Philip of Macedon had failed, curtailing Alexander the Great's career. There are times when one man *can* make a difference, and there are men who will find a way to make a difference. Maybe not so many, but some, I think.

Q: Have you read Stephen Vincent Benét's "The Curfew Tolls"?

This strikes me as a superb meditation on this theme. (It shows Napoleon, born a generation too soon, frustrated because he never got to do very much, and now at retirement age right as the French Revolution breaks out.)

Turtledove: Haven't run into that one. A similar meditation from within our own field is H. Beam Piper's "And He Walked Around the Horses." I wonder if Piper had seen the Benét story you describe.

Q: Well I'm not a big believer in "chaos theory" as applied to human events, but I think that if I were asked to write an alternate history not about war, I'd try to find some subtle but genuine change like the sort of thing they brought out on the TV show *Connections*. Isn't part of the fun of alternate history evoking a reaction of "What?" followed by "Why, of course."

Turtledove: Everything is "Why, of course"—in retrospect. The question is, does it happen cause it's railroad time, as Charles Fort said, or because somebody's foxier than all his neighbors? And the answer, from here, is, I dunno. Both, I suspect. Sometimes the timing is crucial, as when the Spaniards hit the Incas in the midst of the latter's dynastic strife. Of course, one of the things that occasioned the strife was the advent of smallpox, brought from places where the Spaniards had been before. As you say, there is a web, even if the ways the strands connect can be hard to trace.

Q: As for Great Men, my own guess is that in the real world it's a combination of both. There has to be a great man and the correct timing. The revolutions of 1848 were just right to produce another Napoleon, a Lenin, or a Hitler, but didn't. The point of the Benét story (which is in his standard *Selected Works* and also in *Thirteen O'Clock*) is that if the times are not right, the Great Man comes to naught, even though he may have a feeling he ought to have been a Great Man.

Turtledove: "And He Walked Around the Horses" is of similar import. I do wonder if Piper saw the Benét and did a different take on it.

Q: But to pick a couple examples from history: what if Mohammed had been killed by a stray arrow during one of his early battles? Now the rise of Islam could be attributed to a massive and deep groundswell of Semitic rejection of Hellenism, but if there had been no Prophet to focus this, would it have gotten anywhere? Or if Constantine the Great had been hit by an arrow at the Milvian Bridge? What he was doing seems to have been the product of his own personal vision (in more than one sense) and his own personal decisions. No other Roman emperor or pretender was so inclined. No Persian king was so inclined, though there were also Christians in Persia. So if Constantine had not survived, would Christianity have established itself as more than a minority sect?

Turtledove: Well, as you probably know (always the excuse for an expository lump), I've done a series of stories collected as *Agent of Byzantium*, in which Muhammad converted to Christianity on a trading run up into Syria and Islam never happened. The book came out about the same time as Rushdie's *The Satanic Verses*, but I escaped a *fatwa*, for which I'm duly grateful. What you may not know is that I palmed a card. There was another prophet, Musaylimah, active is southeastern Arabia around Muhammad's time and also preaching a monotheistic faith—not Islam, but a monotheistic faith. Had Muhammad not been around, who knows? If it *was* railroad time, the broad outlines of political history might not took too different after all. If it wasn't, they would. But we can't do the experiment and see. In the real world, Abu Bakr, the first caliph, suppressed Musaylimah and his faith right after Muhammad's death.

I don't know what Christianity's fate in an Islamless Iran would have been. Zoroastrianism was well organized, and Christianity was suspect, on the grounds that its followers often favored the Roman Empire. I suspect it would have remained in the minority and been persecuted, as the Manichees were farther west.

Q: Of course here we are back to war and religion, the two great engines for change in history.

But, moving right along, Are you the sort of writer who makes elaborate outlines and takes a lot Of notes? What are your writing methods like?

Turtledove: No, I like telling myself the story, too. I usually know where I'm going, but not how I'm going to get there. I do first drafts in longhand, which seems to make my style tighter. It's a habit I picked up while still working on a typewriter—I'm old enough to go back that far. Typewriters, for those who don't recall, are anything but user-friendly. I started working through hard parts in longhand, then transcribing. After a while, I thought, This is trying to tell me something. So I've done it ever since.

Q: And: what are you working on now and what do you have coming up in the near future?

Turtledove: *The United States of Atlantis* will be out this December, and *Give Me Back My Legions!*, a straight historical about the battle that kept the Romans from annexing Germany. It'll be just in time for the 2000th anniversary of the battle.

Q: Thanks, Harry.

(Recorded in 2008.)

GREGORY FROST

Q: When you started writing, eons ago, you didn't think you were going to make a living at it, did you?

Frost: No, and I don't think I have. When I started out I think I was just desperate to get into print. I wasn't even thinking about moving from that phase into the possibility of making any sort of a living doing it. It was just, *Please, somebody publish my story.* That was really all I was thinking about at the beginning. Breaking into print. Long-term notions of a career were at best nebulous.

Q: That's probably what most of us experience. Don't you think that writing is more of a compulsion than get-rich-quick scheme?

Frost: Yes. I've been teaching fiction now for twenty-some years—adults, high-school kids, college students—and I think, watching all the people who have gone through the various classes with me and knowing all the writers that I know, that it's some form of addiction, or—dare I say?—mental illness. I can't advocate doing this for a lot of people. It's a kind of obsession. You can't help yourself.

I went through a really bad patch in the late '80s and early '90s and I tried repeatedly to throw in the towel and say, "I'm going to do something else. I'm not doing this anymore." That would last for about five days until suddenly I would read something and think, "You know, that's a really interesting idea for a story," and then I was back at it again. So, everyone save yourselves...it's too late for me.

Q: To make matters worse, you have this compulsion to write science fiction and fantasy. Did you know that was what you were going to be doing, from the beginning?

Frost: That I did know. By whatever process I'm hardwired for fantasy and horror probably more than science fiction. Every idea I have just is *bent* in that sense. I've even tried to have ideas that don't bend in that direction, but it doesn't work. I'll start out trying to write something that's not got any fantasy element in it at all, and the next thing I know it's turned left and dragged me over here where something's rotting or something unnatural is about to happen or the resolution incorporates the fantastic. It's where the stories go for me.

Q: This probably is something you have to bring up in writing classes a lot: how much is the writer in control?

Frost: I start off writing classes usually, telling them the way I'm wired and the way I work. I think the writer's in control to the extent that, at least in my process, my unconscious writer, whoever or whatever he is, is in control when I am first-drafting a story. I am in a way not trying to consciously control it. I probably have a sense of where I want to go. I probably have a notion of the structure somewhere in the back of my mind, but it's more of the automatic writing side of me that's run off with the story. Then again I think you're always in control, because all the characters in fiction are some facet of you, being reassembled and re-imagined as somebody else with other phobias, desires, or whatnot, but it still all comes back to you.

Q: But to some extent it has to *not* be entirely you, or else you've only got one character.

Frost: That's true. Hence the re-casting.

Q: What makes Shakespeare so good is that he's got *more* than one character.

Frost: In fact there's an essay by Gore Vidal where I think he says that the average writer has somewhere between three and six stock characters, and that's it, and they're basically repurposing those characters as they write, reintroducing them and pretending at least to themselves that they have more, and there are more voices, a story in their head that they can draw upon. But he says that that actually isn't true. Most people have three or four. Then he goes on to say that Shakespeare, on the other hand, has something like a dozen, and as a result that's why Shakespeare is Shakespeare. He could bring in more characters and a broader swath of humanity than the average writer does. I don't know if that's true, but it made for a great essay.

Q: I think a lot of writers, prolific ones in particular, look back on their work and realize that their standard cast just won't go away, and maybe you have to shoo some of them away.

Frost: [Laughs.] Yes, that's true. I've found that in the last decade I've suddenly started writing with most of the protagonists in my novels being female. That was kind of a shock to wake up and realize, *Gee, why are you doing that?* or *What's happened here?* You're turning to female characters.

Last year at Swarthmore College, I had T. C. Boyle come as a guest speaker and reader. He and I have been friends since the days when he was my instructor at Iowa many years ago. I made a comment to the effect that I was writing all these female characters, and he looked at me curiously and said, "That's very strange, because that's what I've started doing." Now his book, *The Women*, about Frank Lloyd Wright and the women around Frank Lloyd Wright, has come out. He wrote the book from the women's point of view.

So both of us are standing there for a moment scratching our heads, saying, "Gee, why are we suddenly doing this in our dotage?" Are we going, *Ah, let's write female characters. Let's explore our feminine side?* Maybe we're trying not to be us at all, but to be something completely different, to embrace a character we never had before in our ensemble.

Q: I wonder if this isn't a way for experienced writers to avoid a creative crisis and prevent themselves from going stale. If you've written *Huckleberry Finn* four million times, you would have to *stop* at some point.

Frost: That might be. It might be that I've explored this other character already, or it might be what you were saying, that I'm just writing these two bozos over and over again and dressing them in different clothes, and I'm tired of doing that. I want to do something else.

This is sort of my theory as to how Bruce Sterling's slipstream fiction came about—that some mainstream writers felt their material had gone stale on them. So what do you do? You go tromp around in your Wellies in the genres and drag back all this disgusting material that you claim you didn't know anything about or want nothing to do with. Then suddenly you've got John Updike writing science fiction and Margaret Atwood writing science fiction, although she's refusing to admit it, and Paul Auster taking mystery novels and applying those tropes to his stuff.

Q: Isn't this a more familiar phenomenon? There have always been mainstream writers who write science fiction, but for marketing purposes can't admit it.

Frost: Yes, absolutely true. For marketing purposes Harlan Ellison says he is not a science fiction writer. His books are *Fiction.* That is a way he can distinguish himself from the genre itself and to cling at least to a sense of writing pure literature rather than something that can be sneered at by academia, to the extent that academia still sneers at it.

Q: You're still writing something we can call "fantastic," whether you like it or not.

Frost: Yes, one flavor or another of something called fantastic. Like I say, that's the way I am put together, for whatever reason. I grew up devouring comic books, as well as science fiction and fantasy novels. When I was a teenager I thought I wanted to be an illustrator. I went to art school and spent a lot of time drawing figures, and drawing and writing my own comic books. Even starting out in the world of comic books, you're starting out in the world of the fantastic and the impossible, and the horrific, for that matter, EC Comics territory, where I was a lot. So in some sense I was feeding all that fantasy stuff into my head from a very early age.

Q: And no one tried to stop you....

Frost: [Laughs.] No. My parents probably didn't know what I was doing, and I hope they hadn't read the government papers that said that comic books were evil and would destroy your child's brain and do terrible things to them and pervert them. God knows that's all true, of course. Ruined me. But, no, my parents didn't try to put a lid on that at all. I was a voracious reader, and I think comic books just got sifted in with the other books that I was reading. One of the earliest things I read was a retelling for children of Homer's *Odyssey* by Barbara Leonie Picard. I was about nine or ten years old when I read that, so clearly I was seeking out the fantastic even before I knew there was such a thing or realized that there was a category. I was just thinking, *Oh, I really like this.* I gravitated toward the Hardy Boys books that seemed to have supernatural elements in them, even though those all end up like *Scooby-Doo* episodes. It's never supernatural. There's always an explanation involving criminals. What was it...*The Ghost at Skeleton Rock*? I would read any Hardy Boys books that had a hint of the fantastic.

Q: It probably happened to most writers of our generation. There was a teacher in high school or a professor in college who said, "Get rid of all that crap and write literature."

Frost: I managed somehow to bypass those people. As I said I was an art major in college and during my second year in college I took a night course in short-story writing, and the woman who taught it, whose name I cannot remember any more (I'm embarrassed to say), had written a screenplay and sold it to *Voyage to the Bottom of the Sea*. So she was all about the fantastic, even if it was really *bad* science fiction, which, in the case of *Voyage to the Bottom of the Sea* it was going to be. Fantasy didn't bother her at all. So I had somebody there going, "Yeah, go ahead and write this stuff. It's okay. You can do these *Twilight Zone* type stories." That was what I was attempting, terrible imitation *Twilight Zone* stories at that time. I'm sure it was awful fiction.

Q: But you then did sell your first story to *Twilight Zone* magazine.

Frost: That's true. So it kind of came full circle. I met Rod Serling, who came to the college where I was enrolled and spoke one night, and he was very funny, a great speaker. I liked him a lot. Actually, now you mention it, the night I drove to the Clarion writing workshop at MSU was the night that Serling died—I was dozing in the back of the car (someone else was driving) and it came on the radio and woke me right up. So, yes, it was a little weird to sell my first story to T. E. D. Klein at *Twilight Zone Magazine*.

Q: You first novel has definite science fiction elements in it. Did you decide that if you were going to have a novel-writing career, maybe it needed some SF in it?

Frost: The first novel was a kind of odd amalgam of high fantasy and science fiction elements, but by the time I sold that, to Ace Books, to Terri Windling, I was already working on what was for me in the '80s my magnum opus, which was a retelling of the Irish *Tain Bo Cuailnge* in two books. So I was deep off into Celtic mythology at that period, even though the first book had these science fictional elements in it.

I was, however, writing and selling science fiction stories. The early short fiction that I wrote comprised a lot of science fiction. But the novels were gravitating toward traditional fantasy. That became problematic after a while, because I didn't want to be labeled as a high fantasy writer who doesn't do anything else. And so after I finished the Irish books, I didn't want to continue doing that material. Ace was looking to see if I was going to produce another *Lyrec* novel or something to follow up *Remscela*, and I just really wasn't interested in staying in that territory.

Q: They were after what we cynically call the McTrilogy.

Frost: The McTrilogy. Yes, that's lovely. I've never been able to do McTrilogies. I have only been able to do duologies. I jokingly say that my problem with trilogies is that the middle book always sucks anyway, so I just don't bother writing it. But the truth is, that I have stories that just have a two-book story-arc rather than a three-book story-arc. I'm not by nature a series writer. I am not a trilogy writer. I would prefer to keep doing different things, trying out things, which is I suppose in some sense not the smartest career choice to make. The publishing world likes you a lot if you keep doing...you know, *Grandchildren of Dune, Earthworms of Dune.*

Q: The soap opera version, *As the Worm Turns.*

Frost: Ooh, let's tune in. They want you to do the same thing over and over again and that is what they keep shoving big piles of money at you to do. I've never been terribly interested in doing that. That's why I am impoverished, of course.

Q: I wonder if this brings us back to the idea of the deliberate as opposed to the intuitive writer. There is a species of writer you can tell, "I want a story about zombie cheerleaders, set in the Midwest in the '50s, and I want it next Tuesday," they can do it. Not only that, they will be able to tell you that at 3 AM next Tuesday they will be writing the last four pages. I think that's a different talent.

Frost: It's not a talent I think I am graced with, necessarily, although for a number of editors, for Terri Windling and Ellen Datlow, and for you, I've sat down and figured out stories that fit the bill of what was being sought. The first time I ever tried to do that was for Gardner Dozois when he was editing *Asimov's SF*. He gave a reading one night and Michael Swanwick and I were in the audience, and Michael and I were joking around some idea for a short story, and by the end of the evening I'd actually constructed a viable idea for *Asimov's*. Michael said, "You need to go write this story and give to Gardner," so I went home and wrote it overnight and sent it to Gardner, and he purchased it. But that was an anomaly. I don't normally write a story to spec without thinking about it for quite awhile.

For Terri and Ellen, for an anthology coming out next year, they needed a pooka story, and so I am confined to doing a story about pookas. So I figured out one I wanted to write about pookas, in pretty short order, a couple of weeks—that's fast for me. But those are exceptions.

Q: So, if I sell an anthology called *Alternate Historical Vampire Cat Detectives on Mars,* do you think you could write something for it?

Frost: [Laughing.] But of course. How could I say no? I remember that Joe Haldeman, way back at Iowa—I took a class from him; it was the first time I met Joe—one of the things he'd talk about over beers after class was that a lot of writers, back in the late '60s and probably through the pulp era—and he had done this a number of times, too—were approached by the magazine editor, who would say, "I've got this cover art, but I don't have a story to go with it. Would you be able to knock out a story around this cover?" He'd turn out a short story that fit the painting so that they could put it on the cover of the magazine, and in doing it, of course, he immediately got the cover story, so it was a feather in his cap too.

Q: How much of your fiction in some subtle, sublimated way is not deliberate then, but autobiographical?

Frost: I'll pretend none of it is autobiographical, but that isn't exactly true, of course. It's just than when you're not writing stuff that is clearly memoir, or something that can be clearly pointed at and said, "Oh this is your life, this is your family," when you are writing in the fantasy genre, you are *really* disguising the autobiographical material. You can really cover it up with lots and lots of special effects and bandages and so forth, and no one will recognize it.

It's funny. Back to Swarthmore. A writer named Elizabeth Strout was here last week, who has a fine novel out right now called *Olive Kitteridge,* and we were talking about memoirs and such, and I made the comment to her that she probably got letters and phone calls from people saying, "This must be about your life." She said, in fact one woman had approached her at a signing and said, "That's not the way it happened." She was sort of flummoxed and she's going, "But, I made this up. There is no 'that's the way it happened.'" There was no reality attached to it. It's all fiction. It is not autobiography in any way, supposedly.

Then the other people at the table looked at me and said, "Well, you write science fiction, so what about your autobiographical stuff?" I said, "There's none whatsoever in there." Of course that's a lie. But I'm not going to tell you where it is.

Q: Then you get the reader who comes up to you and says, "But magic isn't really like that...."

[Frost makes groaning noise.]

Q: Or worse yet, they say, "Yes, you've described it accurately."

Frost: [Laughs.] It's a little more dangerous when they come up to you and say, "Yeah, you got the werewolves exactly the way they really are." Well, *that's* troubling. You need to get a life. You need to seek help.

There's always somebody who is going to cross the line, but I'm not worried about it. Not yet anyway. If they come up to the table and they actually have the *Necronomicon* with them, then I'll look for the exit.

Q: Which edition? There are so many.

Frost: Is there one written in blood?

Q: Well, I heard a story about something that happened to Clive Barker once. A guy came up to him at an autographing, set down a copy of *The Books of Blood*, got out a razor, slashed his own wrist, bled on the book, then handed Barker a pen and said, "Here, sign it."

Frost: Did Clive sign it?

Q: Yes. What he said afterwards was, "When faced with a lunatic who is holding something sharp, you give him what he wants."

Frost: [Laughing.] Okay...no, I never had anything like that occur. In some ways I think fantasy writers may be better grounded than some of their readers are. We know that we are making this thing up. I am not sure all the people that read horror and fantasy *do* know that you're making it up. There's surely someone who thinks these things are possible in a way that the person writing it probably does not.

Q: This probably the reason science fiction writers tend to be so skeptical about flying saucers. We can do that *better.*

Frost: Yes, *I'll* show you a flying saucer....

Q: Getting back to the point about autobiography, maybe what you do is imagine what your life would be like if one of your family members was an alien or something. You take what might have happened in your life, then allow something to intrude that hopefully *didn't.*

Frost: When I wrote *Fitcher's Brides,* that's about three sisters, each of whom marries the Bluebeard figure in my novel. The first two of the sisters are, as much as I could make them, very much nineteenth-century women. They have the phobias, concerns, and beliefs of the day. The third one, who is the trickster, Kate, who outsmarts the Bluebeard figure, is in a lot of ways a soapbox for me. I get to say a lot of things that I wanted to through her. So there is definitely an element of autobiography in her. There is a story I wrote called "Collecting Dust," which is in the *Attack of the Jazz Giants* collection, and that's about a little boy whose parents who are working themselves to death, and deteriorating, literally crumbling away to dust over time right in front of him. The relationship between him and his sister is very much based on the relationship I had with my sister growing up, except that I was the older brother, so it is *not* autobiography, and yet I was definitely without a doubt tapping into my real childhood with my real sister (sorry, Deb). So, yes, there are elements in there, no question. I can look around and see them.

When I finished *Tain,* I had gotten divorced in the midst of that, and my ex-wife, when she read the book, said she saw a lot of us, of our relationship, in the relationship between King Ailill and his wife Maeve, the king and queen and Connacht. I thought, well, that's pretty weird because I would never have put those things in. I don't know if it's true. I don't know if she was reading that into the book because of what she had gone through, or if I was embedding it unconsciously. I don't think it matters. If it works in the service of the book, that's grand. It doesn't matter if I recognize it or not.

Q: Surely what the fantasy writer does is make something fantastic out of the stuff of life as it is lived. We all have the same emotions. You inevitably put the material of life, however strangely transformed, into the story.

Frost: That's interesting. I was just reading some essays about writing, and one "how to" writer, I won't mention her name, in one of her chapters in her book about writing takes science fiction to task and claims that all sf is nothing more than didactic stories, stories that have a point to make or are trying to teach you something, basically lumping sf in with parables. She's making this blanket statement that all science fiction is like "X", and a result of that is claiming that science fiction doesn't have the richness of characters, doesn't include characters that are based on life that's been lived, and I'm reading this essay and I'm going, *Clearly you haven't read much science fiction, or maybe* any *science fiction. You've taken your impression of science fiction from TV shows or something.* That struck me as unfair, to say the least. Utterly false.

I think that all the relationships and characters you are writing about are based on life lived, and the argument has been made that by the time you are five years old you have already experienced all the emotions that are necessary to write fiction anyway. You've experienced love, hate, abandonment, resentment—everything you can think of—everything you could possibly plug in as far as emotional states. You've already been through all of them. We're all human beings. Those are the only things you get to tap, regardless of whether you're writing fantastic fiction or contemporary American literature set in Poughkeepsie.

Q: What are you working on now?

Frost: Well, in accordance with what I said earlier, I am writing a mystery novel, which is something I've never done. I am going in a different direction. But it has fantastic elements in it because I can't help that.

Q: Is it really a mystery novel, then?

Frost: The difference is it's not a *Scooby-Doo* ending. It won't be that it looks like it's supernatural all the way through the book, and then we get to the end and "Oh, my goodness! It was just this robber dressed up in a clown suit." I promise not to go that way. So it's a mystery, but it's a strange mystery.

Q: What you seem to be describing is a fantasy novel with mystery tropes.

Frost: Yes, that's probably true, but how they market it, I don't know. The borderlines between genres have broken down so much that I don't know which flavor of the week, sub-category this is. Mystery, romance, science fiction, fantasy, horror. I don't know. I don't care either. It will change by next week, as will the flavor of the week.

Q: You could always claim it's Literature, but that doesn't get you out on the shelves unless you're already famous enough to be a brand name.

Frost: I am weeks away from that.

Q: I hope so. Thanks, Greg.

(Recorded at Frost's home, April 2009.)

TOM PURDOM

Q: How does the science fiction field of today differ most obviously from what it was like when you started writing?

Purdom: The magazine science fiction of the period when I started writing, into at least the late '60s, was much more visible. In 1967, I had my first cover story, which appeared in *F&SF*. It was called "Reduction in Arms" and Ron Walotsky did the cover. It was in yellow, with this bull's-eye target on it. It was very prominent. When I walked around downtown Philadelphia, I could see this cover almost everywhere I went. At 15th and Market, where there is now a plaza, there was an old building that had an arcade and two newsstands, one at each end, and there was the magazine, on both stands. If I went down into the subway on Broad Street, there was this huge newsstand that was set up in the subway, and I could see my magazine. I went into 30th Street Station, the railway station, and all the way across the station I could see that issue of F&SF on a newsstand that was right out in the center of the station. That's one of the more noticeable things that I think has changed. If I want to contemplate an *Asimov's* that has one of my stories in it nowadays, I have to visit a bookstore.

Q: Will we look back on this as a golden age from which we have fallen?

Purdom: Right. It used to be when they talked about the

Golden Age, they talked about the 1940s and the stories that were reprinted in *Adventures in Time and Space* and in the Groff Conklin anthologies. Now I notice that people talk about the 1950s as the Golden Age, which was when I started reading science fiction.

Q: Is this because your perception of what science fiction should be is formed by what you were reading when you were young?

Purdom: I think to a large extent that's true. That's what attracted you to the field, certain qualities which were prominent at that point and which remain, for you, perhaps the main thing that keeps the field appealing. But I think the age of the readers is a factor, too. As they get older they retain glowing memories of the things they read when they were young. On the other hand, a lot of younger readers seem to be attracted to the '50s. I notice from the *Asimov's* forum that a lot of them state that they like to read anthologies of stories from that period. I think right in that period you had a big upgrade in literary quality, and in addition the stories retained most of the other qualities that make science fiction interesting to us.

Q: Maybe it was also an age of greater freedom, in the sense that science fiction had not yet become a field of potential bestsellers yet, so there were fewer restrictions on how long the story had to be and what it had to contain. For example, if a book like *The Stars My Destination* were submitted today, it might not be publishable from a major publisher. It would be too short to justify the required cover price for maximum profits.

Purdom: [Laughs] Yeah. Of course you had the opposite problem when science fiction began to break out in the '50s. Publishers like Doubleday had to reach out for some model, and they used the mystery. When I look back, it seems to me the mystery was actually the only other genre the book publishers supported. We talk about genre fiction, but the only other genre that you actually found distributed widely in regular lines of books was mysteries. You didn't find western lines put out by hardcover publishers, as far as I can remember. You saw mysteries, and mysteries were 60,000 words. The standard format was a slim book—it looks slim nowadays; it looked normal then—and Doubleday brought out all its science fiction in the same format, and most of the other publishers did, too.

So for a long time the big complaint among science fiction writers was that they were restricted to 60,000 words. Of course now the big complaint is that they've got to write 130,000 or 150,000 words whether they want to or not.

Q: Did you find the field in the '50s or early '60s confining in any way in the sense of what you were not allowed to do?

Purdom: Well, I didn't, no. Of course there are people who feel that nowadays you can have more sexual freedom and so on, but for the kind of fiction I wanted to do, I didn't feel any great confinement. In the magazines, you could write about just about any idea that appealed to you, and in books you also had the classic space opera type of thing, which Don Wollheim was publishing in the Ace Doubles. Ace was a good beginner's market, or if you wanted to do hack work, it was a kind of hack work—something you knew you could sell. I wrote two or three proposals before I sold my first paperback to Ace. When these first two or three didn't sell, along with a mainstream novel I tried to write that didn't work, I decided it was time I wrote a novel that I was sure would sell. So I sat down and plotted something that was directly aimed at the Ace space-opera market, and it sold in about a month.

Q: But then did you have more of a science fiction magnum opus in mind, which would have to move beyond Ace Doubles? I thinking of something on the order of John Brunner's *Stand on Zanzibar*, which was a real breakthrough at the time, much more complex and lengthy than most SF novels that were being published.

Purdom: Ursula K. Le Guin is a perfect example of this. She did several Ace Doubles, and then finally she did *The Left Hand of Darkness*. If you look at her first Ace Doubles, they were really beginner's work. There was a big jump in quality to *The Left Hand of Darkness*. The thing is that the Ace Doubles gave writers a secure market in which they could learn to write. It was a good beginner's market. You could sell a novel and you could learn something about the art of writing a novel, and then you could move on. Now with my fourth paperback, I moved on. I took "Reduction in Arms," which was a pretty serious story about the nuclear arms race, which had appeared as a novelet in *F&SF*, and turned that into a novel which sold to Berkley. Then I did *The Barons of Behavior*, which was a fairly serious future-political novel, and that sold to Terry Carr for the Ace Specials series.

This was just a natural progression that a writer could go through. I often wish that I had written more Ace Doubles, to tell you the truth. I liked doing them and I would have made money and I think it would have been better for my career as a whole.

Q: Why did your novels stop when they did?

Purdom: I have no idea. No idea at all. I wrote sample chapters and outlines that I thought were just as good as anything else that I'd sold, and they just didn't sell. One possibility is that the competition just got keener.

One thing you have to remember is the way the demographics affected people my age. I was born in 1936. There weren't a lot of people who were born in 1936. Then there were an awful lot of people born in the 1950s, and they started reaching the age when they were beginning to sell novels in the late '60s and into the '70s. So you had a much larger pool of writers to draw on. So I do think that in many ways the Baby Boomers did push things to a higher level of quality and I simply couldn't match the competition. That would be a possibility. I can't tell you. But there was simply more competition at that point.

If I can give you an example of the demographics—remember when John W. Campbell died in 1971?

Q: Yes.

Purdom: Well I did not at first even think of applying for that job, as editor of *Analog*. Then I started thinking. I said, probably these people at Condé Nast would want someone who would stick around for a long time, which meant they'd want someone in his thirties, which I was then. That being the case, I looked around and saw who might be the writers they would choose. Who did you see? I don't think Robert Silverberg wanted to be an editor, and I am certain that Harlan Ellison was not cut out to be the editor of *Analog*, right?

Q: Right.

Purdom: There were two or three other writers in my age group who were borderline or I didn't think were interested. I finally decided there were two possibilities, Ben Bova and me. So I went ahead and applied, and of course they picked Ben Bova, who was so much better qualified, but the point I am making is that I could think of several writers and editors who would have made good editors for *Analog*, but they were all in their fifties. When I talked to the publisher, when I was interviewed, it really became clear that my guess was correct. They liked *Analog* at Condé Nast because they could send it out with their other magazines. It did not cause them any trouble. They made a little money and it didn't cause them any trouble. There was no effort. The thing just published itself. So they wanted somebody else like Campbell, who would sit there and do the magazine for the next thirty years and not bother them. Which meant they wanted somebody in their thirties.

Q: You must have been writing other things too. When I go back and look at how much you published in science fiction, and knowing what the rates were at the time, I can't see how you ever supported yourself that way. Did you ever make a living as a science fiction writer?

Purdom: No. I never really thought I would. That's another difference. I think a lot of people thought of science fiction as something that you wrote because you liked it. You made money, and you wanted to make as much as you could, but I think very few people through the fifties and into the sixties thought of science fiction as something you could make a living from.

When the SFWA was founded in 1965, some seventy people were founding members, and while there were a number of full-time writers on that roster, there were very few full-time science fiction writers. Poul Anderson and John Brunner and Keith Laumer—and they were all high-volume producers. Isaac Asimov, of course, was a founding member, but he wasn't making his living writing science fiction. He was a science writer. If you went through that list and looked at the other full-time writers, you would see that most of them were making their living writing something else. Then you had a lot of writers who were basically making their livings at other things besides writing. I think that most people who set out to write science fiction would not have expected to make a living writing science fiction. Whereas, when I talk to writers younger than me, the ones from the Baby Boom generation, often sometime in the '80s or '90s, they would begin to think, "Things are terrible. The whole field is falling apart." It was because they were used to a world in which they expected to make a living writing science fiction. That was their criterion.

Q: We've heard Robert Silverberg discourse on this subject. He was making a living writing science fiction in the '50s, and then, about 1958, as he put it, he woke up one morning and there was no field. He went on to write other things.

Purdom: Yeah, but that's Silverberg. All I know is that if you look at that 1967 list, which included a lot of people from the '50s, the half dozen people who made livings as science fiction writers were, in general, high volume producers.

Most of the others were doing something else. Frederik Pohl, for example, was an editor for much of his career. So he was clearly doing other things besides writing science fiction. I don't know how many of the older writers in the '50s started to make livings at it, but I certainly did not think of this as something you made a living at. Even Ray Bradbury, who was selling to the slicks, was making his living mostly by writing for the movies, as far as I could tell.

Q: Imagine an alternate career in which you became a full-time science fiction writer. Do you think you could have done it?

Purdom: No. [Laughs.] Unless I had managed a full-time career as somebody writing Ace Doubles. If I wanted to be a full-time producer of action-adventure, space-opera type science fiction, I might have been able to pull that off. I think one of my problems is that I kept weaving back and forth between strictly commercial writing and stuff that I felt was more serious. I never committed myself one way or the other, which reflects my own feelings. I like both.

Q: Very likely you made the right choice. It would seem to me that any number of writers in our field have been wrecked by an attempt to make SF a full-time career. They write a small volume of high-quality material, then turn into hacks and end up writing sharecrops or novelizations, and no one ever takes them seriously again.

Purdom: One of the words that I think gets misused a lot is "professional." Actually, "professional," I feel, should be restricted to lawyers, doctors, people like that. We use it in America to mean somebody who makes their living at something, or, more broadly, somebody who at least gets paid for what they do. The assumption is that if you are working at it full-time, you are better at it than someone who is working at it part-time. That can apply to some things. There are some things that require full-time dedication. For example, being a world-class solo violinist probably does require that you not do anything else. That's it. You've got to devote full time to what that takes.

But when you look at writing, it's not that way at all. Some of the greatest stuff has been written by part-timers. One of the problems with a full-time writer is that they have to do what you said. They have to make sure that they are writing stuff that will sell. They can't do the more risky stuff, or if they do, they have to do it as a sideline. I think one way to divide work up is the degree of risk involved. Some things are more certain to sell; some are more risky; and if you only do the more certain things, you've going to have a very limited career. Often, in the long run, you don't make as much money either.

The classic in this area is Tolkien. Only an amateur could have written, *The Lord of the Rings*, right? But now you've got all these professionals who are imitating him. An amateur created the market. The professionals could never have created that market.

Q: And his estate is still making more money than any of them.

Purdom: Right.

Q: But it ultimately isn't about money, is it?

Purdom: No. If you want to make money, do something else. This is what I've always said, if your major interest in life is making money, then you shouldn't become a writer, or an artist, or anything like that. You shouldn't. That's all.

There are some exceptions. Heinlein always claimed that he wrote for the money and it may have been that writing just happened to suit him, but there are very few people for whom that's going to be true.

On the other hand, if you are a writer, whether a part-timer or a full-timer, the money you get paid does make a huge difference in your life.

Malcolm Cowley, who was a writer from the Hemingway era, wrote a book in the '50s called *The Literary Scene*, in which he discussed American writers, and he pointed out that writers think about money more than most people. It's an insecure source of income. and they don't get a lot of it, so they have to think about it more than most Americans, who have salaried jobs. So, yes, if you're a writer, you are going to think more about money and money is important to you, but you don't go into it for the money alone. That would be a mistake. There are two things I always quote from the beginning of modern publishing. Doctor Johnson said that "nobody but a blockhead ever wrote but for money," and Voltaire said, "One does not write to make money. One makes money so one can write." Those are really the two things you should always keep in mind. Don't write if they're not going to pay you. That's stupid. But on the other hand, don't think you're doing it for the money. You're earning the money so you can keep doing it.

Q: I suppose the way you tell the real writers from the hacks is from the answer to this question: If you were so well supported by a patron or the state that you never had to lift a finger for money again, and you could write, and get published, and reach a large audience with your fiction but not get paid for it, would you still write?

Purdom: I honestly don't know. At my age, when you've been writing for a long time, you've got a lot invested in it. There's a lot of satisfaction in it, too. I suppose I would keep on writing.

Whether I would keep on writing science fiction, I don't know. I am getting a big kick out of writing this memoir I am doing, and clearly that is not a commercial activity. So maybe I would write other things. Writing fiction is very hard work, as far as I am concerned. It would depend on the kind of ideas I got. Suppose I was guaranteed—

Q: You're guaranteed publication, and you are independently wealthy, but you won't be paid for your writing.

Purdom: Yes, then I would do it. That's right. The real thing is would I go through all the effort of writing something that might never appear in print? I don't know if I'd take that risk. If you guaranteed me that I'd reach an audience, sure.

But I don't know if reaching the audience is the thing. There are so many different things involved in writing. They're all important. I wouldn't want to take any of them away.

Q: As soon as I joined SFWA, one of the first bits of SFWA etiquette I learned is that you can't very well go around saying, "Well, I am more artistically sensitive than you, therefore my work is better." The reason that writers talk about money is that it is a safe subject everybody has in common, and it is a convenient wall they can put up to avoid talking about what is really important.

Purdom: I think that you are largely correct. But I do admit that the pursuit of the money has its appeal too. I've done commercial things, and I've enjoyed doing them, and there is something about pursuing money that is fun. Commerce is fun. Commerce is interesting. But I think to a large extent you're right. There's got to be something more to this to keep you going. If you're just interested in making money, there are a lot easier ways to make money. That same amount of energy and time and effort applied to going to college to become a brain surgeon—which is probably comparable—or to become a lawyer, would make you a lot more money obviously.

Q: But you've mentioned in your autobiographical postings that even before you were a teenager, you knew you wanted to be a writer. It's almost inborn.

Purdom: Well, like I said in my memoir, it was suggested to me by an aunt. Somebody planted the idea. But also, it seems to me that at a very young age I recognized that books were written by writers. There was this figure behind the words called the writer. There was a personality somewhere back there. I think I did feel that that would be a nice thing to do, to be somebody like that.

For example, the first book I read was *Bambi* by Felix Salten. That's the book that turned me into a reader. I remember that I was probably about eight or nine when Felix Salten died; and I remember reading this or hearing it and being touched by it at that age. I even knew enough to be aware that he lived in some place called Vienna. I had this vision of this guy sitting in a room writing. I really pictured this person. So there was obviously something going on in my head.

In my memoir, I also mentioned how I got interested in music from hearing Fritz Kreisler on the radio. I think it's interesting that I didn't decide I wanted to hear more violin music. The next morning I told my mother I wanted to take violin lessons. I think that is one of the things that differentiates future artists and entertainers from other people. When they see somebody doing it, they want to do it themselves. A lot of people will say, "That's beautiful, I want to hear more of that." But that sense that you want to do it yourself is perhaps a less common feeling. Since what I was mostly doing was reading, it would seem only natural that I would think that the most wonderful thing in the world you could do is to be a writer. Right?

Q: But you weren't moved to write an animal story first, were you? Did you try to write science fiction from the beginning?

Purdom: I wrote some stuff when I was in grade school. When I was seven I wrote something. I forget what it was. My aunt thought it was great. She told me I should be a writer. I can remember doing a little of that in grade school, even reading something I'd written that made the rest of the class laugh. I also got into public speaking. My father was in the navy so we moved around. After World War II we were in California for a year, and the California schools were out of sync by a year with the Connecticut schools. I had had this class on geography in Connecticut that had a lot of stuff on Africa and the teacher in the fifth grade in California let me give a lecture to the class on Africa. I remember talking to the whole class. It certainly was a fairly long talk. Everybody was awed that I could stand up there and give this lecture. I remember it as very satisfying and appealing. And I did a lot of stuff for class entertainments. I'd write little skits and so on. I was doing all that from a fairly young age.

But I started actually sending stories in to magazines when I was about thirteen, just before I discovered science fiction. Those were varied. I forget what some of them were. I think I wrote something about a pig that became president. I don't know. So I wrote other things before I wrote science fiction.

Q: In other words, it was science fiction that really focused what you were about as a writer.

Purdom: Yes. Most of what I wrote from 1950 on and sent to magazines was science fiction. I did write a couple of western short stories, as I remember it, and a couple of teenage gang-violence stories. Maybe I tried my hand at a light love story. But seventy to eighty percent of what I wrote after that was science fiction.

Q: I note that you mentioned in your online memoir that you were working with agents from the beginning, paying Scott Meredith reading fees, and so on. How much did you work directly with the editors?

Purdom: I started sending stuff in to Scott Meredith about 1955 or 1956. So I had actually been writing and sending stuff in to editors at fairly high volume for several years when I decided that Scott Meredith might be of some value and decided to try their reading fee service.

This is something you're not supposed to do, normally. But in looking at their ads, it was clear that they were an active agency. There was a guy who used to have ads in *Writer's Digest* on how he sold some big thing ten years before that had been made into a movie—and that was all he had ever done. But I could look at the Scott Meredith ads every month and I could see that they were selling new stuff by writers that I'd heard of to magazines and book publishers I was familiar with. I felt that it was at least worth spending a few dollars to see what results I might get. But from my first sale on, everything went through Scott Meredith.

Q: Well I was going to ask you for a good John W. Campbell story. Did you get editors who said, "I want a story about this," and try to use you as their mouthpiece? Or were you too isolated for that, working through agents?

Purdom: I do have a story for you. No, I never ran into that. I have never been that kind of writer. I look at the markets. You could look at Ace Doubles and figure out what Don Wollheim wanted. I didn't have that much contact, personally, with editors. For a long time it was something I did by mail.

But one of my first experiences with Campbell is interesting. During my first months in the army, I wrote a story about a UN police force operating in Africa in the 1980s. I wrote it early in 1959. I got the idea for it because I had been reading a magazine article, in some special issue on Africa. This made me realize that Africa was going to be a fairly turbulent place in the future. So I wrote this story and Scott Meredith sold it to Campbell in three days. They were pretty awed by the speed of the sale, too.

If you want to know how to sell a short story to a science fiction magazine, it's really very simple. Give them a complete plot, at least one or two interesting characters, and an interesting future world, and cram it all into five thousand words.. That's what those of us who learned to write short stories learned to do when the field was young. Nowadays writers tend to think of a short story as a little idea that you throw away. Plot, everything, it was all in the story I sold Campbell, with this African setting.

Then, about six months after the story sold, the Congo erupted into the Congo Crisis of 1960. The UN entered and there was a full-scale civil war. John W. Campbell wrote editorials about the Congo Crisis, and he didn't publish my story until 1961, a year after he bought it. The result was that people reading the story ["The Green Beret," *Analog* January 1961—DS] probably assumed that I had read Campbell's editorials and watched the news about the Congo and written this story. But in fact I had written the story a year before it was published, before Campbell's editorials. He may even have gotten interested in the subject from reading my story. I often wonder how many writers who were supposed to have been pushing Campbell's buttons may have had similar experiences.

Q: I wonder if he wanted to have his buttons pushed, and so he held your story up to make it appear that way.

Purdom: He might have, or it might have been an accident of publishing. But it did seem to me funny that he bought the story in three days but didn't publish it for a year.

Q: One hears about Robert Silverberg and Randall Garrett running races to see who could read a John Campbell editorial and sell a story to him about it fastest.

Purdom: I never did anything like that, and if people think I did, they're wrong.

Q: You didn't sell a lot to him. If you'd published in his magazine every three months, then such a relationship might have developed.

Purdom: I liked *Analog* and I liked Campbell, but I wasn't interested in writing psionics stories, or the other things that appealed to his particular mindset.

There was another story I did which really was based on a Campbell editorial, and that was "Toys," which appeared in the October 1967 *Analog*. The inspiration for that came from a Campbell editorial that I read in 1951, I think, in which Campbell had asked what I thought was an interesting question: what are you going to do when any teenager can destroy a city by twisting a couple of wires in a certain way? It was an interesting thought experiment.

Q: I remember the story. I must have read it within a few years of its publication. What I can remember is that the hero was an extremely educated policeman who is going into what looks to us like luxury accommodations, which by the standards of the story's future setting, are a slum.

Purdom: That's right, but the basic kernel was that these kids have all these gadgets around that are very common, and yet they're lethal if applied in a certain way. So you have all this power in the hands of children. What do you do about this? So that story was based on a Campbell editorial, but it was a Campbell editorial from almost twenty years earlier.

Q: What was your working relationship with Gardner Dozois like?

Purdom: One thing I think everyone should say about Gardner, and since he is now no longer the editor one can say these kind of things without people thinking you're trying to flatter him— Gardner had a wonderful ability to maintain friendly relations with people while maintaining good professional relations. He can reject your stuff and it doesn't damage your personal relationship. We're able to keep the two things going simultaneously. I think that's very important.

I would say that I had a good working relationship with Gardner. There's an editor in Philadelphia, Dan Rottenberg, who I've worked with at *The Welcomat*, which is where I started as a music critic, and I once heard Dan give a talk. He's also a freelance writer. He emphasized the importance of maintaining a good relationship with editors. But he also emphasized that this has nothing to do with going out to lunch with them, drinking with them, paling around with them. He meant a working relationship. That's what you should cultivate. This means getting your work in on time, that you do a good job, and various things like that. This is especially important in journalism but it's important in other fields, too. I felt I had a good working relationship with Gardner.

One thing about Gardner is that, being a writer, he's very sensitive about requesting revisions. He makes it clear that if he wants a change, he will give you a general idea of what he wants, but it's up to you. You may lose the sale, but he's not going to print words you didn't write. That's clear. So several of my stories have appeared somewhat differently than the text I sent to him, but the stories appeared with revisions that I made myself, because he felt that they were needed. In most cases I think they probably worked. In some cases I am not convinced they were necessary, but I felt we had a good relationship.

Q: Did you have any sense there was a distinct Gardner Dozois type of story, the way there was a distinct John W. Campbell type of story?

Purdom: I think all editors have some kinds of stories they're partial to. That applies to Campbell, and it applied to Avram Davidson when he was editing *F&SF*. I think that if you look at a magazine, what you will find is that usually some of the weaker stories play to that side of the editor, because, if he's got two stories and one of them is really good, and it's not the kind of thing he especially likes, he may still buy it because it's good. He's a good editor and he wants variety. But if he's got a certain number of slots to fill, and he's got two stories that are weak, he is more likely to buy the one that fits whatever his bias is. That would be about the only thing that I could say, and I wouldn't try to put a finger on it in Gardner's case. If I had the opportunity to choose between a story that is of higher literary quality but isn't very interesting science-fictionally, compared to one that is more interesting science-fictionally but not quite as well written, I'd probably choose the second. Gardner would probably choose the first. That might be true, but I wouldn't want to be held to that.

That's an interesting question: do literary values bring science fiction down?

Q: Is there a difference? What do we mean by "literary values" other than good craftsmanship?

Purdom: There's a whole class of people, and I think most of them are the people who come out of the colleges with English degrees, for whom literary technique and style and all those things are all that count. They don't care what the story is about. That's the feeling I get.

People like that frequently tell me, "Oh you're not interested in style," or whatever else they're currently emphasizing. Actually I am very sensitive to style and technique, and I finally figured out what the best way to explain my position is. If I'm in a bookstore looking at a book, the first thing I'll look at is what it's about. Sometimes I'll go by the author, because if it's by a certain author, you know what it's going to be about. But the critical thing is what it's about. Then the next thing I do is start looking through the book to see how it's written. If I think it's written insipidly or weakly or thinly, I just put it down. What this means is that I read books on subjects I am interested in that are well written. I do not read books that are well written on subjects I am not interested in. That is a difference I have with a lot of the more literarily-oriented people who comment on science fiction. They are willing to read stuff on subjects that I think are pretty dull, and I can't see how they can be interested in them, but they'll say, "What difference does it make so long as it's good?" But "good" to me means it's got to be about something I am interested in.

Q: There are certain writers, surely, Mark Twain for instance, whose personality is such that you want to read almost anything he writes.

Purdom: I haven't read everything Mark Twain wrote. No. I have to say no. I hardly ever read everything by a certain writer. The writer's name counts for something for me, but I rarely read everything one writer has written. The only two I can name offhand are Ernest Hemingway and George Orwell, and Hemingway didn't write a lot. His output was pretty small compared to most major writers, over his lifetime. And I've only read *A Moveable Feast*, out of the stuff that's been published since he died. Some of his short stories I've read just because I started reading a collection of Hemingway stories and I read all of them. And Orwell I found fascinating, so I went ahead and read all of his novels, as well as all the non-fiction that was available in the United States. But that was years ago, when I was younger. I am less likely to do that now. I want a good writer who is writing about something I am interested in.

Q: There are also science fictional virtues we look for outside of purely "literary" ones. We can see this particularly in writers who aren't otherwise very good, like Edgar Rice Burroughs or Doc Smith. When Smith stepped outside of science fiction, he shed his science-fiction virtues and had nothing else to show. He wrote detective stories but could not sell them.

Purdom: I've read very little of either of them. Again, Doc Smith is a writer I would probably not read, because he just isn't a very good writer, as far as I can tell. Burroughs.... What have I read? I've read *The Son of Tarzan* and that's about it. I've never read the Mars books and I don't have any great interest in them.

Q: It's probably too late to come to them for the first time now.

Purdom: That's right. I'd have to be a kid to read them. I think when you talk about genre fiction, which is what science fiction is, there are certain things that are appealing to the genre audience. If you're writing genre fiction, that's something you can keep in mind. I put certain things into science fiction stories, like ideas about the future, because I think the audience will find them interesting. They should be integrated with the narrative line and all the rest of it, but the point is that one can assume that somebody who reads science fiction wants to read about visions of the future. Likewise someone who reads a historical novel wants to get into the past in some way, and so you include details of the past which you think are interesting in themselves.

This is one of the ways you maintain interest for a genre audience in a genre story. And if people don't like science fiction, which I think a lot of people who read fantasy don't, they don't find this interesting. I've seen criticisms of Charles Stross that complain about his information-dumps, which I find fascinating. He'll insert two or three paragraphs, which he usualy writes with real style, painting a picture of a very original future that's interesting in itself. If the story doesn't have that virtue, then I am not interested in reading it.

Q: I'll bounce a theory off you. I call this the Audience Starvation Theory of Literature. It holds that if the audience really wants to read about something, then they will tolerate a writer who isn't very good. Fenimore Cooper is an obvious example. The public really wanted to read about the West and the frontier. Or, Doc Smith early on was the first person to get out into the galaxy in a big way. Or, Tom Clancy—if he'd tried to write sensitive romances, I doubt he would have gotten anywhere. But the time was just right for a technothriller. So you are right, that content sells books, not style.

Purdom: I am not saying that at all. It's not true for me. It has to have both. And I think you are underselling Clancy. *The Hunt for Red October* was, to my mind, a very crisply written book, well-plotted, with a lot of very interesting characterizations in it, in addition to other stuff. If you happen to be interested in that kind of thing, that's a well-done book. Then there was the one about the Irish terrorist. I forget the title, but I lost some sleep over it. It was a very good suspense novel. I don't claim to have read all of Clancy, but he has written at least two or three novels that you are very seriously underrating, that are much better written and plotted than most thrillers.

Q: I'm not suggesting that he's as bad as Fenimore Cooper but that if he had written, say, westerns, he wouldn't be all that special, because his actual virtues, where he is exceptional, are the technothriller virtues.

Purdom: If he had been writing about a different subject I probably wouldn't be interested in him, sure. On the other hand, Larry McMurty writing about the west, in *Lonesome Dove*, has all kinds of virtues, not only his writing style and his characterization, but the picture he presents of the West, which is different from what other writers do and is fascinating in itself.

Q: This leads us to the point that the western—which is a form of the historical novel—and science fiction have a lot in common. A good deal of what they are about is presenting a world, setting rather than character. I see in your work a great fascination with the eighteenth century, military matters and more. Have you ever tried to write a historical novel?

Purdom: First of all, I have a general interest in history, with a specific interest in military history and political history. The focus on the eighteenth century is something of an accident. I got into it from wargaming, partly. The classic period for wargaming with miniature figures is the Napoleonic era, which is a little later, but I had a friend who was getting into wargaming at the same time. He wanted to do the American Revolution so I picked the Seven Years War so we could combine our forces, because basically the uniforms are the same. So I did devote a lot of time to learning more about eighteenth-century warfare than I might otherwise have. The other thing about the eighteenth century is the music. That's the Baroque period and I'm particularly fond of Baroque music. Plus, I've always had an interest for some crazy reason in Versailles, the culture of it, the bored courtiers and the mistresses and the whole bit. That stuff is like Hollywood gossip, almost. But I do have a general interest in history, yes.

You know, I heard David Brin say something during a radio broadcast which I think was very perceptive. He noted that many science fiction writers read science but almost all of them read history. That is the one thing that we most have in common. He felt that science fiction should really be called "speculative history." I really like the idea, because when you do that you tie together alternate history, time-travel into the past, and all the stuff about the future that constitutes the core of science fiction. They are all speculative history.

I fit right into that speculative history main stream and I think that is true of a lot of science fiction writers. As for writing historicals, I took the time to put together a proposal for a historical novel, which I hope will be a series, but so far I haven't been able to sell it.

My feeling about the whole novel-writing market is that people say, "Oh, yeah, I'm very interested," and you send them a novel and then two years later you still haven't heard from them. That seems to be what happens, even when the editors express interest, and I know other people seem to have the same problem. You hear people talk about two and three year waits, and so, to tell you the truth, I find it hard to stay interested in the whole idea of writing books when I can write novelets and sell them to magazines and see them get into print and get a little money. Why bother? I do have a proposal for a historical novel, a sailing-ship series, and it deals with something that has never really been written about. I first thought about it in the 1970s and then, four or five years ago, when I realized that nobody else was writing about it, I decided to give it a try, and I went and researched the subject. The British fought the slave trade for fifty years, and it's a heroic story—a great epic of the sea. Fifty years of young officers in little ships freeing slaves. It's a great subject, ship-to-ship battles, everything you'd want in a sailing-ship series is there, and it's hardly been touched on. It shows up every now and then peripherally in historical fiction, but nobody has ever written a series about a young officer in the anti-slave patrol, and it's a tremendous subject if you like that kind of thing.

Q: What are you working on these days?

Purdom: Right now I have a story coming out in *Asimov's*, a novella. This will be my first novella. It is a little under 20,000 words, and it's called "Bank Run" and it's basically about banking on a newly-settled planet, and the role of banking in the economy. but done as a thriller.

The other thing that I'm doing is that I'm trying to write a time-travel story about the anti-slavery patrol. I figured that I have this novel which I haven't been able to sell, so maybe I can at least do a science fiction story. It's very hard to do, though, because the impulse to do it is not a science-fictional impulse. I really want to write about the anti-slavery campaign, but I'm trying to shoehorn it into a science-fiction, time-travel story and it's giving me a lot of problems.

Q: If you had your career to start over again, would you have gone the same way, except writing more Ace Doubles?

Purdom: I would have written more Ace Doubles. I'll tell you the other thing I would have done. I would have written more short fiction during the period in which I was writing novels and they weren't selling. I didn't wrote short fiction partly because the short fiction market had shrunk to three or four magazines and it didn't seem worth it. I had this experience back in the early '60s, when the market had shrunk to four magazines: Terry Carr was handling my stuff at Scott Meredith. I wrote this story which I thought was pretty good, a sequel to something else, and it didn't sell. I asked him why. He explained that we had four editors. One of them was Cele Goldsmith, who was a woman, and I knew from some comments from my friends that the idea, which featured a telepathic sex-criminal, revolted women. So I can understand that she didn't like it at all. It had a sexual theme, so they didn't think Campbell would be interested in it, and that left two other editors, and they just didn't happen to buy it. If there had been six editors in the field, the story might have sold. That was one reason why I didn't feel much impulse to write magazine fiction for a long time. Finally I got back into magazine fiction almost by accident and discovered I could still do it. So I wish I had written more short stories and novelets.

Q: Thanks, Tom.

(Recorded at Purdom's home, Summer 2005.)

D. G. COMPTON

Q: You've mentioned that you have a new book coming out—

Compton: Oh, I did not say that. I have written a new book. Whether it is coming out or not is another matter. I already have a couple science fiction novels that haven't been published over here anyway. And to make matters worse, this book isn't even science fiction. So I have few hopes that it will actually be published. It was just something I had to do.

Q: Most American readers probably think of you as a figure of the 1960s and early '70s, for books like *Synthajoy* and *The Unsleeping Eye*—

[Compton shows two books.]

Compton: These two came out in the mid-'90s.

Q: *Justice City* and *No Man's Land.* Are these science fiction?

Compton: Published by Gollancz, yes. They are both science fiction.

Q: They're packaged to look like mysteries.

Compton: That one [*Justice City*] is made to look like a mystery but it's mostly science fiction, and this one [*No Man's Land*] is entirely science fiction.

Q: It even says so. But the Americans have never seen these.

Compton: Which is as it suggests, no wars, no crime, no men, no problem. *No Man's Land*. But one has to have problems, doesn't one?

Q: What got you into science fiction in the first place?

Compton: My publisher. I had been writing some crime novels, and they weren't very good, and I decided I would do something different. I had an idea I liked about population control. This was way back whenever it was, early '60s, I suppose, and I wrote a book. I sent it off to a publisher, the publisher being Hodder & Stoughton in England. They said yes, they would do it, and it was science fiction. And I, who had never even read any science fiction, apart from H. G. Wells, I suppose, and Jules Verne, I said, "Oh, is it science fiction? All right? I don't mind. You can call it what you like, but publish it." So is how I got into science fiction.

After it came out as science fiction and was reasonably well received, it made me think, well, I had better do another, hadn't I? My images of science fiction were so crude at that time that really I thought that I needed a spaceship and mad scientist and a monster. I couldn't do the mad scientist or the monster, but I did the spaceship. It was a utopia set on Mars. So that launched me further into science fiction. I was very lucky because I had entered a ghetto, a very friendly ghetto that has supported me more or less ever since.

Q: Somehow you managed to match the temper of the times in science fiction. I mean a book like *The Continuous Catherine Mortenhoe* or *Synthajoy* were both very much cutting-edge science fiction when they came out, particularly all this material about how media controls our lives, implants, etc. It's almost proto-cyberpunk.

Q: I, you see, am absolutely not a scientist in the smallest way. I had one of those English, very specialized educations, that young men used to have. I don't think it happens anymore. I studied only modern languages and English, really, so science was out. I was simply responding, as you have said, to things that were going on around me, and using science fiction gimmicks, such as the camera in *Katherine Mortenhoe,* as a metaphor for what was going on around me.

Q: I notice that in the Algis Budrys introduction to the Gregg Press edition of *Synthajoy,* that he remarks that much what you wrote about mind-control and electrical implants were almost being supported by experimental science at the time. Were you following any of this at the time? He mentions such things as the discovery that if you put a wire into a rat's brain and hook that up to a button, it will press the button continuously, neglecting food and water and all else until it dies.

Compton: That's very much the sort of popular science stuff that I as a non-scientist would have picked up out of the media or the general press and latched onto as something I could develop. *The Steel Crocodile* grew out of a book I did indeed read—the man's name escapes me [William Sargent, *The Unquiet Mind—DS*]—he was a brain scientist who claimed that, given access, he could indoctrinate any civilization within a couple of years with a new religion. I thought, that's a good idea, maybe I could use that. But anyway, this was all very pop science.

Q: You mean you read things like *New Scientist*—?

Compton: No, no, I never read anything that claimed to be scientific. I have not been interested, basically. I am very interested in society's reactions to what is offered them by science and things that they pick up and the things that they don't, but it's not a subject, basically that I understand. I don't even think I understand the scientific thought process. That's my problem.

Q: How about the science-fictional thought process? As you came to be published more in science fiction, did you develop a more conscious sense of being a science fiction writer?

Compton: I have to be honest and say that since even when I became a science fiction writer, I did not research the media. I should have gone out and read a lot of science fiction, but I never thought of myself as any sort of a writer. I was writing what was interesting me, and the science-fiction convention, which I only understood in a very clichéd and obvious way, gave me metaphors, a way of talking about things in, I hope, an interesting an unusual fashion.

Q: What got you writing at all? Have you always written for a living?

Compton: I always thought of myself as a writer. From a very early, school-day age, I had a facility on the page. I was glib. I was literate. As soon as I left school, basically, I went off to become a writer. I went to a rural cottage somewhere and I was going to be a writer. I was twenty-one years old and just out of the army and I sat down at my desk, armed with my facility, but rapidly discovered of course that I had absolutely nothing whatever to say. I then realized, of course, that there are two aspects of being a writer. One has to be able to write and one has to have something to say.

This was a very disheartening thought, because that meant I had to go out and get a job, various shit-jobs. I was a postman, a window-dresser, a bank guard. I worked on the docks. I just did things and things and collected *en route* a wife and two children. I did ten years of that, and then I got a very small inheritance, and then my wife, brave, brave, crazy woman, said, "Look, you've always said you were going to be a writer. Come along, do some writing." And I packed my job in. I was a door-to-door salesman at that time. Very bad at it, with my stammer apart from anything else, I didn't make a very good salesman.

So I sat down and wrote radio plays. And for two or three years I wrote and sold avant-garde radio dramas in England and then in Germany. I got myself a German translator and I think he made me much better than I actually was. He was a very good man.

And while I was doing that I started writing the crime novels, and after that, as I told you, I drifted into science fiction. The radio-play-shaped ideas stopped coming.

Q: Sometime after the end of the 1970s, I stopped noticing new books from you. Were you actually silent for a while?

Compton: Yes, I think I ran out of science-fiction-shaped ideas. I was working in the condensed book department of the *Reader's Digest* by day, and I was condensing popular stuff, and I was therefore understanding the market tastes a little more. This was the time when the gothic romances were very popular, and I though, My God, I can do this. Victorian pastiches, very heavily plotted. I have always loved plot. So I did half a dozen of those, under a pseudonym, as a woman, Frances Lynch. It isn't a secret. Those basically failed. I never achieved the sort of takeoff into big-sellerdom that I had hoped for. People who understood the business said, "The trouble with you is the fact that your tongue is in your cheek shows. It shows on the page that you're really not quite taking this seriously. Conviction isn't there."

So after doing a half a dozen of those, which probably was the six years you're talking about, of my absence, I did nothing at all, being very disheartened, until my agent found me a collaborator. I did one book with John Gribbin, *Ragnarok,* which is a political thriller dealing with terrorists, good terrorists who were holding the world to ransom. John Gribbin is a volcanologist. He is a scientist, a physicist, and had a theory that if you exploded a very small explosive device in the right place off the shores of Iceland, this would create a vast atomic eruption that would bring a long winter, a three-year dust cloud, so you could hold the whole world to ransom. We did out thriller along those lines, which did all right. That was sort of science-fictionish, so I got back into science fiction after that.

Q: Now that you are writing science fiction consciously, as opposed to when you were doing it without knowing it was science fiction, does this change your expectations of what the book should be?

Compton: Never. Absolutely never. These are books of character, of personality, of an individual who is changed. It's the classic structure that well-made novels have, but I'm centered in this. I'm interested in the evasions of people's lives, and the things that happen to make them recognize the evasions, and possibly cling to them nevertheless. I don't often have happy endings. There has always been a feeling, I gather, in fandom, in America anyway, about my books, "Oh, he's all right but he's so depressing."

Well, that's probably fair. I probably am, and my latest non-science-fiction one is probably the most depressing of them all, which is why I have a suspicion that it will never find daylight.

Q: You mean it won't be published here in the States, or anywhere?

Compton: Anywhere. I have become very involved, politically almost, in the assisted suicide movement with Oregon's record over here, and I became involved up in Maine when we had a referendum. My latest book grows out of that interest and concern. Not exactly a thigh-slapper.

Q: I see this in some of your earlier work, such as *The Continuous Katherine Mortenhoe*.

Compton: Indeed, so it isn't new.

Q: What I think we can say about that book is that it might be genuinely prophetic. It seems to be describing reality TV. It is probably only a matter of time until somebody does a reality TV show with the dying.

Compton: With the dying, yes. Did you ever pick up the movie?

Q: No, I didn't.

Compton: Ah, I am not surprised. It came and went.

Q: Was it called *The Continuous Katherine Mortenhoe*?

Compton: It was called *Death Watch*. Bernard Tavernier the French director did it with Harvey Keitel, Romy Schneider, Harry Dean Stanton, and Max Von Sydow. There were nice people in it. A lovely movie, in fact. But it was early and it had a downer at the end, and it never gained universal release. It went around the art houses. At Brown Bear Festival a couple years ago in Milford Pennsylvania they featured it. I was pleased. It's, what? Thirty years old now? Yes, thirty years old.

Q: Is it available on DVD?

Compton: No, only on VCR. That's a problem.

Q: If it's VHS, at least you can still find it.

Compton: Yes, sure. I have a copy. I am very fond of it. I was very lucky. It was early on in Harvey's career, and he gives a very nice performance. It was a film that I think stuck perhaps too reverentially to the book. I think maybe some more liberties ought to have been taken. But I like it.

Q: You're very fortunate as far as authors go. Most authors bemoan what is done to their books in the movies.

Compton: My favorite story, which luckily you haven't heard so I will tell it again, is that after I had heard from the director, who I didn't know anything about, that he wanted to make it, and my agent said, "Yes, he's reputable, so go on and have a talk." I went along expecting a clichéd, cigar-chewing guy, I and I was going to cry all the way to the bank after he had signed the contract, you know. First of all the image was completely wrong. It was a lithesome young Frenchman, rather elegant and thoughtful. I finally came down to the classic cliché question, "Tell me, why do you really want to make a film of my book?" He said, "There was one phrase in it that told me I had to make it, and it's when there's this dying woman and you write that 'she has the possibility of joy'."

I tell you this is utterly true. That sentence was the most important thing in that book for me and he had picked those six words out as his reason for making it. You can't get much luckier than that, can you?

Q: No, you can't.

Compton: Utterly phenomenal. [Laughs.] They believed in it and they all worked for peanuts, because they couldn't get any decent, major Hollywood funding. And I've a feeling that if they hadn't been so reverential and had picked it over a bit, it might have been a better film. But there you go.

Q: It might have been a worse film. It might have starred Arnold Schwarzenegger and had an upbeat ending.

Compton: That was why Hollywood wouldn't have it. They told Tavernier, "Yeah, we love it, but you really have to give it a happy ending." They really did.

Q: This gets back to the whole subject of downbeat endings. Wouldn't you agree that the reason you have a downbeat ending in a story is that it's the honest ending?

Compton: Usually, that's my experience. But then that isn't the reason that people go to the movies, is it? They go to the movies to feel good. I can understand this. You read books, probably, if you don't mind having to pick yourself up and dust yourself off afterwards after you've finished the final page. It *is* a different medium.

Q: Surely if you just say, "I'm going to write books with upbeat endings because they are more commercial," what you are going to produce is lies.

Compton: I would certainly say that, only maybe you and I have a view of the world that isn't generally shared. It's very interesting that you should say that. I have always been an admirer of Ursula Le Guin. And the other day I saw that she has a new book out. That heartened me because I think she's older than I am and I'm beginning to feel a bit written out, and what else is there to say, all that stuff, but I think her new book is very fine, and she is as positive-thinking as she always has been. It's a book with an upbeat ending. It's lovely. I was so hoping that she would be here, but she never travels now. [The new Le Guin book being referred to is *Voices.*—DS] I would have loved to have talked to her with the problems I have. There's enough doom and gloom out there. Do I really want to add to it?

Q: Maybe you want to add some understanding of it.

Compton: Maybe.

Q: As opposed to merely bemoaning.

Compton: I know. I know. Maybe helping other people. Yes.

There you go. But I certainly have problems now with justifying covering more pages with more depressing squiggles.

Q: I am thinking of that scene in *Shakespeare in Love* where the Queen says of his latest play, "That's very nice, but something more cheerful next time."

Compton: [Laughs.] Right. Yes. That's where I've gotten. My wife once got rather worried looking at my *oeuvre* in general. Most of them end with the woman dying or being put in a mental home or being carted off, or whatever. One reason for that of course is simply because I use so many strong central women characters. I was a feminist almost before the word was invented. I have always been pro the woman's place in the intellectual and power-structure world. I do remember early on over the first three or four, I read several reviews speculating on whether D. G. Compton was a man or a woman. I was really very pleased that I fooled them. [Laughs.]

Q: Budrys talks about that in the introduction to *Synthajoy*. He cites a line in which female protagonist notices she is sweating under her bra, and something about worrying about her shoe size, and this is not something that would come from male observation.

Compton: Well, there you go. I am glad I fooled him too.

Q: You only did it briefly. Is this all from a sense that women aren't empowered enough in society, or that women aren't represented enough in fiction? There was a time in which science fiction notably did not have a lot of women in it.

Compton: When Hodder published *Katherine Mortenhoe* they said, "You can't have a woman's name in the title. It's science fiction. You can't." As simple as that.
   I am simply a great admirer of...Oh, God...womanliness. A

woman's views, a woman's position.

I suppose I cannot think of a novel that has a really strong, but at the same time rounded and real woman as a lead character. Perhaps that's my ignorance.

Q: You mean a science fiction novel?

Compton: No, novel, period. I haven't read any science fiction. I really haven't. Four or five books in thirty years. It's not a genre that I have ever, I suppose, found all that—I should be saying this—comfortable.

Q: It's all right. You can be contrarian.

Compton: [Laughs.] I can be contrarian. No, I do not read science fiction. Certainly my generation of science fiction, as far as I can discern, they all came out of reading the field and graduating there. Of course growing up in England during the Second World War, there weren't any SF magazines going on there. I do remember that we had an a couple American soldiers billeted on us, a couple of the nicest guys. And my only experience with science fiction up until adulthood was, I think, a single episode of "The Incredible Expanding Man," in one of their comics.

Q: I can't place what that is.

Compton: But I remember it well. And at eleven years old I was absolutely enchanted with the idea of the *incredible expanding man.*

Q: I've heard that they used to use American pulp magazines as ballast on ships, and then they were sold very cheaply in London, and a lot of English science fiction writers of your generation read old American magazines that they picked up for a penny or two. Didn't you have access to this? Did you grow up in the country or in a big city?

Compton: What I've left out is that I come from a theatrical family. My father and mother were both in the theatre, and my initial thought was always that I would write plays. Therefore most of my literary interests as a young man were dramatic. That of course is why when I finally settled down to write, I wrote plays. I wrote radio plays because by then I had recognized the extreme difficulty in getting stage plays performed, whereas there was a wonderful, inexhaustible market at that time for radio drama.

Q: What were your radio plays like? Were they at all fantastic or were they realistic stories?

Compton: They got called avant-garde. They were very odd pieces, literary fantasies, literary games-playing I suppose. Gosh, it's all a very long time ago now. [When the small press, Kerosina, published Compton's *Scudder's Game,* they produced a boxed Collector's Edition that included two of his more accessible radio plays –DS] One of the more successful ones dealt with a man having to choose between a fantasy girl he was living with and a real one. Of course by the time he had hemmed and hawed and chosen the fantasy one she'd given up on him and pissed off, and so he got nothing. It was odd stuff.

Q: But she was a real person?

Compton: Oh, no.

Q: He created her.

Compton: He lost her by a loss of faith in her. I didn't know what I was talking about. I was twenty-nine years old. But people did them, and particularly, as I said, the Germans at that time were very snobbish about their radio. It was *kultur.*

Television had come along, only that was for the masses, and the Germans looked for their culture on the radio. My translator handled Beckett and Ionesco and all the people of that time who were writing very odd plays, not exactly realistic, and I fitted in to that sort of thing. I wasn't Samuel Beckett obviously, but I fitted in with *Waiting for Godot, Rhinocerous,* Jarry's Theatre of the Absurd and the Theatre of Cruelty, all the odd things that were going on at that time in Europe. All these early plays. In America too—Albee's *Zoo Story.* I was in that genre.

Q: We can see in retrospect that this was a step toward science fiction, without you knowing it.

Compton: Yes, indeed. And I always had a very serious intent. I must have been a very earnest young man. I was concerned by moral imperatives, so I brought to my plays that urge toward thoughtfulness that has continued ever since, certainly. Every one of my books has a moral center, I would say.

Q: Thank you, Mr. Compton.

(Recorded at the Nebula Awards weekend in New York, May 12, 2007, where Compton was present to receive SFWA's Author Emeritus award.)

ROBERT J. SAWYER

Q: So, what's your background? What brought you to the SF field?

Sawyer: Well, skipping over all that boring stuff between the Big Bang and April 1960, I was born in Ottawa, Canada's Capital city. My father was an economist, and shortly after I was born he was offered a teaching appointment at the University of Toronto, so we moved there, and Toronto, or environs, has been my home ever since.

I was first introduced to science fiction through kid's TV shows, most notably Gerry Anderson's *Fireball XL5,* which started airing in Canada in 1963, when I was three; I still consider the music played over the closing credits of that series—"I Wish I Was a Spaceman"—to be my personal theme song.

When I was twelve, my older brother and my dad noted what I was watching on TV, and they got me some science-fiction books: *Trouble on Titan*, a YA novel by Alan E. Nourse; *The Rest of the Robots*, Asimov's second robot collection; and David Gerrold's first novel, *Space Skimmer.* I'm still enormously fond of all three, and am thrilled to now be friends with David. In fact, we collaborated on editing an essay collection entitled *Boarding the Enterprise* last year in honor of the fortieth anniversary of classic *Star Trek*, which, as anyone who has read my books knows, was also a big influence on me.

Indeed, with all due respect to those book authors, I've got to say that it was media science fiction—the original *Star Trek*, the original *Planet of the Apes,* and, to a lesser degree, the original *Twilight Zone*—that really opened my eyes to SF as a vehicle for social comment, for looking at the here and now.

Fast-forwarding: I knew from very early on that I wanted to write science fiction, and I'd been captivated by Gene Roddenberry and Stephen E. Whitfield's book *The Making of Star Trek.* So after high school I did a degree in Radio and Television Arts at Toronto's Ryerson University. Ironically, in doing courses in English literature there, I discovered that print, not film or TV, was were I really wanted to be.

I made a living after I graduated in 1982 for the next decade mostly doing nonfiction writing, plus the odd SF story on the side. I somewhat precipitously became a full-time SF writer in 1990, when my first novel, *Golden Fleece*, came out.

For the record, anyone who says major awards have no financial value is full of beans—I made more money off of science fiction in the six months following winning the Best Novel Nebula Award in 1996 for *The Terminal Experiment* than I'd made in the six years preceding that. John Douglas, one of my editors on that book, put it just right the day after I won the Nebula, I think: "Overnight, you've gone from being a promising beginner to an established, bankable name." I've made a comfortable living ever since, and now have seventeen novels under my belt.

Q: What difference does it make, in terms of writing SF, that you are a Canadian? Sure, it probably means you get more local media coverage, but I note that all those books and TV shows you cite (except for *Fireball XL5*) were American. Do you think that a Canadian perspective produces a different kind of SF? Did you find it necessary to learn to "fake American" in order to sell to American markets? Did anybody try to pressure you to do this?

Sawyer: Honestly, the difference it makes is principally financial. I make about double what I'd be making if I lived in the

States. First, science fiction actually is quite popular in Canada, and people aren't such genre snobs here—plus they like to buy Canadian. That means, even though the population is only one-tenth as big, I sell as many copies in Canada as I do in the States, and that makes me a national mainstream bestseller here, and that directly translates into money in my pocket.

Being a big fish in a small pond has other advantages: I've got a lucrative sideline going as a keynote speaker at conferences up here, doing about one major gig a month. And there's a long list of paid library residencies and so forth; as we do this interview, I'm sitting rent-free in Canada's north, being paid a stipend of $2,000 a month to write a book that I'm already being paid by the publisher to write. And although the really big bucks are doubtless in Hollywood movies, the Canadian film industry is significant, and options tons of properties. Right now, I've got film rights to ten of my novels under option, nine of which are to Canadian producers.

As it happens, I'm a dual US-Canadian citizen—my mother is an American who was temporarily in Canada when I was born—and someone asked me recently if I'd ever thought of moving to the States. The implication was that, like actors leaving Toronto to try their luck in L.A., that that should be my next move. But he had it backwards, and I had to say to him, "Sorry, I couldn't afford the cut in pay."

Now, what about the impact on the words I write? Well, being a Canadian resident hugely affects my perspective. Canada is a middle power, a nation of peacekeepers, and a country that looks for compromise. There's no doubt that my politics are liberal by American standards, and that my heroes are much more pacifistic than most Americans would write. The most often quoted remark from all my books is something an alien said in *Calculating God*: "Honor does not have to be defended." To a Canadian that seems right: honor is something you have, it can't be taken away by anyone; to a lot of Americans, though, that line seems nonsensical.

Anyone familiar with both Canada and the United States is

aware that I criticize both countries—hell, the Government of Ontario gets ripped a new one in *Calculating God*. But some of the commentary on Canada goes unnoticed by some American readers, because they don't get the references, and so they think I'm only taking swipes at the US government, and they get testy about that.

But I make no apologies. When the Soviet Union invaded Afghanistan in 1980, and Jimmy Carter reactivated Selective Service, I could have said screw that, I'm in Canada, but I went and registered for the draft, and to this day I file a tax return with the IRS. I'm an American citizen and criticizing both the countries I love is not just my birthright, it is, I honestly believe, my patriotic duty—God love the Dixie Chicks! And, yes, just like them, I do love the United States: I don't think anyone who has read the speech by the American president that appears in segments at the beginning of each chapter in my *Hybrids* could think otherwise. Right after 9/11, we put an American flag on our car in solidarity; it's still there and it's the only flag on our car.

And, sure, lots of Canadians told me to Americanize my books if I wanted to sell them to publishers in the Big Apple; they kept saying that Americans wouldn't get what I was saying. But I refused to believe that Americans were that provincial, if you'll forgive the pun. I've had books published by Warner, HarperCollins USA, Ace, and Tor, and never once have any of them ever asked me to tone down the Canadian content on my books. And why should they? Americans love Canada, and Canadians, honest to God, love Americans.

Q: So, do you get your ideas from the secret P.O. Box in Schenectady that American writers use, or another one somewhere in Canada?

But, more seriously, I should think that an important difference between Canadian and American SF (and writing in general) is that may topics which are controversial in the USA are not in Canada. I doubt Evolution is a big deal in Canada, whereas in the US school system it's almost a taboo. I can see two ways this could affect things. First, it could mean that you have more freedom writing in Canada. Or it could mean that in order to make satirical or controversial points in the US, you might seem to the Canadians to be belaboring the obvious. Any sense of this? I imagine we have more flat-earthers in the US too. Or do I have a greener-pastures view of Canada?

Sawyer: No, no, there's no doubt that intellectually, these days, the pastures are greener in Canada. Our prime minister is only a moron; your president is an idiot...[laughs]. Seriously, of course there's a reactionary right wing here in Canada, and religious fundamentalists, too, but they don't hold much political sway, to which I'll say, advisedly, thank God.

But one very valid reading of my Neanderthal trilogy is that the Neanderthal culture I portray is emblematic of Canadian ideals: full acceptance of alternative lifestyles including the whole GLBT gamut and polygamy, plus secularism, pacifism, and environmentalism, topped off with the willingness to give up personal liberty for the common good (for the actual common good, not trumped-up threats). It's significant that many American critics have termed the portrayed world utopian. It isn't—it's not no-place; it's that big honking land you get to if you just keep driving north.

But, you know, I have had troubles with the US market, now that I think about it. Back in 1994, I submitted *The Terminal Experiment,* as a finished manuscript, to my then publisher, who had an option on the book—and the publisher rejected it, despite the fact that my previous books for them had been doing well (and, indeed, they eventually bought five more books from me).

Now, there's no doubt that *The Terminal Experiment*—which is about a biomedical engineer who finds proof for the existence of the human soul—is in part about the abortion issue; it's not even subtextual; I say it directly in the book. And the editor in question said they feared their ability to sell this material in the Bible Belt. Yes, changes and cuts were suggested, but I refused to make them, and my agent at the time, the redoubtable Richard Curtis, supported me in that.

So, we moved on to another publisher with a new imprint that I think really was trying to draw attention to itself, the HarperPrism line, and they published the book verbatim as the previous house had rejected it...and, of course, *The Terminal Experiment* went on to win the Science Fiction and Fantasy Writers of America's Nebula Award for Best Novel of the Year. So, I guess it paid to stick to my guns...which, of course, is something we Canadians only do metaphorically!

My great friend Robert Charles Wilson has recently come up with a definition of what science fiction is (my own, incidentally, is "the mainstream literature of an alternate reality"). He says that SF is "the literature of contingency"—and he very much is intending a Gouldian evolutionary reading of that. And, yes, damn it, from *The Time Machine* on, SF has been, at its core, about evolution: how things could have been different; how things might turn out. That America is turning its back on the single greatest scientific truth we know—natural selection resulting in speciation—is painful to me. It's no coincidence, I think, that the major SF novels about evolution of the last several years—my own *Fossil Hunter* and *Calculating God*, and Stephen Baxter's aptly titled *Evolution*—are by non-Americans.

As for getting the ideas, actually, the fount—and I think this is true for many of us hard-SF writers, regardless of nationality—is really in Britain: the weekly magazine *New Scientist*. How can you not love a magazine whose subtitle is "The Week's Best Ideas"?

Q: There's a certain type of American (who probably vote Republican; which I do not) who might say that the reason Canadians have this more utopian view is that someone else has always looked out for them. They've spent their entire history either under the protection of the British Empire or the

Americans. Is there any validity in that, or are Canadians just as good at staring Hitler, Stalin, or Osama bin Laden in the face as anyone? Or does Canadian SF look at things through rose-tinted glasses?

Sawyer: I would invite this hypothetical "certain type of American" to actually read some history, old boy. First, Canada has been an independent country since 1867; we've hardly been relying on the Brits since then. As for the United States protecting us—when and from whom, one might ask? The wars the United States has fought during my lifetime—Vietnam and Afghanistan and Iraq—were not particular threats to Canada, and Canadian peacekeepers are still in Afghanistan, mopping up the mess made there. NORAD, the North American Air Defense Command, is a joint US-Canada effort. In fact, a Canadian officer, Canadian Forces Major General Rick Findley, was in charge of the battle staff at NORAD's Cheyenne Mountain complex on September 11, 2001.

As for staring down Hitler and Stalin, Canada joined the Allied Powers and sent our boys off to die in Europe starting September 10, 1939—just nine days after the invasion of Poland. The US, on the other hand, sat on the sidelines until after the attack on its own facility at Pearl Harbour on December 7, 1941, over two years later.

Parenthetically, my favorite film is *Casablanca*, and I recently had someone refer to it in my presence as "wonderful escapism." It's not: it's a pointed commentary on the United States's failure to join in the fight against Hitler. The American Rick Blaine says, "I stick my neck out for no one," and the European Ferrari has to say to him, "My dear Rick, when will you realize that in this world today, isolationism is no longer a practical policy?"

And as for Osama bin Laden, well, politely, he hasn't attacked Canada, although we share in the outrage over what he's done. But I think its regrettable that all that can be said is that perhaps he is being stared down, rather than apprehended, and it's not been particularly effective leadership going after

Saddam Hussein instead of the real threat. But Canada faced its own home-soil terrorism crisis in October 1970, and then Prime Minister Pierre Trudeau so effectively and swiftly dealt with that event that it is no coincidence that there's been no act of terrorism on Canadian soil in the thirty-seven intervening years.

Canada's foreign-policy record (including our Prime Minister, Lester Pearson, winning the Nobel Peace Prize in 1957), its foreign-aid record, its record of vigorously joining battles in just wars, and its peacekeeping record speaks for themselves. Canada doesn't have rose-colored glasses on—but, if I may be so bold, your hypothetical American of a certain type has on blinkers.

Q: I wonder why the publisher even worried about how *Calculating God* or any of your novels would sell in the Bible Belt. Do they really think that Fundamentalists buy anything more SFish than the *Left Behind* books?

Sawyer: I never claimed to understand my publisher's decision; I merely report it—but the book in question was *The Terminal Experiment*, not *Calculating God*; Tor, who published the latter book, has been nothing but 100% supportive in letting me tell my stories my way.

But, in fact, having been guest of honor at many SF conventions in the South—Albuquerque, Houston, Memphis, Chattanooga, Knoxville, Orlando, and Richmond, to name some—it's clear that there are lots of SF readers down there, and, yes, some of them do have a sensibility that varies from that in the north.

A fellow from Bethlehem, Georgia, wrote this of my *Hybrids* on Amazon.com: "I mentioned in an earlier review that with respect to Sawyer's Liberalism, he let the nose of the camel come peeking under the tent. Well, in *Hybrids* the camel is all the way inside the tent and it has taken a dump in the middle. I'm going to have to hold my nose if I read any more of his stories. Points include the old Military Industrial Complex as the boogieman, and universal homosexuality being apparently espoused."

Well, first, of course, neither of those things actually happen in *Hybrids:* the villain is a sole terrorist acting alone, but I am very proud of the fact that the book was nominated for the Spectrum Award, which celebrates positive portrayals of gay, lesbian, or bi characters in SF. More to the point, though, it stuns me that the quality of my book, or any book, is being judged not on its execution but rather on its politics—an astonishing way to review a book, in my view. In fairness to the reviewer, though, he did give my book four stars—but I've seen other examples of people sorting SF into "good" and "bad" based simply on the underlying politics not on the effectiveness of the storytelling.

Q: We've had a lot of people in our field bemoan the apparent retreat of science fiction itself, Gregory Benford most notably. Just as the "future" has arrived, we have space travel, exo-planets are being discovered by the dozen, we have robots, the internet, etc.—now so many writers and readers are no longer interested in the future, and alternate histories and fantasy seem to outsell anything that resembles real SF. What do you make of this?

Sawyer: Oh, yes, I've been decrying this for years. In 1999, I gave a talk at the Library of Congress entitled: "The Future is Already Here: Is There a Place for Science Fiction in the 21st Century?" And I'm just reading William Gibson's latest, *Spook Country*, and he's given up totally on writing about the future, finding, as many others do, wonder enough in the present.

Certainly, for my own career, I've moved my work much closer to the here-and-now. You can divide my career into two parts: the first phase included my off-Earth spaceships-and-aliens novels: *Golden Fleece, Far-Seer, Fossil Hunter, Foreigner, End of an Era,* and *Starplex*. Now, I'm very proud of all of those, and *Starplex* was the only 1996 novel to be nominated for both the Hugo and the Nebula, not to mention winning Canada's Aurora and being nominated for Japan's Seiun. But, as a group, they are my worst sellers. My best sellers are all the others, starting with *The Terminal Experiment*: near-future or present day, and exclusively on Earth.

It's a mode I intend to continue in, because I've found that I can still do all the things I want to do artistically and philosophically in that milieu. And I use that term "philosophically" advisedly: if I had my druthers, this field would be called philosophical fiction, not science fiction—phi-fi, not sci-fi.

But I am still very much a hard SF author: actual, real science is the backbone of my work. That it's a field that draws fewer and fewer readers each year saddens me. I used to say, man, I wished I started selling novels a decade earlier, in the early 1980s, with the wave of writers that included the last bunch to become really rich writing SF: Greg Benford himself, William Gibson, David Brin, Greg Bear, Kim Stanley Robinson.

Now I say I'm so glad I didn't start a decade later: my first book came out in 1990, and I make a good living, but the guys who are starting out in the first decade of the twenty-first century are facing a much smaller audience, with vastly reduced print runs. The era of any appreciable number of people being full-time SF writers is coming to a close, and that's bad artistically for the field.

Q: Why *not* continue to write of a spacefaring far future? If we haven't given up on those Heinleinian vision of out species expanding outward, isn't *now* more than ever the time for someone to write a really compelling, intelligent far-future, outer-space story, if only to capture the audience back from Harry Potter? You may have seen the exchanges I had with Gregory Benford over this. If hard SF is losing its market share, surely the only possible solution is *better* SF to bring those readers back.

Sawyer: Nope, I disagree. It's the disconnect between our here-and-now and the far-flung outer-space story that's driven people out of SF: no human has left Earth orbit for 35 years now, and yet we tell people they should give up their precious reading time to space opera because it's somehow important, relevant, and true?

The reason I'm prospering is that I have managed to bring in large numbers of readers who don't habitually read SF, while not alienating the core SF audience. The outsiders care not one whit for magical post-singularitarian or transhumanist worlds, but find the "what does it mean to be human" theme of my work to be of interest.

It's a tricky balancing act: appealing to the hardcore SF readers and to mainstream readers alike, but I seem to be managing it. *Calculating God* was a national top-ten mainstream bestseller in Canada, meaning it was being widely read and enjoyed by people who don't read science fiction, and it hit number one on the bestsellers' list in *Locus,* which is based on a survey of science-fiction specialty stores, meaning it was appealing to hardcore SF readers, too. *Hominids* was used for a major "if everyone read the same book" program in Canada, and was hugely popular there with people who had never read an SF novel in their lives—and it also won the Hugo, voted on by the absolute hardcore of SF fans, those who are members of the World Science Fiction Convention. The future of SF isn't narrowly focusing on distant tomorrows, but broadening the appeal to bring in readers from outside the shrinking core.

Far-future SF has gotten increasingly esoteric, and increasingly magical rather than grounded in reasoned extrapolation. Remember Homer Simpson, when he became an astronaut, looking lovingly at an inanimate carbon rod, and saying, "Is there anything it can't do?" Substitute "nanotech" or "post-singularity science" or whatever your favorite synonym for Clarke's "indistinguishable from magic" is, and you get a lot of so-called science fiction today—and 99.999% of humanity has no interest in it, not because they don't believe great advances in technology may someday be possible but because they're being wielded like magic wands in these stories, and, frankly, the actual fantasy writers do a better job of combining magic with rousing plots and compelling characterization. Even if far-future SF writers rose to the challenge of adding those missing elements, they'd still only be producing an oddball variant of fantasy, not something unique and special in its own right.

Q: About your new novel.... Describe a little of what it's about and how you came to write it.

Sawyer: *Rollback*, my seventeenth novel, out now from Tor, is a good example of what I've been talking about in terms of trying to appeal in and out of genre. Canada's national newspaper, *The Globe and Mail,* called it "a novel to be savored by science-fiction and mainstream readers alike," whereas *Publishers Weekly,* in its starred reviews, recognized that the core SF reader should like it, too, saying "Sawyer, who has won Hugo and Nebula awards, may well win another major SF award with this superior effort." And, indeed, it is hardcore, hard SF: heck, it was serialized in *Analog* prior to book publication: you can't get any more hard-SF than that!

Rollback started with a pure high concept: a man and a woman, both in their eighties, are offered a chance to be rejuvenated, each becoming physically twenty-five again. They accept—and it works for the man and fails for the woman.

The book just grew organically from exploring the ins and outs of that concept: all the heartbreak, all the joy, all the wonder. Of course, I had to find a reason why someone might want to live for a very long time that wasn't petty and self-serving, and I soon settled on making the woman a SETI researcher who had been instrumental in decoding messages from aliens, and that the dialog, because of the light-speed delay, was going to take many decades if not centuries. And then that made me start thinking about morals and ethics, and how our view of right and wrong might change if we lived for a very long time, and the novel's philosophical backbone is exploring what morals might actually be universal, transcending species boundaries. A novel accretes—a plot point here, a grace note there, a flourish, an ironic touch—but that was its genesis.

It really was a Hollywood-style high-concept pitch, by the way. I was actually under contract to Tor to write a different novel—a single, standalone volume to have been called *Webmind* about the World Wide Web gaining consciousness. And I was finding as I was working on it that the idea was too big for one book. But I had a contract to fulfill, and so I actually had a power lunch—I felt so Hollywood! I went out to lunch with Tor publisher Tom Doherty and my editor at Tor, Dave Hartwell, and said, look, I want to set aside *Webmind,* and do another book for you instead: and I gave them the high-concept pitch, and they green-lit it, as the saying goes.

Rollback was an emotionally draining book to write, I must say: I had to face a lot of my own thoughts and fears about aging and death; I freely confess that I cried while writing parts of it. But the response has been wonderfully positive from readers. Many of them have told me they cried in the right places, too—and, of course, laughed a lot, too: I always have lots of humor in my books.

I've now gone back to the conscious-Web idea, and have sold it as a trilogy: *Wake, Watch,* and *Wonder*—collectively, the WWW series. I'm well into *Wake* now, and it's coming along nicely.

Q: Thanks, Rob.

(Recorded in the Summer of 2007.)

CHARLES STROSS

Q: Charles, let's start with the really obvious stuff, who you are, your background, how you got into writing.

Stross: How I got into writing? I don't even remember. I think I first tried to write a short story when I was about seven. Around the time I was in high school I got my hands on an old manual typewriter and I began churning out the regular million words of crap. I was certainly far from being able to write. The sad fact is that despite the introducer's talk about my illustrious career as the hot new thing, I am a breakout success after about twenty years.

After my first professionally published short story, which was published in *Interzone* in 1986, it took me seventeen years to actually have a novel come out.

Q: How long had you been writing before you sold the story to *Interzone*?

Stross: I do remember actual that my first successful attempt at writing a science fiction novel—successful for values of "I'll burn it if I can ever find it"—was when I was fifteen. It ran to about 40,000 words and it was dire, so I redrafted it and redrafted it again. Then, by the time I was sixteen the keys on that little manual typewriter began snapping from metal fatigue. So one manual typewriter later, I was still writing rubbish, but more proficient rubbish in large quantities.

Around the time I was twenty I got my first word-processor. You shouldn't underestimate the advantages of a word-processor for revising text. I was getting better at what I was doing, which was just as well at the time. It was around the time I was around twenty-one that I actually sold that first story. It's probably a damn good thing that nobody offered me a three-book contract at that point, because I would not have been an overnight success, to put it mildly. There's a reason most writers don't really break big until they're in their thirties. It actually has to do with life experience.

But if I had actually realized this when I was younger, I probably would have given up, if I had known how long it would take. But I was too stupid to wait.

Q: You had succeeded in the sense that you'd sold a story in your early twenties. There are many people who are still beating their heads against the wall at fifty.

Stross: Yes. I had begun getting that positive feedback reinforcement loop where they actually pay you by the word for what you're doing. A lot of writers basically give up after a while, if they've been trying hard at selling stories and have failed.

I was not quite sure what I was doing right at the time. It took me a while to learn how to write consistent short stories, and then a significantly longer time to master what I needed to do to write an adequate novel. One of my later early novels is on a website, where I sort of left it. It's a trunk novel that's not really good enough that I would want to see it on paper these days, but it was good enough that I didn't think it needed to molder in a desk drawer. It came within a couple of inches of being sold in 1994. It was a couple of books after that that I got the process of writing a novel down sufficiently well, with a sufficient understanding of the processes involved in writing, that I could replicate it and do better.

Q: Were you in touch with any other science fiction writers in Britain at this time, part of any discernable scene, or were you in a garret working by yourself.

Stross: I was pretty much in touch. Around the time I was eighteen I got in touch with an amateur writers' workshop working out of Northampton, called the Cassandra Workshop. Several writers in the UK scene have come out of there, notably Simon Ings, for example, who some of you may have heard of. I also discovered fandom about the same time. I have been going to SF cons since about 1984. So I have been a fan since before I was selling any fiction. And I have workshopped quite regularly with other writers. I was a regular at the Milford writers' workshops in the '80s and '90s in the UK, residential one-week workshops. So, yes, I haven't exactly come out of a vacuum. By about the mid-1990s I had sold about fifteen or twenty stories in various venues. I came fairly close to selling a novel in 1994 except for a three-way cluster-fuck involving myself, an agent, and an editor and a comedy of misunderstood intentions.

But around 1989 I also discovered that I could line my pockets reasonably well doing freelance journalism, on a subject I knew a lot about, namely computers. This was while I was doing a computer science degree, having I decided that I was *not* cut out for life as a pharmacist. I was a student and this was a great way to get free copies of software. You'd write to a magazine and say "Give me a copy of X and I'll review it for you." And they would, and they'd even write you a check afterwards. By the mid-'90s I was writing pretty regularly for a magazine called *Computer Shopper,* not for sale in the United States, but it was about the second-highest circulation newstand magazine in the UK. This began to eat into my time.

Around 1995 I moved to Scotland and joined a start-up web company. I was writing a non-fiction web-book for Addison-Wesley at the time, and I suddenly realized in about 1995 or 1996 that I had sold one short story that year. It was a reprint of one I had sold the year before. I also realized at that time that I hadn't been working on a novel for a couple years, and it began to look to me as if I were actually on the edge of giving up writing fiction. So I decided that I had to either give it a real shot or just give up. It was at this point that, having pretty much failed in the preceding decade to do anything other than sell short stories to *Interzone,* I sat down and tried to figure out what I had learnt the hard way, by running at things—by writing the proverbial million words of crap, bouncing off things, learning how *not* to do things.

If any of you want to be a writer, don't follow editors around at conventions with a carrier-bag full of manuscripts. [Laughter from audience.] It doesn't work. It just annoys them. I found that out when I was seventeen.

So I decided I needed a strategy. The strategy is very simple. If you want to succeed as a writer, you need to write. You need to finish stuff, you need to send it out to places where it is conceivable the editor might want to publish it.

I meant to take a fairly commercial approach. I decided I was going to start writing science fiction novels. I wanted to start with a space opera, because it struck me that a) I had something interesting to say about that area and b) it was saleable. In other areas I had something to say but they were somewhat less commercially viable. Start a novel, finish it, send it out. It would take years to get off an editor's desk, because there are few publishers who will now read stuff that is unagented, and they're all chronically behind schedule in reading for the slush-pile. Start another book, but not a sequel, one in a separate sub-genre. Hopefully I would be blanketing the target. At the same time I was going to do the *traditional* thing, which I had up till then discounted as completely impossible. I gather that at a Clarion workshop some years ago, somebody asked Gardner Dozois what the trick was for success in science fiction publishing. He said, "There's no secret about it. What you do is write a kick-ass series of short stories and you sell it to one of the major magazines, get a major critical following, get nominated for awards, and then you place a novel."

This isn't secret. [Laughter from audience.] John Varley did it. William Gibson did it. This happens all along. And yet I'd known perfectly well that this was complete rubbish. I couldn't possibly do that. But why not try?

It worked.

Q: When you started writing in the '80s, we had something called Cyberpunk. Did you feel that you were standing on the shoulders of that movement?

Stross: If I mention that when I was a spotty seventeen-year-old I was getting copies of *Cheap Truth* through the mail from Bruce Sterling, then yes, I was unhealthily interested in the cyberpunks. I've grown out of it. I think most of them grew out of it as well. You can't write the same thing all the time. You have to move on. I think some some of the cyberpunks have turned out to be very, very interesting writers indeed.

But yes, they were definitely influential. They weren't the primary influence on my SF, not in isolation.

Q: We also see strands of H.P. Lovecraft in your work, including a recent novel which has been described to me as "Ian Fleming meets H. P. Lovecraft." Would you describe your interest in Lovecraft?

Stross: You haven't met my wife but she specializes in collecting photographs of authors having their brains eaten by him. [Laughter from audience.] We have a slight Lovecraft problem in my household. [Louder laughter from audience.] Yeah, H. P. Lovecraft is very influential.

But one of my secret vices is that I am also an aficionado of spy thrillers, primarily the traditional British spy thriller. I had read my way through all of Ian Fleming by the time I was about twelve, and that can warp you for life. I also have a weakness for secret histories. So, some time ago, I think in the mid-1990s, I started working on a novel. It has a long history, but to sum it up at the end, it was never published, but it was cannibalized in chunks that have come up in different contexts.

I was very interested in Vernor Vinge's idea of the Singularity at the time, and I came up with an interesting hypothesis, which was: What if artificial intelligence is actually fairly easy to develop, but we can also anticipate a hard-takeoff singularity when it emerges. Why hasn't it happened? Well, what if there organizations out there dedicated to *suppressing* it? So I worked on this thriller in which we have a rather strange spy organization whose job is to suppress outbreaks of artificial intelligence. This didn't work terribly well, for one reason or another, but I had an idea: hell, I'm going to write a spy-thriller, and let's go back and grab H. P. Lovecraft, or, as Terry Pratchett parodied it, the Dungeon Dimensions. And let's backfill an explanation, because what the hell, I want to do a slashdot reading, sandal-wearing computer nerd who has fallen into a Len Deighton novel and can't get out. And Lovecraftian horrors as backfiller. There's an old trope that has been used a lot in science fiction, or science fantasy actually, in which magic is merely applied higher mathematics. Computers are machines for doing an awful lot of mathematical operations very fast. Therefore computer hackers are natural recruits for any such security organization. That's basically where *The Atrocity Archives* started coming from. It came more from the spy-thriller roots, but more with Lovecraftian horrors from beyond space-time as an adversary rather than the Soviet Union. Some people would say there's not much difference there.

Q: We all have the feeling that our computers are alive, capricious, and magical. Possibly that comes from real life.

Stross: Possibly. I know they're out to get me.

Q: A lot of things you have written, particularly *Accelerando,* give the impression that no only will science fiction be obsolete faster than we can read it, but *so will we.* The obsolescence of the human being.

Stross: *Accelerando* started out as a short story, which was my attempt to avoid a nervous breakdown. I mentioned that I wasn't really cut out to be a pharmacist, so in 1989 I went back to university to do a one-year conversion degree to computer science, which is basically when they drop an entire undergraduate computer science degree on you in one year. You either fail or you survive. I survived and by 1995 I had gotten sucked into the swirling vortex that was the World Wide Web and the dot-com boom. In 1997 I was recruited, as a contractor initially, by a company that was formed about two weeks earlier to do e-commerce bank clearing things in the UK: a company called Datacash. I was there for about three and a half years writing the main software which their business ran on. The company went public successfully. It IPOed at the tail-end of the dot-com boom.

Now, life as lead code-monkey inside a dot-com which is growing at thirty percent compounded growth per *month* is a bit hairy. I was doing my nut. We really needed an entire software development team to do my job, but we didn't have the funds to recruit them because we were being paid a month behind the growth curve, which at thirty percent was quite steep. I was stuck holding together what had been originally written as a proof-of-concept demo—this company had just $50,000 to fund it. (This was a shoestring operation initially.) I was holding it together with string and baling wire while it was handling what at one time appeared to be about twenty percent of all the e-commerce transactions in Europe. If anything went wrong, I'd get the blame. I was doing my nuts on this, to begin with, dealing with British clearing banks. Banking IT is an oxymoron. [Laughter from audience.] I know far more than anyone should have to know about the workings of British bankers and the level of their psychology. And then I met the *French bankers...* [Laughter from audience.] Because word came down from on high, you must plug in to this e-commerce operation being offered by a subsidiary of Bank Paribas.

You know what they say about French computer programmers? Let's just say French computer programmers are notorious in the industry. There are good ones, but they usually get the hell out. The bad ones always will start working for the really large enterprises, and the banking programmers in any country are bad. Having to tie into a French bank's idea of what an e-commerce system should look like *is* a Lovecraftian horror. [Laughter from audience.] It got its tentacles into me, good.

One Thursday I was grappling with my to-do list, which at that point was eight and a half man-years long, and things just came to a head and I turned to my boss, the chief technology officer, and said, "Look I am going to Amsterdam for a weekend." They just stared at me. They didn't mind I had an eight-and-a-half-year-long to-do list: they took one look at my expression and said, "Okay."

So Feorag and I headed off to Amsterdam and I lay awake in bed until four o'clock in the morning that night mentally drafting my letter of resignation. You can tell how bad this was. The next day we were wandering around Amsterdam in the rain, when I get a phonecall from the office and it was my boss. "Yeah, what is it Dave?" "It's about Kleline"—the French e-commerce operation. [Stross speaks in a low, grim voice.] *"What is it now?"*

I don't want to get into the technical explanation of just why this company was so bad, but let's just say it was nightmarish. "It's about Kleline, there's a problem." "Yes," I said. "We've just heard Bank Paribas"—their parent company—"are *winding them up!* For incompetence!"

I heard a burst of applause from around the office in the background. [Laughter from audience.] So I headed to the nearest pub to get very drunk indeed. I suddenly realized that all of this had to come out somewhere, because I was living through, basically, five years worth of normal time compressed into each year, the equivalent of about a year's worth of change every two and a half months. It was doing my head in. The sense of rapid change that comes out in the first part of *Accelerando* externalized what I was feeling living in the back end of a successful dot-com in 1998 or 1999. That is where that came from, the blistering pace of change. It took me some years to slow down and calm down after I left that business.

Q: Getting back to the concept of Singularity, if the near future will become incomprehensible due to the rate of change, how do you write about it?

Stross: With difficulty. On the other hand, I'm not convinced by it. On the subject of the Singularity I'm an agnostic. It might happen. It might not. I certainly don't hold with the "Rapture of the Nerds" interpretation that some people have. [Laughter from audience.] There is a tendency for it to get conflated with messianic, millennial fervor, which I should denounce very thoroughly. This happened around 999 A.D. as well, this idea that the world was going to come to an end and things would be weird and incomprehensible afterwards and we're all going to go flying up into cyberspace—I'm sorry, Heaven. No. Let's not go there. Keeping to the issue of whether or not artificial intelligence will be around, we do actually have a metaphor, a handle in our culture for how we relate to such transcendent intelligence. Go back and look at any mythological system trying to explain gods, entities that are anthropomorphic in the face they present to us, but are of incomprehensible power and capriciousness.

Q: Isn't it true that it's the nature of technological change to go through these stages? First, the general public has never heard of it. Then they will say it's ridiculous. Then they will say it is too expensive. Then it happens and they take it for granted and life goes on pretty much as before.

Stross: That's if you think of the Singularity as technological change, rather than if you think of it as we are relegated to the status of pet cats or dogs. That's actually a step-change. We've had a number of step-changes in the way we've existed where what happens afterwards is not something you could predict from life as it was before. For example, I'd cite the development of agriculture. Adopting agriculture is a one-way process. You can't go from being a hunter-gatherer society to being an agricultural society and back again without experiencing a massive die-off, a lost of ninety to ninety-five percent of your population and most of your knowledge. Agricultural societies can support a much higher population density, and natural population growth will in time bring the population up from hunter-gatherer level up to agricultural densities—if they develop agriculture.

I could also point to the development of language. Before there was a language-and-tool-using species on this planet, things were very different to how they have been since then. I suspect that if the Singularity does happen, involving strong artificial intelligence, then what comes after will be as easy to predict from now as now is from the context of a world in which there was no actual speech-capable intelligence.

Q: I can't help but feel that a lot of people will still go to McDonald's and play their videogames, and as long as the artificial intelligence which runs their lives does so in an unobtrusive manner, they'll never notice.

Stross: Yeah. People have an amazing capacity to ignore stuff. [Muted laughter from audience.] Just look at the whole climate-change issue.

Q: The other question about writing about an incomprehensible future is how you make it comprehensible to the reader without going, "That's amazing, professor, how does it work?" and then the professor goes on lecturing for umpteen pages.

Stross: Here we are getting into literary technique and questions of showing, not telling. But the handle I took on it in *Accelerando* was you hit on human protagonists or weakly post-human protagonists—human beings who have been augmented and tweaked, but are still recognizably human. It's very hard to do non-human protagonists in fiction, because fiction is fundamentally, when it's not just pure entertainment, about the study of the human condition. Mainstream literature focuses on the human condition in a strictly contemporary or historical circumstance. Science fiction expands the envelope to include scientifically feasible conditions, including possible futures. Fantasy expands it even further to include mythic archetypes and things which are frankly *not* plausible. But this is all about the human condition. It is very difficult to write a novel in which there are no human beings. I think it has been done a few times, but it's pretty darn rare.

Q: Usually they're anthropomorphized in some way. They're squids, but they're really human inside, that sort of thing.

Stross: You can probably anthropomorphize artificial intelligence or transcendent entities in fiction. The way I approach the problem is to assume that such an intelligence would have a very powerful theory of mind. That is, its ability to develop mental models of other entities would be much stronger than our own. You've all had the experience of holding a mental conversation with somebody you know quite well, or of projecting your mind into the mind of somebody in a book you're reading. We do this by having a theory of mind which allows us get an idea how their behavior will happen, to treat this as a black box with a mind in it, to say, "Well if I say so-and-so it will do something else in return." One suspicion is that a strong AI will have a theory of mind that is better than out own, possibly one that is good enough to simulate our actual likely reactions in advance so that they can figure out what our goals are and do an end-run around us so that we end up doing what they want us to do. As far as we're concerned they'd be nice, friendly, reasonable people and, funnily enough, everything we did would end up being for their benefit. We wouldn't even recognize the way in which we are being manipulated.

Q: I would like to bounce an idea off you. It's my new ending to *Childhood's End* by Arthur Clarke. This bulging-headed kid is saying to his parents, "Mom, Dad, I'm a member of the new, post-human species and you're going to have to die to make room for us. Sorry about that," and both parents have pistols behind their backs and they nod and say, "That's nice, dear." I can't help but wonder if the masses might not resent being transcended over or otherwise replaced, and there could be a Luddite reaction.

Stross: Obsolescence doesn't mean that stuff gets done away with immediately. What we seem to have found during the twentieth and twenty-first centuries is that with progress in new technologies, old technologies very seldom go away completely. What happens is that the new stuff is layered on top of them. The development of the silent movie didn't make theatre obsolete. The development of the talkie did make the silent movie obsolete, but you can view that as an upgrade and a bolt-on to the previous movie technology. Television hasn't killed movies off. Computer games haven't killed television off, and so on. They all co-exist.

Now the flipside of this is that we have far more choices of technologies, media, and lifestyles available to us. Things are a lot more confusing. We have far less time to devote to any one aspect of stuff. But it actually an increase in the complexity of the sphere we live in rather than everyone updates to the new technology. Again, in ecosystems, the advent of a species that occupies a *new* niche doesn't necessarily mean an extinction of someone in a different niche.

Q: I still think there'd be some resentment if there really were enhanced superior people out there. How would you feel meeting a post-human?

Stross: By the standards of our ancestors a couple centuries ago, we probably *are* post-human. Don't underestimate the ability of a graduate student today with Google, a web-browser, and a high-speed internet connection to do library work at a pace that would have been just mind-boggling to their predecessor just thirty years ago. Again, we have not so much artificial intelligence as intelligence augmentation. We use computer technologies and networking to bring information to us, to allow us to do things more effectively than before. As for the issue of whether there are post-humans about and whether or not people will feel resentment toward them, yes, that happens, but again, look at the current world situation and the horrible mess in the Middle East which is caused by resentment of western interference in those countries. You can have an analogy there, but that does not mean that one side or the other is going to ultimately render the other extinct.

Question from Audience: You've mentioned the influence on your work of Cyberpunk and Len Deighton and H. P. Lovecraft. How does P. G. Wodehouse fit in?

Stross: I decided I wanted to do P. G. Wodehouse in the twenty-seventh century. It seemed like the right kind of thing to do after *Accelerando,* because I couldn't go back to *Asimov's* and do more of the same. So I picked something completely different.

From Audience: Whatever happened to that dot-com company you were working for?

Stross: It was doing pretty well until two weeks ago when the US government decided to ban offshore gambling, because they had a headlock on the British online gambling industry. They were the main credit-card clearing system for this. I think their shares dropped seventy percent in one day. They're still in business.

From Audience: Could you tell us something about the origins of your Merchant Princes series?

Stross: Hidden inside that science fiction series is a thinly veiled metaphor about globalization and the economic development of undeveloped nations. It also started out as an attempt to do a juxtaposition between *Nine Princes in Amber* and H.Beam Piper's Paratime series. I am showing a bit too much here.

Q: I gather you are quite well-read in science fiction and went through the usual massive-immersion phase we all do at about age fourteen.

Stross: The golden age of science fiction is seven.

Q: You were precocious. It's usually more like eleven or twelve.

From Audience: Why haven't you done a sequel to *Singularity Sky* yet?

Stross: Confession time. I wrote *Singularity Sky* and it was sold to Ace and they wanted a two-book deal. It's very difficult to only write one book because editors often want to buy one just like the one before, only different. It's predictable, it's easy to sell to marketing and sales, it minimizes the risk of the author failing to turn in something acceptable. Also I had begun writing a sequel, *Iron Sunrise,* before I had a rush of common sense and realized it was stupid to write a sequel before I'd sold the first book. So I had part of a sequel, and my publisher wanted a sequel much more eagerly than a stand-alone. So I sat down and wrote *Iron Sunrise* in about 2002. The problem I have is that it was the sort of the Charlie Stross action/space-opera universe that I started designing in 1994, and by about 2003 I realized that I had lost my inability to suspend my disbelief for the setting, which is a bit of a crippling problem if you want to write more fiction set in it. Also, I had a whole lot of new things

I wanted to say, and with only one science fiction novel slot per year, I could either try and write a sequel to something I had invented ten years earlier, or I could try and produce something new, which is why I haven't actually done a sequel. I haven't ruled one out in the future, if I find that I have something to say in that setting, or if I am short of things to say in other settings, or if I get additional science fiction book slots.

From Audience: What media have you written for besides stories and novels?

Stross: I hate to say I have none. I actually did have an approach from one of the major comics companies last year about taking over one of their projects, but it is not going to be a creator-owned thing; it is going to be one that they own; and in the final analysis I didn't have enough time to take the time to learn a whole new skill. While I believe a lot of my skills in writing and characterization are transferable, I would have to take quite a lot of time out to learn the basics of doing a script. So I decided to become somebody who only does one thing, rather than spread myself too thinly.

From Audience: Tell us more about that P. G. Wodehouse book.

Stross: It's not a P. G. Wodehouse book, but it is a long novelet in the current issue of *Asimov's SF* [January 2007], entitled "Trunk and Disorderly." I wrote it because, of course, there was this line going through my head after one pint of beer too many. [Laughter from audience.] "I want to you to know darling," said Laura as she flounced over to the front door, "That I am leaving you for another sex robot, and she's twice the man you'll ever be." With an opening like that, I just had to write the story, and it had to be a farce, and it had to be a farce that could plausibly involve sex robots. Another couple of pages and it involved... uploaded aunts and a grand vizier and a wooly mammoth with a passion for beer and an evil sense of humor. What are you going to do? You've got to turn to the masters.

Q: Just imagine how H. P. Lovecraft would have written that story.

Stross: One of the possible sequels I have in mind is Jeeves and Wooster meet Cthulhu. [Laughter from audience.] And it's not *Scream for Jeeves*.

From Audience: In *Accelerando* you turned a bunch of stories into a fixup novel. At what point were you just writing them as stories and what changes did you have to make to make them parts of a novel?

Stross: Initially I wrote "Lobsters," which was pretty much a standalone story at that time, and it ended on a rather weird note. It was a pretty obvious that Manfred's marriage wasn't going to be happy so I decided a couple months later to ask myself, what happens in five years' time? Well, it's a divorce story, and a quarter of the way into it I had a moment where in one flash I saw the structure of the novel, that it would be a trilogy of trilogies, each story dealing with one generation of a post-human family, three generations, each generation so effectively distant from the previous generation that communications are difficult. The stories would be set at roughly five-to-ten-year intervals, and they would go through a period in which a hard-takeoff singularity occurred. So from the second story onward, I was writing with the eventual structure of the book in mind. Having said that, the stories were ground out over a period of about four years, and I had to do an awful lot of cutting and polishing to make them fit together properly as a novel.

From Audience: Do you prefer writing novels, or short stories?

Stross: Not every author is successful at selling stories as well as novels. Sometimes you go through a period in which everything you turn out is golden, but sometimes you don't. I've currently had three stories in a row rejected by *Interzone,* which used to be my stomping ground. But what I do find these days is that I get a lot of requests for short stories, and I can't write fast enough to keep up with them, not by a long way. And my novel-writing schedule is going to be a bit of a train-wreck this year, so I have to put a big moratorium on writing short fiction. Quite probably I will do no more short stories over the forthcoming couple of years. You are only as good as whatever you are writing.

From Audience: Earlier you mentioned a crazy idea about a giant ship made out of ice.

Stross: It is one of the ideas in the folder marked "Merchant Princes novels? 5-6." You really wanted to know that, didn't you? Actually it's a pretty good historical thing. There was a guy called Magnus Pyke, who was a mad British inventor. During World War II he was fairly notorious for discussing business matters while in the bath. He came up with an interesting material called Pykrete was twenty percent sawdust in water, then frozen. This stuff was of about the same tensile strength as concrete and ridiculously cheap to make, and it didn't take much of a refrigeration plant to keep it frozen because it was in Arctic or northern waters. His proposal was quite simple. During World War II he proposed that the allies should build an unsinkable aircraft carrier by making a one to two million ton aircraft carrier out of Pykrete, which would sit in the middle of the North Atlantic with a refrigeration plant and fly heavy anti-submarine aircraft from it. When he came up with this proposal, the H.M.S. Habbukuk, I believe it was called, the German submarines could torpedo this thing. The torpedo would make a dent in the Pykrete wall, and they'd just spray more Pykrete into it. Meanwhile, it's got seriously heavy bombers flying off it to hunt submarines. It was to close the air-patrol gap during World War II, and later he suggested it would be possible to build a battleship that would be effectively immune to nuclear weapons. Nuclear weapons would not be something that could make a hole in deep-frozen concrete thirty feet thick. It was one of those weird ideas I decided I had to investigate for the alternate history novels. Alternate history novels are always the stomping ground of baroque technologies that never took off in the real world...especially Zeppelins. So, that was just one of those questions.

From Audience: Who are some of your favorite new writers who you are keeping your eye on?

Stross: One of the real problems I've got is I am writing so much I don't really have time to read at present. So I'd rather not answer that question right now. But I will state, keep an eye on Elizabeth Bear. She is showing amazing breadth and range in the stuff she has coming out. I think she is very, very hot right now.

From Audience: Has Hollywood or TV come snooping around yet?

Stross: I have been programmed with the magic words which one uses when asked about media rights, which is, "Thank you for your interest. I will put you in touch with my agent." However, in answer to your question, there has been a short film made of one of my short stories, made on a shoestring in Scotland, and it's not terribly available right now.

From Audience: Which story?

Stross: "Rogue Farm." Other than that, there have been various slips, but no, I haven't actually sold anything.

Q: If you wanted to pick something of yours to be filmed, what would it be?

Stross: I would actually say a television series the Laundry books. [Applause from audience.]

[An exchange follows in which someone from the audience asks Stross a technical question, which he answers. The interviewer then admits that he himself must be on the wrong side of the Singularity because he found the entire exchange incomprehensible. Stross then continues.] Someone asked me about the influence of Cyberpunk on my life. In early 2000 I woke up one morning and had an existential crisis, because I realized that I was living with a girlfriend who had three-foot-long purple dreadlocks; I was sleeping on a futon and eating Japanese and Chinese junk food, in an apartment about as old as Texas, with roughly eighteen computers in various states of repair in it, and I was plotting the defection of a development team from one corporation to another. Basically my life had imploded into *Neuromancer,* and not in a good way.

From Audience: What special perspective has being in Scotland given you?

Stross: I should admit that I am not Scottish originally. I am from Yorkshire. Polish-Jewish by way of Yorkshire, now living in Scotland. Scotland is a very interesting country. Its legal, financial, and other infrastructure is at least as different from England's as Pennsylvania is from any state in the Bible Belt, if not more so. It has a separate parliament. It has a separate legal system, and arguably it has a separate language, or rather a language which has converged with English so that some people can translate from one to the other without thinking about it. It is actually a quite interesting place to live.

It also has a political culture that's been very radicalized. There are only eighty Scottish seats in Parliament (in London) out of six hundred and fifty in total. During the Thatcher years, the Conservatives had only about twenty seats north of the border anyway, so Thatcher calculated that by following policies that completely alienated Scotland but fed money down south, she would pick up more seats than she would lose in the north. So for about ten to fifteen years, Scotland was run almost as a foreign colony from Westminster. It got to the point where the largest tax rebellion in British history occurred around 1990, the Poll Tax Rebellion, at the height of which fifty percent of the population were not paying their property taxes. There were demonstrations in London with over a million people marching on Parliament. That's actually what brought down Thatcher in the end. Her own party didn't want to have to deal with the fallout. Subsequently, pressure in Scotland for complete independence from the UK began building up. Part of the reason why the Blair administration held a referendum on devolution and Scotland acquiring its own parliament so rapidly was because they figured it was the only way to guarantee that Scotland would remain in the union. At the point of the elections of 1997 in which Labour took power from the Conservatives, polls were showing that opinion in Scotland was running fifty-five percent in favor of outright independence. The stresses of the Thatcher period weren't felt as much down south, but up north they very nearly split the United Kingdom. The result is that it does feel very much like a different country.

Q: No talk of restoring the Stuarts? [Laughter from audience.]

Stross: I suspect that if Scotland did get independence it would become a republic very rapidly. This is a country where not only the governing party but the two largest opposition parties are all left-wing. And the fourth one is green.

From Audience: So how has that affected your fiction?

Stross: To the extent that I am writing against the background in which I live.

From Audience: People have asked about movies. What about audio adaptations of your works?

Stross: Possibly. But there is not that much of a slot on the BBC for audio adaptations of books these days, certainly not genre titles. They've only got a limited number of hours they're broadcasting. The switch the digital radio in the UK, which preceded the switch to digital TV, hasn't caused the same flowering of content and spoken word stations that you'd have expected. We have a very nice digital radio structure, but an awful lot of it is commercial pop stations. We don't have clear-channel disease, but we're not far off. As for audiobooks, there is, I believe a talking-books for the blind adaptation of *Accelerando* out on the way out soon.

From Audience: I was thinking of the BBC 7 adaptations of Terry Pratchett.

Stross: Terry Pratchett is responsible for one percent of all the books sold in the UK, behind the four percent that J. K. Rowling has.

From Audience: Have you ever met him?

Stross: Terry Pratchett? Yes, I've known him since the mid-'80s. He's a fixture in British fandom.

Q: I think we're out of time. Thanks, Charles.

[Much applause.]

(Philcon Principal Speaker interview, November 2006)

BRIAN HERBERT and KEVIN J. ANDERSON

Q: Hello. I am Darrell Schweitzer and I will be the interviewer tonight. Tonight we are here to talk about *The Winds of Dune* and our guests are Brian Herbert and Kevin Anderson. Brian Herbert is the son of Frank Herbert, the creator of *Dune*. Brian is the author of numerous books that have nothing to do with Dune. He had quite a career on his own before became involved in continuing the *Dune* series.

His credits include *Sidney's Comet* (1983), *The Garbage Chronicles* (1985), *Sudanna, Sudanna* (1985), *Man of Two Worlds* (a collaboration with his father, 1986), *Prisoners of Arion* (1987), *Race for God* (1990), and then numerous *Dune* books which we will be discussing. He also edited *The Notebooks of Frank Herbert's Dune* in 1988.

Kevin Anderson published his first story in 1982 in *Space and Time* magazine. He is the author of *Resurrection Incorporated,* the *Game Earth* trilogy, *Lifeline, The Trinity Paradox,* the *Saga of the Seven Suns* series, and many more, so he is indeed eminently qualified to collaborate with Brian Herbert on further extensions of the *Dune* series, of which *The Winds of Dune* is the latest volume.

Q: We are here to talk about the latest book. How many have there been in the series now?

Herbert: It's the eleventh, and also our second sequel to Frank

Herbert's *Dune Messiah*.

Q: Brian, I checked the chronology, and as you were born in 1947, that means you would have been about sixteen when *Dune* started to appear serially in *Analog*. You were presumably about fourteen or fifteen when your father was writing it. So, did you grow up with *Dune*? Did your father take you aside and say, "Hey, look at this," and show you new chapters?

Herbert: Paul Atreides was fifteen at the beginning of *Dune*, but that's about the only comparison with me. I did grow up with it. My dad would read chapters of it to my mother. My mother had been a creative writer and she had given up her writing career to support out family. So she gave him professional advice. She was his intellectual equal.

That's the short version of that answer, but I can go a lot longer.

Q: Go ahead.

Herbert: Actually, my mom got terminal lung cancer when I was in my early twenties. Prior to that I didn't think I liked my father at all, but Dad went into another gear. He became her maid, her cook, her nurse. He built an incredible house for her at Hana on the Island of Maui, where she could breathe easier with lung cancer. She was a miracle survivor. Instead of six months, she lived for ten more years. Dad and I became absolute best friends on the planet. So, from a really rocky beginning with my father, I am really pleased that we had the time to get close.

Anderson: Let me add something, because he's not going to gush over his own stuff much, but Brian spent years writing this wonderful biography called *Dreamer of Dune*, and he went through this whole span of Frank Herbert's life, and it's really the story of Brian growing up in the household with this incredible dynamo of a guy. He sent me a copy of the manuscript when he had finished writing it, and because he is my friend I've got to read it and tell him it's a great book, but I'm not really a big biography guy. I like things with a plot, and people's lives do not usually follow the standard story structure.

But I read this biography that he wrote, and it's incredibly captivating, the best biography that I have ever read. It was nominated for the Hugo the year it came out. For any of you who are *Dune* fans, and I am assuming there are a couple of you in the audience, you really will understand a lot more, not just about Frank Herbert, but also about Brian too. It's a really excellent book.

Herbert: Thank you. It's a love story between my parents too, and about what they sacrificed for each other.

Q: Brian, were you led to being a science fiction writer by having it in your genes, or having it in the air?

Herbert: My wife noticed that I was writing really good letters. I would write complaint letters and I would defeat attorneys for big corporations, and I would get rebates on products and small-sized settlements. So she said, "Why don't you go to your father and he'll help you with your writing. You are basically a good writer," she said, "but he can help you put stories together." Just about that time he and I were getting close. So I am only writing because my wife encouraged me to do it.

Q: At what point did you decide to extend the Dune series?

Herbert: When Dad died in 1986, he had just been beginning *Dune 7*. I saw him use a yellow highlighter on *Heretics of Dune* and *Chapterhouse Dune,* but I didn't know there were any notes. My mom died while that book was being written, and she titled the book. That is her title, *Chapterhouse Dune.* There is a three-page tribute to her at the end of the book. I felt emotionally that that was where the series should end, but I knew on the logical side of my brain that there were more stories to be told. Dad had tried to publish mystery stories in the 1950s, and they were all rejected, but he left his series on the edge of this cliffhanger, this huge mystery. It was up to Kevin to convince me. Other writers had approached me, well-known writers. I had turned them down. I do manage my father's business, the estate and I felt it should end. But Kevin convinced me otherwise. He had I have had like a ten-minute argument in eleven years and one of us apologized, and we went on from there.

Anderson: I can be persistent sometimes.

Q: Kevin, where did you enter into all this? How did you become the Collaborator of Dune?

Anderson: Let me back up a little bit. I was a *Dune* fan since I was about eleven years old. That was where I first read the original *Dune*. I loved it. It was this big adventure story on a science-fiction planet with this young hero banding with desert rebels against the big empire and riding giant sandworms. It was this great story. Then I read it again when I was in college and got all these other layers. I didn't notice them at all the first time I read it, the politics, the economics, the religion, and all kinds of interest, deep layers that are in *Dune*. I just fell in love with it and I started reading of all Frank Herbert's other books. Not just his Dune books, but *Hellstrom's Hive* and *The Dosadi Experiment* and *The White Plague* and *The Eyes of Heisenberg* and everything. I really studied how Frank Herbert wrote, because I admired what he did so much, and I learned vicariously how to be a writer from how Frank Herbert did it, because I didn't think anybody could do better than *Dune*. I wrote stories and published them in small presses. I sent them to various places. Darrell Schweitzer rejected a bunch of them. [Looks to audience.] Yes, he really did.

Then when I sold my very first novel I decided that I wanted to send the very first copy of my very first published novel to

Frank Herbert. By selling the book to Signet Books I was able to get the Science Fiction Writers of America membership directory, so I had Frank's home address. I had planned on doing this to thank him for everything that he did, but between the time the book was accepted and it was published, Frank Herbert passed away. So I never managed to get in touch with him and I never managed to meet him. But I managed to have a relatively successful career of writing my own fiction. I was nominated for a bunch of awards, and then I started working for Lucasfilm and *The X-Files* and finally I got to the point where Brian was going to edit with Ed Kramer, the man who runs Dragoncon, an anthology of Dune short stories. I was one of the people invited to do it. But as a Dune fan, I wanted to know how the Dune saga ended. After *Chapterhouse Dune,* Frank Herbert just left this cliffhanger. When this idea came up, I just thought, *All he can do is say no.* It was pretty much a shot in the dark. I wrote a letter describing how much my interest was in Frank Herbert, my passion for the Dune universe, and I asked if Brian was ever going to finish the series himself, or if he had plans to work with somebody else, or if he would be willing to work with me. He kind of sat on my letter for a month or so, and then he called me out of the blue.

As Darrell can tell you, most science fiction people know each other. I already know most of the writers. We know most of the big fans, but I had never met Brian. He was an enigma to me. He was the son of my literary hero. And he called me up out of the blue and we started talking. Like I said, I've read everything Frank Herbert wrote. Brian's read everything Frank Herbert wrote, and within like three minutes—my wife was in the room and she said, "You guys just started speaking a different language." We were riffing off of each other and talking about nuances in *Whipping Star* or *The Heaven Makers,* or obscure Frank Herbert books, and finishing each other's sentences. We just clicked right away.

Herbert: Sort of like a jazz performance.

Anderson: Yeah. Like a jazz performance. We were just going from there. I flew up to Seattle to spend some time with him. My wife and I went up, and we were brainstorming, and we off and running. We had climbed up on the wild Shai-Halud and we were running off.

Herbert: I tried to dig up some dirt on Kevin before I called him, and I couldn't find any. Just the other day I met Bob Salvatore for the first time, and Bob said I should have called him. [Laughs.]

Anderson: I spread around bigger bribes.

Q: Brian, I notice that the first five or six books you published had nothing whatever to do with *Dune*.

Herbert: Well, actually they do.

Q: All of them?

Herbert: *Sidney's Comet,* my first novel, was my third book. The first two were humor books. But that is about a world that is too much consumerism and there is no room for garbage, there's no room for bodies and burials, so everything is catapulted into deep space. Garbage is littering the cosmos, but it is all coming back as a garbage comet, to wipe out the planet. So that's kind of an environmental theme, albeit funny. *Futurama* did something on that. I didn't know anything about it in time to take any legal action. But I think it was a satire. I think they did a half-hour cartoon show on Saturday morning on it.

Q: I can also remember a TV show called *Quark,* which was about galactic garbage collectors. So there is a garbage mythos in science fiction, if we think all the way back to *Garbage World* by Charles Platt—but maybe we don't need to.

Herbert: My Time Web series is also on an environmental theme. I made it bigger than a planet. It's an entire galaxy that's an ecosystem, and there needs to be a galactic expert that can take care of all that. The galaxy is disintegrating and we can't just let it go.

Q: You must be in a position like Alexandre Dumas the Younger, in that in a hundred years people will be confusing your work and your father's.

Herbert: I doubt that.

Q: Did you feel any need to distance yourself?

Herbert: That's why I wrote two humor books and lots of satires. But then, in the 1990s I spent five years writing that biography of Dad, while I was doing other publishing projects. So I was on a path to write a Dune book. I knew too much about it not to.

Q: When you take up a series like that, how do you sense where you need to expand as opposed to where it is too much? I might be controversial and suggest that George Lucas was profoundly mistaken to make the second set of three Star Wars movies—the prequels—and should have left that part to the imagination, because all we had was a trilogy in which we already knew how things were going to turn out, and a story-arc that involves a cute kid who grows up to be Hitler. It just did not work. So, how do you avoid this problem?

Anderson: Did it not work because that was the story, and you had this little kid who was going to grow up to be Hitler, or did it not work because Lucas didn't do it as well as he should have? I would argue that, although it's going to be dark, the concept of this cute little kid, who had everything going for him, whose life goes so tragically wrong that he ends up being the most hated man in the universe, Dark Vader—or Paul Atreides, depending on which one you're talking about—I would say that can be an incredibly compelling story.

One of the books I published a year ago was called *The Last Days of Krypton.* It's the story of Superman's planet and how it comes to its end. Yes, you know the planet blows up at the end and one little baby gets out, but that doesn't mean that there's no story that you can tell that's interesting. And what we did with the House books was tell the immediate prequels, the love story of Duke Leto and Jessica, the first battles with the Baron, the planetologist being sent to Dune. I think that when you have an immense universe that people care about, and they have characters that they love and want to revisit, we didn't need to have a Romulan ship and Spock coming back to reset the timeline to make it interesting. I loved that movie, but I wanted to go back and just see young Kirk and Spock. I didn't need to have any reason to go back.

Herbert: We actually can see an end of the series as far as the major novels go. But with the House series, we are staying right on the Frank Herbert timeline. We found a chapter that Dad had written that he didn't include in *Dune.* It would be back-story of when Duke Leto and Lady Jessica met. Well, Kevin and I found that deleted chapter and we put it into *House Harkonnen.* So we have really stayed on course on Dad's story. We have two more under contract and then we have three more after that. All of them either go back to the history of the founding of the great schools, or other stories that Frank Herbert laid out, either in his notes or in his appendices, or just comments that he made. For example, in one of his sequels, he said that Tio Holtzman, a man, was not the one who invented the foldspace engine. Instead, it was a woman, Norma Cenva. So, since we knew that there strong women in the series, in the Butlerian Jihad series we developed Norma Cenva as the founder of the spacing guild, and all that.

Lady Jessica, by the way, is modeled after my mother, Beverly Herbert. So the strong female characters that you see in the series—there's a lot of expansion you can do there, and it is exactly what Frank Herbert wanted.

Q: At what point do you feel free to invent rather than follow his notes?

Herbert: He had an appendix describing in outline form the Butlerian Jihad and he said that Abulurd Harkonnen had been a coward 10,000 years before. I thought that was interesting, but what we did was go back to that period, and all we had was a name like that and a couple of other names, and then we added all the other framework. But that was the time about which Frank Herbert had said that thinking machines had ruled mankind and we rose up in this great jihad. Well, Frank Herbert had been a reporter, and he was flipping over the myth that smiling robots are going to make our lives easier and save time. So I don't think we are inventing things. We are really explaining them. Dad had spent twenty years trying to explain why Paul Atreides went dark in *Dune Messiah*. We did it in a novel, *Paul of Dune*.

Anderson: So Frank Herbert gave us the road map, but we're doing the cross-country road trip. We can stop and see things along the way and explore little side-roads, but we know the main structure of the road system.

Q: But he's always there as the third collaborator.

Herbert: Absolutely. I hear his voice when I'm writing.

Q: You said you see an end. Are you going to stop, or just go in another direction after that? You've got a whole galaxy full of people and all these minor characters. It could go on indefinitely.

Herbert: But it won't, at least not in the big door-stopper novels like Kevin and I write. Our next book after this one will be in two years. We are alternating years now. It will be *The Throne of Dune*, where Shaddam Corrino comes back and tries to retake the throne. Then there will be *Leto of Dune* or maybe *The Golden Path of Dune*. It will be the first years of the God Emperor. After that, maybe three novels about the founding of the great schools, thousands of years before *Dune*. That would be *The Sisterhood of Dune, The Mentats*, and *The Swordmasters*. Beyond that, there are other stories, but we don't see them as major novels. Maybe some graphic novels that aren't dumbed down. You know, you have to keep up the intellectual level of the series.

Anderson: That's the real answer. On every one of these books that we do, while are names are on the cover, the biggest word on the cover is Dune. There's a certain brand identity, that people expect something when it says Dune on the cover. You don't want to do, like, *The Paperclips of Dune*. It shouldn't be a little off-the-cuff adventure or small book. It needs to have the *gravitas* that a Dune book has. If we can't come up with stories that have that much to them, then it doesn't belong in the series.

Q: You don't want to turn out the soap opera version, which would be called *As the Worm Turns*.

Anderson: Or the musical comedy with dancing sandworms.

Q: Or the horror version, *Charnel House Dune*.

Herbert: Well how about *Gunga Dune*?

[Rising laughter from the audience.]

Herbert: Are we Dune yet?

Anderson: We just want to make sure that we don't water down *Dune*.

Herbert: That would destroy the ecosystem.

Q: At this point I think we've gotten silly enough that we should turn for sensible guidance to the audience.

Audience Member: I remember reading that Frank was a lay psychoanalyst. Toward the end of the sixth book—you said he was writing the seventh?

Herbert. He had started to make notes on it that I didn't know existed. I saw him using yellow highlighter, and it turned out eleven years later that there were notes.

Audience Member: Towards the end of the series, when Duncan Idaho—not the real one, but the ghola—has a quasi-fight with a reverend mother, and then I'll skip ahead to where they are taking off, and there are all these pictures, *American Gothic* and other masterpieces, and then there's this pregnant woman—Did your father explain any of that in the notes, where he was going with that? Was he going to go in to the reverend mothers more?

Herbert: The estate of Frank Herbert was still open in 1997, even though he had died in 1986. My mother had died in 1984 and her estate was still open. It was very complicated, and an estate attorney named Walt Tabler called me and said there were two safe-deposit boxes, so what did I want to do of them? I had been an insurance agent for years and I always told my dad always to keep copies of important manuscripts and documents off-premises in case there is a fire. Well, I didn't know he did it. So we went down there, and an estate attorney named Jan Cunningham had a yellow legal pad and started writing everything down. We had to break into the boxes legally. We had no keys. We found country and western lyrics. Dad had written some songs. That would be good, huh? We found some recipes, some letters, and a Tandy Radio Shack floppy disk that said "Dune 7 Notes." For the nay-sayers, I actually put that up on our website. We actually had an NSA security guy check to make sure there was nothing else on there except what we found with it, which was a thirty-page printout. It was the arc of the story, of the plot. It was various character analyses, and various focal points of what he thought were important. So that's what we wrote.

But Kevin and I had written the Butlerian Jihad series and the House series, so what Frank Herbert had envisioned in one novel, Kevin and I couldn't do in one novel. So we did it in two novels, *Hunters of Dune* and *Sandworms of Dune.*

Anderson: So that's what answers all those *Chapterhouse* questions. It picks up right after that. If you will notice in the later books that Frank Herbert wrote, when you read *Dune* it's this big adventure story and it's got all kinds of great things in it, but it has all these other layers; but as he got to other books, he got more interested in other things. The later books are a little more didactic. They're a little more dense and political. Frank wanted to talk about these issues that were interesting to him. So he would just fast-forward past things. In fact in *The Heretics of Dune,* when the Honored Matres wipe out the planet Dune; they turn it into a charred ball; he does that between chapters. He doesn't even show it. The ships are closing in and they are powering up their weapons, and then in the next chapter there are a couple people sitting around in a garden talking about what a shame it is that Dune was destroyed. So when Brian and I started writing his outline of *Dune 7,* well, we like to blow up planets and destroy things, so we wanted to flesh out and show all the action that Frank Herbert just alluded to, because he wanted to speed ahead and get to the next concept he wanted to talk about.

Herbert: It was sort of jumping from *Dune* to *Dune Messiah*. In the meantime hundreds of billions of people are killed but he starts *Dune Messiah* off by saying that it happened.

Anderson: But we like the gaps, because they give us novels to write.

From Audience: Can you speak a little bit about your collaboration and how you write?

Herbert: To sell the first three books, the House series, Kevin and I talked for four months, and then he flew to Seattle, and we brainstormed in May of 1997. We produced a 140-page book proposal. Normally when you well a proposal you're going to have, like eight pages, and maybe a chapter or two that you send in to the publisher. We sent in this huge thing, because we had so much energy surrounding the project. So we come up with very big proposals for each of the trilogies that we put together, or other sets of books, and then, once we have sold the project to a publisher, Kevin and I will brainstorm again, and we will divide it up into, say, 100 chapters. Kevin will take fifty based on his strengths, and I will take fifty based on mine. He has a physics degree. He worked at Los Alamos and Lawrence Livermore. I am a sociology guy with a degree from Cal. Berkeley, so I'll do the philosophy, the sociology, the Bene Gesserit type things.

Then we start rewriting each other's chapters, so Kevin, for example, would send me all his fifty, and I will go through all hundred chapters and start adding philosophy to his action, that kind of thing. Then he'll do the reverse when he gets it, in the next draft. It goes through about ten drafts.

Anderson: But we do it all on the computer, so I never see what he's marked and changed in my chapters, and he never sees what I've marked. That's what a collaboration's all about. You check the ego at the door. I trust whatever he's going to do to my prose and he trusts whatever I'm going to do. We go back and forth and back and forth so that what emerges in book form has been gone over so it has a unified voice that we think is better than either of us could have done individually.

Herbert: But Kevin and I have collaborated before, and I have collaborated with my cousin Marie Landis to write a couple of horror novels. She and I just wrote odd and even chapters. It probably wasn't the best way to do it, but it turned out great. We had a lot of fun. But with Dad he was always so busy, that I collaborated on the last novel that Frank Herbert wrote, called *Man of Two Worlds*. I gave him the book proposal as a very serious novel. I had written a lot of satires before that. Then Dad was so busy that I spent thirteen months writing the entire first draft. Then Dad took it for six or seven months and added a lot of the humor to it. So people think that humor is mine, but it actually isn't. It was Dad's. But the situation was different with Frank Herbert. He was so busy that we had to just block out some time that he had to work on it. With Kevin and me, I think we have the idea way to do it.

Anderson: It depends on how your partnership works. This works for Brian and myself. Especially in science fiction, there's a lot more collaboration than you would ordinarily see in—I don't know—mystery historical novels. But in science fiction, a lot of writers like to hang out and brainstorm.

Herbert: Well, Niven and Pournelle have done very well.

Q: Are you the kind of writers who can talk about a story at great length before you write it, or, if you talk about it too much is there danger of losing it? There seem to be two schools of thought on this.

Anderson: We are definitely of the same school of thought, especially because we are collaborating. These are very complex and intricate books, and each one of them has six or seven main storylines and main characters going back and forth, that we feel that if we just started off without working it out together, it would be like trying to build a grand skyscraper without bothering to do a blueprint first. We really want to map it out in great detail, so I know what he's doing in his chapter and he knows what I am doing in my chapter. But in no way does that stifle the creativity, because we've spent days doing the creative stuff, and drawing up the blueprint. We feel that designing the architecture is the creative part, not putting the bricks down.

Herbert: Dad and I would talk about it without taking notes. I know he did that with Bill Ransom too on the collaborations he did with Bill. At some point somebody said, "We'd better get this written down, before we forget it."

Anderson: I find that it really energizes me to do brainstorming with Brian. It doesn't make me tired of the project at all. It makes me all fired up because I'll come up with this really good idea, and then he'll give something that makes it take a left turn and becomes a really *great* idea. That's how you just add to each other. It only gets better.

From Audience: I wonder if you could tell me something about the linguistic aspects of your dad's work. I was introduced to it on a rainy weekend in Cape Cod, never having heard of the Dune series, and I couldn't put it down. One of the things I remember very sharply is the linguistic originality, or borrowings as the case may be.

Herbert: There's a poetic beauty to the words that he chose. Sihiya, a desert springtime, and some beautiful words. He based a lot of it on Arabic, at least the Fremen language, but then he would add Navaho and languages from the Gobi Desert. He was just able to absorb a lot of information. He did speak Latin and Spanish. He made up a lot of things. He liked to combine words, combine languages, combine concepts. He said that in the future—I was writing a story once and he said this—you can have a character named Ichuro Munoz. He's got a Japanese first name and a Mexican last name. You don't have to explain it. It's just detritus from the past, the way Dad put it. Look at the religions that he created, Zen Sufi, a combination there. The Orange Catholics. That's the Protestants and the Catholics. And others. Buddislamic. So he wasn't sticking to any one language. He was making things up. But there are actually some real words in there too, as certain experts have pointed out to me. There are some real Navaho words, for example.

Dad believed that the Native American view of the universe was the better, as opposed to the way we live. So, for example, the character he identified with most was Stilgar, the leader of the Fremen. Dad's very best friend in the world was a Native American. By the way, that Native American said—I have to go to a little bit of a different subject—but Howie was his name. A Norwegian family had adopted him, and he was a full-blooded Native American, and Howie said, "The Frank Herbert that you know would not have existed had it not been for Beverly Herbert." He was there, the Native American best friend, when Dad met my mother at the University of Washington in 1946. That's a little off the question you asked, but that's how it is with answers about Frank Herbert.

Anderson: Let me throw something back at you, when you're talking about the linguistics of *Dune*. Didn't you once tell me that *Dune* itself first started as a haiku?

Herbert: It was a haiku. Seventeen syllables. Most of the haikus that I've seen are about nature, these Japanese poems. The original haiku has not survived, but it was taped to his desk for a while. I have the desk, and I've looked all over it, and I can't find it.

Q: That may be the most expanded haiku in the history of literature.

[Laughter from audience.]

Herbert: Absolutely.

Anderson: Especially if you count all the seventeen volumes of the Dune books.

Q: Compared to that, my rewrite of *The Lord of the Rings* as a limerick is nothing.

Herbert: You can read *Dune* for the poetry, and then you can go back and read it for the philosophy, the politics, all these layers. Or you can just read the adventure story.

From Audience: Do you think we will ever see another release of a theatrical film in the Dune universe, and, if so, who would you want to helm it?

Herbert: I usually answer that question, but I think Kevin knows the answer.

Anderson: Well, funny you should ask. You are all aware of the David Lynch movie from 1984, and then the Sci Fi Channel did two six-hour miniseries. They each had their own advantages and disadvantages. But Paramount has now acquired the rights to do a big-budget, big-screen version—I hesitate to use the word "remake"—of the original *Dune*.

Herbert: It's a classic interpretation.

Anderson: Right.

Herbert: This is why I answer the question, not him, because we've been told what we can say.

Anderson: Instead of a remake, we want it to be done correctly in the first place. Thanks to Peter Jackson, who has proven with *The Lord of the Rings* that you really can do a movie of that big of a book and do it successfully, right now Peter Berg has signed on to be the director. He did *Hancock* and *Friday Night Lights*, *The Kingdom*. We've got some big name producers on it. We've met with the team and we're involved in some of the creative stuff. But right now it's still in the scriptwriting phase, and it's Hollywood, so don't hold your breath, but it's sort of moving along.

Herbert: Peter Jackson raised the stakes, so it has to be a good movie. You can't get everything in *Dune* into a movie. So that's the challenge. But we do have Richard Rubenstein as one of the producers, and he did the two television series, where he followed the plot very faithfully. So we have a good team.

From Audience: A little background on the Bene Gesserit.

Herbert: Dad said they were like female Jesuits.

From Audience: Do you have any more information on how that concept came to be?

Herbert: My Dad had, I think it was, eleven Irish Catholic aunts. They tried to force Catholicism on him, and Dad rebelled. My mom similarly didn't have all those aunts, but they tried to force Pentecostalism on her. So I had no organized religion when I was growing up. Ultimately Dad was a non-practicing Buddhist, as it turns out. But the Bene Gesserit came from his Irish Catholic aunts. He saw them as a cluster of women who had this power about them and he somehow resisted it. But also, as was mentioned previously, my dad was a lay psychologist. That was in the early 1950s, the late '40s, when we lived in Santa Rosa California. At that time, good friends of our family were the Slatterys. He was a professor at Sonoma State, and he was a well-known psychologist who had studied with Carl

Gustav Jung in the 1930s. Jung and she had notes that she brought to Dad and talked to him about. Jung had the concept of the Collective Unconscious, and so the Bene Gesserit with their genetic memory going back for thousands of years and the voices that are heard from within to guide that particular living sister is all based upon Jung. Then, the strong women. My mother was an incredibly strong woman, and Dad felt that we needed more female energy in the universe, because men have pretty well messed things up for about ten thousand years. But I think that before that, some of the Goddess beliefs were unbalanced too. So, Dad wanted the pendulum to swing. In books Five and Six in the series, women are running everything.

As they should.

[Laughter from the audience.]

From Audience: I have a two-part question. You mentioned how your mother was the inspiration for the strong women in *Dune*. But has there been anyone in your life who has been the inspiration for characters in your books, or for you Kevin?

Herbert: We dedicated this novel to our wives. We phrased it in such a way that we appreciate what they've had to put up with when Kevin and I vanished. Dad was like that too. He would vanish into his study. She was a very brilliant person, but she would wait for him to come down out of his science fiction universe and then they could go do something.

But in one of my early novels, *Sudanna, Sudanna,* I have this futuristic world that is all covered with goo, and there are these ships floating across through the goo, and one of the characters has problems with his wife because she keeps pulling the covers off, and that's my wife Jan. I had a rebellious daughter at the time, and there is a rebellious daughter in that story. But Kevin and I both have very supportive wives and very intelligent wives, who give us a different way of thinking, so when we write a female character wrong, they'll let us know.

Anderson: Very clearly. My wife, Rebecca Moesta, and I have written over thirty novels together and we're still married, which is kind of an amazing thing. We do have a guest bedroom that sometimes I've had to go through after brainstorming. But we've been married eighteen years, and even when she is not collaborating with me, she brainstorms with me all the time, and reads the whole manuscript. She gives me the really, really tough copyediting of the manuscript that copyeditors are scared to do. She'll just take a page and write BORING! on it.

I haven't yet gotten that from a New York copyeditor, which is good, I suppose. She makes me be a much better writer. I think it's impressive I've been married for eighteen years, but that's nothing. He's—

Herbert: Forty-two years. I met her when she was very young and I was very young. It's not so much whispering, "You are mortal," because we are not pharaohs or anything, but one time I was talking to an audience like this and I was talking about the female characters that I have in my other books, and I felt like I was becoming something of a women's liberationist, and I heard my wife out there snickering in the audience, and deservedly so, because I didn't know anything.

From Audience: First of all, guys, being a writer, you intimidate me whenever I read your work, because it's such great writing craft. But being a Norwegian myself, I don't have the Native American background. I see Rachel Carson coming through very strongly.

Herbert: That's true.

From Audience: Could you guys talk a little more about the environmental influence here?

Herbert: Obviously, Rachel Carson. Her great book had been published before *Dune,* and so Dad was aware of it. But Dad said to me that he had a lot of messages. If you look at *Dune,* the *Whole Earth Catalogue* referred to it as an ecological handbook. That is the message that catapulted *Dune.* It took until about 1970. The book was published in 1965. By 1970 there was a groundswell because of the environmental issue. Frank Herbert spoke at the first Earth Day in Philadelphia. Ira Einhorn organized that, by the way. He's got kind of a star-crossed history, there. Then Dad spoke on college campuses all over the United States, just on that environmental issue. There's so much more in there, the politics, and the religion, and all these incredible things. But Dad set up a detailed ecosystem. So, for example, at the end of the first movie of *Dune* it rains at the end. Well that can't happen or it would destroy the cycle of the sandworms. Frank Herbert explained that very carefully.

So, he understood from when he was growing up as a nine-year-old boy. My grandparents were alcoholics and they spent all the money they had on booze. So Dad went out fishing and brought in the dinner for the day. In the process he met a Native American who had been an outcast. This was on Fox Island, near Tacoma Washington. Dad said the outcast had been a murderer in his tribe, and they sent him out to the island. Well Dad kind of embellished things sometimes, so I don't know if he'd been a murderer, but it made a good story. So here's this nine-year-old kid adventuring, and this Native American taught Dad how to live in the woods, how to eat grub-worms and red ants, and how to fish, just totally another world-view. Dad would sometimes take his nine-foot rowboat out and he would hitch it on to tugboats that were towing barges, heading for Alaska, until he got caught and they would cut him loose. So he was always out there in the environment. That really comes through. Some people read *Dune* and they get thirsty. Well, Dad never lived in the desert but he certainly figured out how to write about it.

Anderson: There is a background in it from where I come from.

I live in Colorado and I spend most of my time when I get free time out hiking or mountain climbing. I have climbed to the top of all fifty-four of the fourteen-thousand-foot peaks in the state of Colorado. I have done three hundred and twenty miles on the Colorado Trail. For years I have been a member of the Sierra Club, the Nature Conservancy, and The Colorado Trail Foundation, The Continental Divide, all these different things. Any chance that I get, I get out and do my writing with a tape recorder, so I am out in the mountains, in the forests, and that's where I am dictating things. In fact I have written a lot of Dune stuff in the Great Sand Dunes National Park in Colorado or in Death Valley in California. My wife and I donate a lot of money to various charitable organizations, and it's always a tug-of-war between the two of us, because she wants to donate money to soup kitchens and feed the orphans and save the children and all that, and I want to spend money on The Sierra Club and The Colorado Trail, and she tells me that's being kind of cold-hearted because that's not helping people. But it's helping the whole world and the environment. Those are the nights that I sleep in the guest bedroom sometimes.

Herbert: The Sierra Club comment is interesting, because Dad was a Republican speechwriter in the 1950s. I think I mentioned that he was a non-practicing Buddhist. He was an anti-war leader in Seattle, and war is the biggest destroyer of the environment that there is. He was in the World Without War Council. So here is this big, bearded Republican speechwriter leading thousands of students in Seattle taking over the freeways. But Dad felt that The Sierra Club had gone too far. They had been too extreme. What Dad said is that they were so radical—this was back in the '60s—that a bunch of loggers just went in and clear-cut a whole, huge area because they were afraid of what would happen when The Sierra Club got their rules in. So Dad was a pragmatist and he believed in negotiating things from a reasonable standpoint.

From Audience: I think one of the things that makes your collaboration so great is your adherence to the original. When we read one of your books, it is almost the same as reading the original by Frank Herbert. It sticks so much to the theme and the style of writing. That doesn't work with other writers. In particular I am thinking of Arthur Clarke and Gentry Lee, where if you read any of their collaborations, you can almost tell what Clarke wrote and what Lee wrote.

Herbert: As Kevin mentioned, we set out egos aside at the door. But we also have the same vision. If any of you have gone to Europe, for example, and one of you wants to shop and one of you wants to see the history, it doesn't work. Well Kevin and I are on this huge journey through the Dune universe, and we have the same vision. Sometimes he will come up with an idea that's the same idea that I've had. I've already had the idea, but I got my fax on his desk before he was able to fax me. The last one, I beat him too. But we are coming up with the same ideas in parallel. We don't try to outshine each other. We've talked about shining a light on each other, but ultimately we are shining a light on Frank Herbert. That's what it's about, going back and reading *Dune* again.

Anderson: Somebody asked us a couple days ago at a booksigning, "Did you write this part or did Brian write this part?" We looked at each other. We can't even remember who wrote which part, because we rewrite each other's parts so much. But as far as the adherence to Frank Herbert, we really need to please the toughest Dune fans. And we are the toughest Dune fans. Brian and I, we live and breathe everything about Dune. We have immersed ourselves in these books and in the notes that Frank Herbert left and in our own stories. We're not just picking up an hors d'oeuvre. We're there for the whole banquet.

Herbert: Also, before I wrote a word with Kevin, I spent a year doing a concordance of all six Dune novels. So I know all the page references for the Sisterhood, the eye colors of all the characters, all the details, and so we refer to that all the time.

Question from audience: You refer to the Bene Gesserit as strong characters, but yet you have them with a computer.

Herbert: That's a secret of breeding records—

Anderson: Shh! It's a secret!

Question: I am not saying it's bad, but they still have a computer, which is something they're not supposed to have.

Herbert: But it's secret. By the time of *Dune,* computers are illegal because of what they did to us 10,000 years before. But in the novel *Dune,* we don't know that yet. It's like Paul Atreides—you think he is a heroic figure by the end of *Dune,* and it turns out that there is a dark side to him. Well there is a dark side to the Bene Gesserit too. If you just take a look at the Honored Matres, which are the dark side of the Bene Gesserit, and they are coming back and destroying all our heroines. And Dune. They have destroyed the planet Dune. Dad was not naïve enough to think that heroes or heroines would be pure.

Anderson: They're also very pragmatic. They have their end-goal in sight and they are willing to bend some of their own rules to achieve it.

Herbert: But the Bene Gesserit, though, are many times talking about what it means to be human. That's an important theme to Frank Herbert. You can see that not only in the Dune series, but in his others books. And since there are no computers, for example, in the time of *Dune,* what do you have? You have mentats, which are like Frank Herbert characters all over the place. They're computerized brains. He's talking about human potential. Look the potential for women, too. That's why the series has really lasted, as opposed to other big series, nineteen or twenty-book series that were hinging on technology. This is not hinging on any aspect of technology or science. It's about people.

Question from audience: When you talk about how hard you work to follow Frank Herbert's whole universe, you do more than that. I've read all of your father's works and all of your works, and it's hard to tell the difference between Frank Herbert and your writing. How did you come up with the ability to write in that style? Okay, fine, they're different. You've created these books and you have the barest outline to go on, but then you've created a style which blends so perfectly with the original. How did that come about? Did you work at it deliberately?

Herbert: No. Partly it's admiration for Frank Herbert, but Dad believed in the oral tradition, and stories being passed on from generation to generation. I heard him reading all the Dune novels to my mother. So somewhere in my subconscious, I hear his voice reading to her. I hear his voice speaking to me, plus the details of what he taught me about writing. He taught me the care and feeding of editors, how to build suspense. The care and feeding of editors was kind of amusing. It was how to send a manuscript in so it won't get thrown into the slush pile.

I sent him my *Sidney's Comet* novel. It was three hundred pages at the time. He edited twenty pages, sent them back from Hawaii, and he said, "This is how editing tightens the story. Go now and do likewise." So he was telling me from the beginning that I had to do the hard work. But I appreciate that comment.

As for our style—Frank Herbert changed his style. As Kevin mentioned, *Dune*, is one style. It has this wonderful poetry and this great adventure, and beneath it are all these messages, but by the time you get to *The God Emperor of Dune* and on, the characters are talking a lot and politics and big things happen in the background. So he changed his style too, but he was exploring the layers he had set up in the novel *Dune*. As Our style—we like to look at *Dune* as an example Kevin and I never hope to match.

Anderson: When we started out, we discussed this, and we said that we were *not* going to imitate Frank Herbert's style, because he has a distinctive style, and we were both well established as professional writers before we started writing together or we started writing in the Dune universe. So we didn't want to be imitating the way someone else writes. If someone is going to be writing new Conan novels, you don't want to them imitating sentence by sentence the way Robert E. Howard wrote. But perhaps it comes across just because it's so many years of constant exposure and immersion in the Dune universe. We go back and read the Dune books, and then turn around and read them all again. So it's constantly in our minds what Frank Herbert wrote. So when we were doing *The Winds of Dune,* we both practically memorized *Dune Messiah.* Maybe it's just osmosis, but we do try to write something that is respectful, and in that universe.

Herbert: And I think that we feel like the characters are really alive. Sometimes I have to remind myself others.

Q: We've just run out of time. Thank you to you both.

(Conducted at the Free Library of Philadelphia, Aug 11, 2009.)

HOWARD WALDROP

Q: Let's start with something of your background. Who is the guy who writes all these neat things?

Waldrop: I'm Howard Waldrop and I was born in Mississippi in 1946, but I moved to Texas with my family in 1950, so I didn't have much chance to develop a real Southern accent. People from Texas can tell can I am not from Texas. Most other people think I've got a Texas accent, but that's not what I have. I have a Texas laid on a slight Mississippi accent.

I lived mostly in Arlington Texas, which is halfway between Dallas and Fort Worth, growing up. I went back to Mississippi every summer, for periods ranging from six weeks to three months, the whole summer sometimes. I grew up in Arlington, graduated from high school there. I went to University of Texas, Arlington on and off for five and a half years but never graduated. I was drafted out of college into the army in 1970. I was at Fort Ord and Fort Gordon and Fort Bragg. I got out at Fort Bragg and moved back to Texas, and as soon as I could, I got to Austin. I spent a little time in College Station, but I moved to Austin. I lived there until 1995, moved to the Pacific Northwest for seven and a half years, then moved back to Austin two years ago.

Q: Was Austin where you first made contact with science fiction and fandom? I've always associated you with the Austin and College Station scene, with Joe Pumilia, Lisa Tuttle, Steve

Utley, and that lot.

Waldrop: It was amazing. I'd sold my first story when I first went *into* the army, but it came out when I was *leaving* the army, in 1972. In six months, around that time period, Lisa and Joe and Steve Utley and George Proctor and Bill Wallace and all these people had sold their first stories. So that's why we started the Turkey City Writers Workshop in 1972. The first one was at mine and Buddy Saunders's duplex in Grand Prairie, Texas, next to Arlington. For a while we were doing the workshops *every two months,* and moving it around the state. Everybody ended up eventually in Austin for one reason or another, but we all started somewhere else. It took anywhere from a year to two or three years to get to Austin, but Austin was *the* place where everybody was.

Q: You ended up collaborating with most of these people, so there must have been a lot of creative cross-fertilization going on.

Waldrop: I explained it in *Custer's Last Jump,* which is a book of collaborations. We would work and work on our own stories. Sometimes they would sell and sometimes they wouldn't. They would go out and come back. For a while there, *everything* we were collaborating on sold *first time out, every time.* So this is an incentive, when you're starting out as a writer. As I said in the book, one plus one isn't two, it's two point one five or something. The collaboration you do becomes a third thing, which is smarter than both of you. It's working against your weaknesses and with your strengths, with what each of you can do. Mainly we were young and full of piss and vinegar and we had time and energy leftover when we finished our own stuff. You'd give somebody a story you were having trouble with and you'd say, "I'm having trouble with this? What's wrong with this?" and they would say, "I know how to fix this." So you'd say, "Well *fix* it," so they would sit down and write another draft and figure out how to fix the story.

Mainly, we were young, and we had a lot of time and energy. That was the main reason we were collaborating.

Q: There certainly was a kind of crazy fusion going on. Typical of your collaborations is "Custer's Last Jump," with Steve Utley. Didn't you say that started with each of you trying to top the other?

Waldrop: Yes. I called Steve up and I read him a short section that I'd written about Crazy Horse's airplane, and an hour later he called me up with part of the Mark Twain stuff. We essentially wrote that story *in five days on the phone,* back and forth. We did our own parts, and—neither one of us remembers it—but evidently we got together at some point and put the drafts together. I think Steve typed up the final draft and sent it off.

Q: It's quite an innovative story in many ways. It is one of the few I can think of that works in the form of a history lecture and notes, rather than a conventional narrative.

Waldrop: That's one reason it was easier to write, because it is in the three sections, and one is a magazine article, one is a *Smithsonian Annals of Flight* volume, and one is Mark Twain's notes for his interviews when he took a zeppelin trip out West. But it was easier to write that way because each of us was writing a different section. That was written way early. It was written in 1972, although it was not published until 1976. Terry Carr and Silverberg each had it at one time for *New Dimensions* or *Universe,* and they kept *losing* publishers, and then they'd give it back to the other guy who had a publisher. He'd lose his publisher. It ended up exactly where we sent it the first time, and for the book it was supposed to be in, but meanwhile, a couple of other people had it or tried to get it.

Q: My point about the form of the story is that it's not in dramatic scenes, but as exposition and notes. I can think of few successful stories like that. Borges did a few.

Waldrop: Yeah, but that *seemed* to be the way to do it. We were smart enough then, in the second or third year of our writing careers, to know that you had to do something like that to get all the background stuff in. When it was printed in Germany in 1977 or so, the German editor added a few references to the bibliography, and we've always kept those in the American reprints since then. A couple of book references, because he liked it so much that he made up his own and stuck them right in there in the middle of ours.

Q: A lot of people writing a story in such a manner would just be dull. I think what makes it work is the humor. You are one of the few people to write funny alternate history. Did you do this deliberately, or did it just come out that way?

Waldrop: Essentially it just came out that way. I have never thought that for something to be important it has to be long and dull and boring, which is what most people expect of something important. Real life has funny things in the middle of terror. If you've seen the movie, *The Gods Must Be Crazy*. The gun-fight in the banana plantation between the helicopter and the Communist bandits. The machine-guns are shooting down bananas all over the place. One guy is running and slips on a banana. [Laughs] Here in the middle of this horrible firefight. Stuff like that happens in real life and we put in humor in just because it's part of it.

Q: A lot of your stories are striking that way. I think if "Fin de Cycle," in which Marcel Proust is a bicycle soldier.

Waldrop: No, it was Jarry who was the bicycle soldier. Proust was in the artillery *in real life* when he had to do his national service, as we say. But they're telling Melies how to make a movie, in the story.

Q: You seem to have been drawn to the alternate-history form well before it became a fad. You may have helped make it a fad. What makes you want to screw around with history?

Waldrop: Someone once said that at one time alternate history stories were so rare that all the examples were good. All the examples, like *Remember the Alamo* by Fehrenbach and *Bring the Jubilee* by Ward Moore, *The Lost Years* by Oscar Lewis, the one about Lincoln retiring to California. When we started doing it, mostly in the early '70s, it was still an oddity in the field. Alternate-history stories were fairly rare. But by the end of the '70s they weren't rare anymore. I don't know if we're responsible for part of that, or if it was just time for everybody to start realizing what a great thing alternate history was.

The reason I do it is because there has got to be a better world than *this* one. You know what I mean? Deep down inside that's essentially it. It's not a constant, nagging thing, but if you look at *all* the possibilities, you say "Why did we end up with *this* one?" You start taking the steps backwards, and there's no point at which a step one way or the other would have changed *everything*. The small changes start adding up. Other people write the alternate histories about the big battles, the big political stuff, and I think it's the small, incremental changes along the way that would have produced a widely divergent world from the one we have now, without having a change in a big battle like the South winning the Civil War or Hitler winning World War II. It could have been small things started changing in the '20s and you'd have a wholly different present.

Q: So you are not a big believer in the Great Man theory of history, but more in the Accumulation of Circumstances theory.

Waldrop: For want of the nail, as Ben Franklin said, the horse was lost, and for want of the horse the messenger was lost, and for want of the messenger the battle was lost. I think it's *even smaller* than that. It's like "The Sound of Thunder" before the movie destroyed the story. [Laughs.] "The Sound of Thunder" is like, a guy steps on a butterfly seventy million years ago, and the whole world's changed from the time he left. It's like that. I think it's small, incremental changes along the way that would tend to accumulate. Of course as somebody said, how would you *know* it's different if you were in a *version* of the world. You *wouldn't*. It would be the one you're in. It would be the timeline you're in. One thing had changed two hundred years ago that leads to a *different than now,* you would have no idea that the one *we* experience *now* exists, because that possibility would have been cut off.

Q: That's the "Bring the Jubilee" principle. The hero accidentally changed history into the one we know. He didn't intend to.

Waldrop: There's a difference between time-paradox stuff and alternate history. Both have the same idea. It's an existential thing. You're inside the timeline, so you have no view outside of it. Our view right now is that everything outside is speculation. Is there a timeline right beside this one where Hitler did win World War II, and we're talking in the Nazi Silver Springs, Maryland? If you get into that and time paradoxes, like if you killed your grandfather before he met your grandmother, would you be alive? There have been stories in which a number of people pop out of existence as soon as a guy gets in a time machine.

Q: If there's an infinite number of possibilities, most of them probably aren't very interesting. Somewhere there is an alternate universe in which this coffee cup is over there...and nothing else has changed.

Waldrop: [Laughs.] Exactly. And, like I said, it doesn't make any difference in life. But one of the two novelets I wrote for the Capclave book starts out with some things that happened to me and my sister when we were kids, and it goes off completely differently. It's a time-travel thing, but the changes that the character affects aren't that big. He comes back and his sister has moved a couple of miles from where she is now. [Laughs.] He's changed history but it doesn't amount to much. He *knows* he's changed history, and nobody else in the whole world does.

Q: It occurs to me that if you were traveling between parallel universes like this, there would be no way you could possibly know that you have come home. The coffee cup on the other side of the table could be in China. That might be the only difference. But it's not *your* time-track.

Waldrop: I don't know if you ever saw the "Treehouse of Horror" episode of *The Simpsons,* where Homer is trying to fix the toaster. It is every time-travel paradox in the history of the universe. That thing should have won a Hugo, because in seven and a half minutes they go through the *whole thing.* He keeps coming back and trying to figure out if he's home or if he's in this other timestream. You hear him running back in to short the toaster some more to get back to another timestream. It's brilliant. It should have won the Hugo that year, it really should have, because they knew *exactly* what they were doing. They refer to every time-paradox story there's ever been. There's a "Sound of Thunder" segment.

Q: This does get back to the idea of serious science fiction ideas presented as humor. You have probably seen a lot of science fiction novels that would be a lot more entertaining if they were funny, and possibly should have been.

Waldrop: Like I said, for a long time they felt that to be important they had to be long *and* dull. In other words, to get across any serious idea at all, they had to be just deadly, *deadly* dull. But all the great stuff has had some humor in it, or has been humorous, to get it across. Like the scene in "Remember the Alamo!" [by Fehrenbach] in which Travis gets up and makes a great speech and draws a line in the dirt and says, "Texas or liberty, God or death!" and Crockett and Bowie say, "That's talkin' awful big, Bill." Of course they end up surrendering the Alamo, but it doesn't change things in the long run. They delayed what was going to happen for two weeks. They say, "That's talkin' awful tough, Bill. I'm not sure this death thing is a good idea." It's a wonderful story.

Q: Do you start out with a neat idea like this? Do you regard yourself as a notion writer?

Waldrop: It's happened before. I don't sit down and toss around ideas and stuff. Either the ideas will just come to me for *no reason* at all, or I will start with a scene or something, visualizing a scene, and I will say, "How did these people get here? What led up to this? What happens next?" You know, all that kind of stuff. It's usually like that more often than not. A lot of people get ideas first and figure out a character to go with it. Damon Knight always used to say that if you get an idea first, ask yourself, "Who does this idea *hurt* most?" There's your character. You write about the character whom this idea is messing up the most.

Let's say...what? I don't know. Free fusion energy in every house. Who would that hurt most? So you write the story about him. Exactly. There's your viewpoint character.

Q: You don't seem to be the sort of writer who writes on the basis of what's popular in science fiction now. I didn't see you try to jump onto the Cyberpunk bandwagon.

Waldrop: No. In fact, I was talking about this with somebody last night. I said, "I am so tired of being the avatar of the zeitgeist," because I'll write a story, and ten years later or so, *other* people will start writing stories about *that* subject. Like when

I wrote "Us," five or six years ago, you know, the one about Lindbergh Jr. and the lives he could have had. Now Philip Roth comes and writes a book and makes a ton of money, *The Plot Against America.* My story should have been out in a collection a year before it was. I've written a lot of stuff, and other people have written about the same subject area ten years later, both in and out of the field. I've already been through with that for ten or eleven years and suddenly the idea gets hot again. Remember when Doctorow wrote *Ragtime,* that was the first time that had ever been done, incorporating all that detail, and it wasn't more than two or three years later that there were all these alternate New York City type novels out, set in the end of the nineteenth century. As George Martin said, he didn't write *Black and White and Read All Over,* his book about the Yellow Journalism period, but now you can read *The Alienist* by Caleb Carr, which is set in exactly the same era with exactly the same people in it.

People do tend to write books like the hottest book around. Gibson's *Neuromancer* came out of nowhere. There were a couple precursors, but it was like a year later there were fifty cyberpunk books out on the stands. That book has *such* an influence on people. It was a new SF trope. Up until *Neuromancer,* the use of science was the *official* use. In other words, it was technocrat-approved scientific discoveries being used in the way they were *supposed* to be used, unless there were mad scientists. But when you got to *Neuromancer,* it was inappropriate use of approved technology. That was the thing. It was ground-level use. Kids would look at some new development and say, "What can we do with this?" Like encrypt all their friends' stuff so their parents couldn't spy on them. It was unapproved use of approved technology.

Q: It's a proud and lonely thing, but it is an honorable thing to be ahead of the curve, but it is probably better to be ahead of the curve than *behind* it.

Waldrop: Right.

Q: Walter Moseley has just brought out his Cyberpunk novel *now*.

Waldrop: There are some things where if you get the idea for it, you're going to do it no matter what has been done, or where or when. I think that novels have a certain time in a writer's life in which they *should* be written, and if they go past that time, they shouldn't be written. You know what I mean?

Q: Yes. You shouldn't write your novel of adolescence when you're seventy.

Waldrop: Exactly. That kind of thing. Or let's say you're going to write a novel involving certain parameters, and the time for those parameters goes by. You can still write the same novel, but you have to refer to it, as if there'd been a paradigm shift. You'd have to refer to it in pre-paradigm-shift terms, from the viewpoint of somebody *past* that, rather than from *within* that paradigm.

Q: You're looking back on the subject-matter.

Waldrop: You're looking back, narrating it from the viewpoint of somebody who *has been through it* all or is older and wiser. The "Wonder Years" approach.

Q: Judith Berman has raised the point in a celebrated essay that there is a kind of paralysis in science fiction right now. Nobody is addressing the future anymore. Maybe the way to do it is with humor.

Waldrop: I was talking to someone about *that*. I said the hardest novel in the world to write right now is the one set within the next ten years. We used to be afraid of history in the last ten years, because we hadn't got enough distance. But looking into the future, you can figure out some things. We're still going to be having terrorism. We're going to be in an energy crisis, and all that kind of stuff. But looking ten years in the future: are we going to Mars? Maybe not, but for a while we're going to *pretend* we are. Are we going *back* to the Moon? Maybe. We probably will a few times. But trying to predict, socially, what is going to happen, the closer you are, the harder it is. It used to be, in the old days, the further it got, the harder it was.

Q: But it would also be longer before anybody caught you being wrong.

Waldrop: Exactly. That's the thing. If there's a paralysis it's because the writers are looking for, but haven't hit on anything that could *actually* happen, or that could be posited from what you got now. What you've got now s scared people who won't admit they're wrong.

Q: In film terms, the difference is between the dreadfully earnest movie *Mission to Mars* and something like *Red Dwarf* or *Futurama*. Now those last two make sense. They're good science fiction. The other wasn't very convincing.

Waldrop: Right. You're in the far future. You've got 'droids and all that—and it's funny. They're making fun of all the things that *could* go wrong. As somebody said, melodrama dates less than any other form. Good vs. evil, that sort of thing. It dates less, no matter where it's set because people are still interested in the conflict and it's almost timeless. You can watch a movie from the '30s and you can apply it to up to about ten or fifteen years ago. Nobody has cell phones. What's going on in there? In other words, you have to use a car to get from one place to another, or a plane—that dates less than something keyed in exactly, like a World War II movie. They take place in a period of five years. But a melodrama from the '30s was still valid in

1970 or 1980, what was going on in the melodrama.

Q: I suppose the writer can't *really* obsess about this too much. But how long do you think humor holds up over time?

Waldrop: Good, basic Aristophanic humor holds up forever. It's always easy to hit somebody over the head with a bag of *merde*. That gets a laugh even now, if you set it up. Certain kinds of humor don't date at all, and certain kinds are keyed *right to* their time. Those date, but the basic slapstick and stuff like that doesn't change. Verbal humor, although humor is based on somebody else's pain or discomfort, of course, that never changes.

Q: A story of yours, "Mister Goober's Show," strikes me as a wonderful story, but it's very specifically for Baby-Boomers. It's about a certain time in which television was still new and unique. I suspect that an eleven-year-old today would not understand that story.

Waldrop: It was set in a time when TV was unique and just catching on, but it refers back to a time twenty years before that, when TV was first really new, right when they had just figured out the concept and started constructing the first early sets. The technology had already changed completely twice since the time they started making televisions and the time the story takes place, in early 1951. Then it follows the characters up until the late '80s. But, yeah, it is a Boomer type story, but it refers back to the flapper generation. That was when the mechanical TV was first made. I was trying to get those two eras together into one story, because it's all about outmoded technology.
  Did you read "Major Spacer," the one that starts in the '50s and then has the fifty-year space-break, and ends in the year 2000? It's about a guy who had a TV show in the early '50s, and there is a Y2K type thing, although it is not Y2K, it's a terrorist thing, right after the turn of 2000. I wrote it to show the

difference between the technology we had in 1950 and the technology of 2000, which everybody takes for granted. They *didn't* have actual videotape in 1950. They shot audiotape through a stationary head at *10,000 feet a minute.* You had to put a refrigerator box there and shoot this tape through it. So that to have a thirty-second commercial you'd have to have a mile of tape. It would all be in the box when you got through, because there wouldn't be a reel that could turn fast enough to take it up. They were just first developing that. But I wanted to show the differences that fifty years have brought in TV technology.

Q: Just like a real hard-science fiction writer, you have a real preoccupation with technology.

Waldrop: *Dream Factories and Radio Pictures,* besides being all the stories, is a history of motion picture technology through the past century. You're right about that. People don't even think that motion pictures are a science and a technology besides being an entertainment medium. Especially the changes that have come in the past ten years are as phenomenal as anything that has happened. They've been used wrong, just like the first innovations were used wrong in most cases. Like the moving camera and the pan-shot and all that stuff—they knew they could do it but they didn't know what to use it for yet. It took another fifteen years until they figured out how to use a tracking-shot or a zoom-shot or whatever else they needed. Right now they're trying to figure out what to do with CGI. The answer is, like, stick it in your eye, most of the time, because they can. They can make it come and get you. That's what they've been using it for, for special effects they couldn't have gotten any other way.

Q: I also note your great interest in movies....

Waldrop: I was talking about the appropriate use of CGI on the panel today. It was like what Billy Crystal did in *1961,* which is about Mantle and Maris. You know the home-run thing between Mantle and Maris. It's just that there wasn't any special effects, but every time you looked outside of Yankee Stadium, it was *1961*. The right buildings, and all that. That was a very restrained use of CGI.

Q: The best example I can think of is in *The Devil's Backbone,* which is a Spanish ghost film made by Guillermo del Toro, the guy who made *Hellboy.* There is the ghost of a kid who's been drowned. As he appears to people, he doesn't look all that well, but there are always little bubbles floating around his face. They could have had exploding guts, but they settled for bubbles.

Waldrop: That's restraint. Usually when they pay money for CGI, they want something big and splashy that you can see up on the screen to show where the money went. But the *little bubbles* are just as hard to do as making *the whole screen explode.* Very few directors have the restraint to do just what they need to do and then quit.

Q: Have you ever been involved in films?

Waldrop: Like I was saying at the panel today, we made a short movie in 1966 at a convention, about a theft at a comic convention. It goes on from there. The usual stupid thing.
 People have tried to option my stories and make them and adapt them to TV but nothing has ever happened. You get the first six-month option money, and that's the last time you hear from them.

Q: I note that you once "discovered" a lost screenplay of Mortimer Morbius Moamrath, *Cthulhublanca.* But beyond that, have you ever written screenplays?

Waldrop: Me and Tom Reamy wrote a screenplay together that he took to Hollywood when he moved there in '69 or '70 or whenever that was, and he later turned that into the story "The

Detweiler Boy," which appeared in *F&SF*, and I think it was up for a Nebula. But you can see what the screenplay was about from that story. Essentially it's *Basket Case* ten years before *Basket Case*. We thought that the easiest thing you could get produced then was a cheap horror movie, so we wrote a horror movie you could film cheap.

Q: Do you still yearn to do this? Do you feel Hollywood calling?

Waldrop: No. I don't even get excited anymore when they first get ahold of me, like you do when you're younger. Like I said, the most you're going to get is the first six months option money, and then you'll never hear from them again.

Zelazny used to say, "Just take the money. If they ever actually make the movie and it turns out good, you can say, 'They had such wonderful material to work from,' and if it turns out bad you say, 'I just took the money.'" [Laughs.] Right.

Q: So what are you doing these days.

Waldrop: I'm writing my butt off. I got to turn in *The Search for Tom Purdue* to Subterranean by December 1st. It's a short novel I've been working on for a long, long time. It'll be about 40,000 words, something like that. Real long for me. Then I hope to get back to *I, John Mandeville?* and *The Moone World*, which eventually *will* happen. Those are novels I have been working for about twenty and thirty years apiece.

Q: As we were saying earlier, if you've been working on a novel for twenty or thirty years, it'll be a different book from when you envisioned when you started.

Waldrop: Even *Tom Purdue*, which is a short novel, has changed two or three times. I've been working on that for about twenty. It's changed in concept in even the last ten or twelve years. But *Mandeville* has essentially stayed in the same form in my mind.

But then again I conceived it in a weird form that doesn't *seem* weird by now. The way I was going to narrate it doesn't seem weird at all anymore. So that's holding its own with my aging brain. The stuff that changed, obviously I didn't have it right when I thought of it. If it stays the same, then you had it pretty much the way it should be.

Q: You're not one of these guys who writes a novel in two weeks then? Not fast.

Waldrop: No. [Laughs.] Typing is the hard part. I hate typing and I am a two-fingered typist and it takes *forever* to type something as long as a novel. But the actual writing of *The Texas-Israeli War,* our first book, we wrote that end-to-end in ninety days. But that was because there were two of us. I wrote a complete first draft in thirty days. Buddy wrote a complete second draft in thirty days, and we each rewrote half of the third draft, so we had fifteen days apiece. And we sat down with that time-table when we started writing the book. That's what we knew we *had* to do, and then turned it in. I *can* write the first draft of novel in thirty days if I *really* want to hurt myself. But I don't want to do that.

Q: I guess this is the difference between quality and career.

Waldrop: [Laughing.] It's not much of a career.

Q: A careerist has to turn out a book about every year.

Waldrop: If I wrote novels I would have a lot more money than I do right now. I can guarantee I would have *some* money, which is more than I do right now. But I work too hard on short stories. It would have been wonderful if, the older I got, the faster and easier they would have come. But it's turned out the exact opposite. The older I get the slower and the more difficult they come to me, the actual work of getting the story done, I mean. The ideas are coming to me all the time, but I am just not doing anything with most of them.

Q: Are you at least keeping notes?

Waldrop: Yes. I make notes on stuff and put them in the thing called "the undeveloped file," which gets thicker and thicker as time goes on. Then I will look back through that occasionally, when I'm looking for a piece of information that I wrote down, and see if I can find it and if anything happens. But, yeah, I work too hard on short stories.

Q: It's not too hard. Not everybody can be an Avatar of the Zeitgeist. That would make a good book title, maybe for your next collection.

Waldrop: Yes, I think so. [Laughing.] But I will have to write a *story* called that. Then of course if you name the thing, you scare it away. You know the old superstition that if you talk about it beforehand, you won't want to write the story. That's why I will usually refer to the story titles while I am thinking about them by a general term, not what becomes a real title, but "the Africa story" or whatever. Only in the last stages does it get a title, though some times I have thought of the title first. I've held off putting it on a manuscript until I was almost done. It's not a superstition. It's just that most of them didn't have a title until the end.

But like I said, the stories are getting harder and harder all the time. I'm getting into them further every time, I think. This would be easier if you were reading the two novelets [for the delayed Capclave book—DS], because they're the freshest on my mind. They were just really hard to do, because I was trying to do two totally different kinds of writing.

Q: Do you find it more rewarding if you put more effort in? You get, presumably, a richer story.

Waldrop: This is what we all *hope* for. This why I keep doing this, right? As I asked myself on the panel the other night, "Are you getting better or are you just getting weirder? Are you just talking to yourself louder?" You can become recursive, and you have to say, "Am I doing this because it will make a better story, or am I doing this because it's easier to do this?" You keep questioning your own motives. Why am I doing it *this* way instead of *that*? Why am I telling it this way? Is there a *better* way to tell it? Like I said, one of the two novelets starts as a dialogue, an interview, turns into a monologue, and finishes up with a letter being read for about seven or eight pages. So it's three different styles of narrative all in the same story and two-thirds of it in half the same voice. I don't know if it worked or not. We'll see.

Q: Sounds interesting. I will look forward to it.

Waldrop: Great.

(Conducted at Capclave, in Silver Springs, MD, Oct. 16, 2005.)

INDEX

Abu Bakr, 137
Accelerando (Stross), 208-208, 209, 211-212, 214, 217, 222
Ace Books (publisher), 145, 155, 192
Ace Doubles, 155, 156, 165, 175
Ace Specials, 156, 159
Adams, Douglas, 122
Adventures in Time and Space (ed. Healy & McComas), 154
The Adventures of Huckleberry Finn (Twain), 142
Aeneid (Virgil), 118
The Age (magazine), 42
Agent of Byzantium (Turtledove), 129, 137
Albahari, David, 94
The Alienist (Carr), 257
The Alteration (Amis), 134
Alexander the Great, 135
Amazing Stories (magazine), 97
Analog (magazine), 13, 15, 18, 20, 61, 66, 109, 110, 123, 157, 166, 167, 200, 224
Anderson, Gerry, 189
Anderson, Poul, 158
"And He Walked Around Horses" (Piper), 136, 137
Andrews, V.C., 108
The Aristocats (film), 101
Asimov, Isaac, 82, 100, 133, 158
Asimov's SF (magazine), 97, 98, 121, 146, 153, 154, 174, 214, 216

The Atrocity Archives (Stross), 207
Attack of the Jazz Giants (Frost), 149
Atwood, Margaret, 142
"Audubon in Atlantis" (Turtledove), 133
Auster, Paul, 142
Bad Medicine (a.k.a. *Counting Coup,* Dann), 55
Bambi (Salten), 163
"Bank Run" (Purdom), 174
Banks, Iain, 77
"Barbarian Confessions" (Rusch), 121
Barker, Clive, 148
The Barons of Behavior (Purdom), 156
Basket Case (film), 263
Bear, Elizabeth, 219
Bear, Greg, 198
Beckett, Samuel, 188
Bedford-Jones, H. 131
Belmont-Tower (publisher), 129
Benford, Gregory, 122, 197, 198
Benét, Stephen Vincent, 135, 136, 137
Berg, Peter, 240
Berman, Judith, 258
Best American Mystery Stories 2009), 121
Bester, Alfred, 80-81
"The Best Known Man in the World" (Pearlman), 85
Betancourt, John, 100
Bey, Turhan, 34
Big Bang Theory (TV), 120
Bin Laden, Osama, 195
"A Birthday" (Friesner), 106
Bisson, Terry, 82
Blackwood, Algernon, 92
Boarding the Enterprise (ed. Gerrold & Sawyer), 189
Bonaparte, Napoleon, 136
The Book (Zivkovic), 86

The Books of Blood (Barker), 148
The Book of the New Sun (Wolfe), 18
Borges, Jorge Luis, 89, 252
Boucher, Anthony, 126
Bova, Ben, 13, 18, 157
Bowie, David, 11
Boyle, T. C. 141
Bradbury, Ray, 159
Brave New World (Huxley), 121
The Bridge (Zivkovic), 96
Brin, David, 173
Bring the Jubilee (Moore), 253
Brooks, Terry, 126
Brunner, John, 21, 158
Budrys, Algis, 178, 185
Bulgakov, Mikhail, 89, 90
Burks, Arthur J., 131
Burroughs, Edgar Rice, 107, 170, 171
Bush, George W., 36
Cabell, James Branch, 126
Calculating God (Sawyer), 191-192, 196, 199
Camelot (musical), 125
Campbell, John W., 12, 17, 18, 157, 165, 166, 167, 168, 175
Campbell, Ramsey, 51
Camus, Albert, 39
Candide (Voltaire), 39
Carr, Terry, 156, 175, 251
Carson, Rachel, 242, 243
Carter, Lin, 125, 126
Casablanca (film), 195
Cassandra workshop, 204
The Caves of Steel (Asimov), 82
Celestial Matters (Garfinkle), 132
Chaney, Lon, Jr., 34
Chapterhouse Dune (Herbert), 225, 227, 234
Cheap Truth (magazine), 206

Childhood's End (Clarke), 213
CIA, 69
Clancy, Tom, 172
Clarion workshop, 61-63, 205
Clarke, Arthur C. 64, 199
Clement, Hal, 20
A Clockwork Orange (Burgess), 121
Clute, John, 76, 80
"Collecting Dust" (Frost), 149
Compton, D. G., 13
Computer Shopper (magazine), 204
Conan series (Howard), 248
Condé Nast (publisher), 157
Conklin, Groff, 154
Connections (TV) 136
The Continuous Katherine Mortenhoe, 177, 178, 181, 182, 185
Constantine the Great, 137
Cooper, James Fenimore, 171, 172
Cosmos (magazine), 128
Covenant series (Donaldson), 24
Cowley, Malcolm, 161
Crane, Stephen, 79
Crime and Punishment (Dostoyevky), 39
The Crucible (Miller), 27, 35
"Cthulhublanca" (Waldrop), 262
Cunningham, Jan, 233
"The Curfew Tolls" (Benét), 135
"Custer's Last Jump" (Waldrop & Utley), 251-252
Custer's Last Jump (Waldrop et al.), 250
Cyberprep, 99-101
Cyberpunk, 99, 206, 214, 220, 256
The Daily Planet (newspaper), 11
Dangerous Visions (ed. Ellison), 50
Dark Tower series (King), 24
"Da Vinci Rising" (Dann), 44
da Vinci, Leonardo, 42, 44, 49

Darwin, Charles, 32-33
Datlow, Ellen, 146
Davidson, Avram, 168
Dean, James, 43, 44
"Death and the Librarian" (Friesner), 111-112
Deathwatch (film), 182-183
de Camp, L. Sprague, 129
Deighton, Len, 214
del Rey, Lester, 129
Del Torro, Guillermo, 262
Depp, Johnny, 109
Derleth, August, 23
"The Detwiler Boy" (Reamy), 263
The Devil's Backbone (film), 262
"The Diamond Pit" (Dann), 60
Dick, Philip K., 80
Dickson, Gordon R., 20
The Dictionary of the Khazars (Pavic), 88
A Different Flesh (Turtledove), 133
Diving into the Wreck (Rusch), 127
Doherty, Tom, 201
Donaldson, Stephen R., 24
The Door into Summer (Heinlein), 75
Doubleday (publisher), 154
"Double Visions" (Dann), 46
Douglas, John, 190
The Dosadi Experiment (Herbert), 226
"Down in the Bottomlands" (Turtledove) 133
Dozois, Gardner, 11, 42, 146, 167-168, 205
"Dragonet" (Friesner), 97
Dream Factories and Radio Pictures (Waldrop) 261
Dreamer of Dune (Herbert), 224-225
Dreaming Down-Under (ed. Dann & Webb), 42, 50, 52
The Drummer (newspaper), 11
Dumas, Alexandre *fils*, 229
Dunsany, Lord, 126

Dune (Herbert), 223, 224, 226, 228, 235, 238, 239, 240, 243, 245, 246, 247-248
Dune (film versions), 239-240, 243
Dune Messiah (Herbert), 235, 248
Dune series, 225-226, 233, 245-246
Dune 7 (Herbert), 234
Edison, Thomas, 67
Einhorn, Ira, 243
Elkin, Stanley, 83
Ellison, Harlan, 43, 45, 50, 142, 157
The Encyclopedia of Science Fiction (Zivkovic), 88
End of an Era (Sawyer), 197
Escher's Loops (Zivkovic), 86, 96
Etchison, Dennis, 51
Evolution (Baxter), 194
Exodus (Biblical book), 28
Extra Duty (Dann), 60
The Eyes of Heisenberg (Herbert), 226
F&SF (see *The Magazine of Fantasy & Science Fiction*)
Fantastic (magazine), 15
Far-Seer (Sawyer), 197
"The Feast of St. Catherine" (Wolfe), 19
Fevre Dream (Martin), 15, 21, 22
FForde, Jasper, 118
The Fiction Factory (Dann et al.), 60
"Fin de Cycle" (Waldrop), 252
Findley, Major Rick, 195
Fireball XL5 (TV), 189, 190
Fitcher's Bridge (Frost), 149
Fleming, Ian, 206
"Flower Fairies" (Rusch), 115-116
Flowers for Algernon (Keyes), 120
Foreigner (Sawyer), 197
Fossil Hunter (Sawyer), 194, 197
Fort, Charles, 136
The Forever War (Haldeman), 78-79

Four Stories Till the End (Zivkovic), 93
The Fourth Circle (Zivkovic), 86, 88
Franklin, Benjamin, 36, 253
Futurama (TV), 228
"The Future is Already Here: Is there a Place for Science Fiction in the 21st Century?" (Sawyer), 197
Galaxy (magazine), 15
"A Game of Crola" (Friesner), 97
Game Earth trilogy (Andrson), 223
A Game of Thrones (Martin), 13, 18, 19
The Garbage Chronicles (Herbert), 233
Garbage World (Platt), 228
Gardner, John, 117
Garfinkle, Richard, 132, 133
Garrett, Randall, 166
Gathering the Bones (ed. Dann, Etchison, and Campbell), 51
The Ghost at Skeleton Rock (Dixon), 144
Gibson, William, 197, 198, 206
Give Me Back My Legions! (Turtledove), 138
The Great Steamboat Race (Brunner), 21
Globe and Mail (newspaper), 200
Glory Road (Heinlein), 16
"G-Men" (Rusch), 121
The God Emperor of Dune (Herbert), 247
The Gods Must Be Crazy (film) 252
Golden Fleece (Sawyer), 190, 197
Goldsmith, Cele, 175
Gollancz (publisher), 176
"The Green Beret" (Purdom), 165-166
Gregg Press (publisher), 178
Gribbin, John, 180-181
Guns of the South (Turtledove), 134
Haldeman, Jack C.II. 77
Haldeman, Joe, 12, 146-147
Hamlet (Shakespeare), 118
Hancock (film), 240

Hardy Boys series, 143-144
Harrison, Edward, 28
Harrison, Harry, 55, 133
Harry Potter series (Rowling), 198
Harold Shea series (Pratt and de Camp), 17
HarperCollins (publisher), 43, 51, 192
Hartwell, David, 124, 128, 201
The Heaven Makers (Herbert), 227
"Helen Remembers the Stork Club" (Friesner), 103-104
Heinlein, Robert A., 12, 15, 16, 69, 81, 82, 84, 89, 161
Hellboy (film), 262
Helprin, Mark, 44
Hellstrom's Hive (Herbert), 226
Hemingway, Ernest, 47, 57, 161, 170
The Hemingway Hoax (Haldeman), 84
Herbert, Beverly, 231
Herbert, Frank, 107, 223, 224-227. 230-231, 233-234, 236, 237-238, 240-241, 244, 245, 248
Herbert, Jan, 241
Heretics of Dune (Herbert), 225, 234
Heydrich, Heinrich, 135
Hitler, Adolf, 136, 195, 229, 253, 254
Hodder & Stoughton (publisher), 177, 185
Homer, 12
Hominids (Sawyer), 199
House Harkonnen (Herbert & Anderson), 230
House of Dracula (film), 30
Howard, John, 56, 58
Howard, Robert E., 15, 92, 248
Hoyle, Fred, 78
The Hunt for Red October (Clancy), 172
Hunters of Dune (Herbert & Anderson), 234
Hussein, Saddam, 36, 196
Hybrids (Sawyer) 192, 196-197
Iliad (Homer), 12
Impossible Encounters (Zivkovic), 96

Impossible Stories (Zivkovic), 86, 93
The Incomplete Enchanter (Pratt & de Camp), 125
I, John Mandeville (Waldrop) 263-264
Ings, Simon, 204
Interzone (magazine), 13, 86, 94, 202, 205, 218
The Internet Review of Science Fiction (e-zine), 116, 117
Ionesco, Eugene, 188
Iron Sunrise (Stross)
James I (King of England), 28, 29
Jarry, Alfred, 188, 252
Jefferson, Thomas, 36
Johnson, Samuel, 161
Jubilee (Dann), 48
Junction (Dann), 43
Jung, Carl G., 241
The Jungle (Sinclair), 32
Justice City (Compton), 176
Justinian (Turtledove), 129
Kafka, Franz, 89, 90
Keitel, Harvey, 182
Kennedy, Robert, 43
Kerosina (publisher), 182
Kim Possible (TV), 102
King James Bible, 28
King, Stephen, 24
Kipling, Rudyard, 84
Klein, T. E. D., 144
Knight, Damon, 50, 256
Koran, 36
Kornbluth, Cyril M., 93
Kramer, Ed, 227
Kreisler, Fritz, 163
"The Lady or the Tiger?" (Stockton), 86
Landis, Geoffrey, 13
Landis, Marie, 236
The Last Days of Krypton (Anderson), 230

The Last Witchfinder (Morrow), 26, 28-31, 32, 33, 34, 35, 260
Laumer, Keith, 158
Laundry series (Stross), 220
Lawrence, D.H., 107
Left Behind series (LaHaye and Jenkins), 196
The Left Hand of Darkness (Le Guin), 156
Le Guin, Ursula K., 94, 156, 184
Lem, Stanislaw, 90
Lenin, Vladimir Ilyich, 136
Lest Darkness Fall (de Camp), 128
Lewis, C.S., 126
Liberating Atlantis (Turtledove), 133
Lifeline (Anderson), 223
Limbo (Wolfe), 124
The Literary Scene (Cowley), 161
Living with the Dead (Schweitzer), 93
"Lobsters" (Stross), 217
Locus (magazine), 199
Lonesome Dove (McMurtry) , 172
The Lord of the Rings (Tolkien), 118-119, 126,160, 239
"The Lost Years" (Lewis), 253
Lovecraft, H. P., 15, 22-23, 91-92, 95, 206, 207, 214, 217
Lucasfilm, 227
Lucas, George, 229
Lucian of Samosata, 90
Lynch, David, 239
Lyrec (Frost), 145
Madame Bovary (Flaubert), 39
Machen, Arthur, 92
The Magazine of Fantasy & Science Fiction (*F&SF*), *122, 126, 153, 168, 263*
"Magic, Incorporated" (Heinlein), 16
"Major Spacer" (Waldrop), 260-261
The Making of Star Trek (Roddenberry & Whitfield), 190
Malleus Malificarum (Kramer and Sprenger), 27
The Man in the High Castle (Dick) 130-131

Man of Two Worlds (Herbert & Herbert), 223, 236
The Man with the Iron Heart (Turtledove), 135
Marsbound (Haldeman), 81
Mars Crossing (Landis), 70-71
McCarthy, Cormac, 118, 121
McCarthy, Joseph, 101
McMurtry, Larry, 172
Mindbridge (Haldeman), 75
Martin, George R. R., 13, 46, 257
Masks of the Universe (Harrison), 28
The Master and Margarita (Bulgakov), 90
Melies, George, 252
The Memory Cathedral (Dann), 42, 44, 48, 49
Merchant Princes series (Stross), 215
Milford workshop, 204
Mission to Mars (film), 259
"Mister Goober's Show" (Waldrop), 280
Moamrath, Morbius Mortimer, 262
Moby Dick (Melville), 111
Moesta, Rebecca, 242
Mohammed, 137
Monroe, Marilyn, 43
Moone World (Waldrop), 263
Morrow, James, 45, 124
William Morrow (publisher), 33
Moseley, Walter, 258
"Moso" (Turtledove), 133
A Moveable Feast (Hemingway), 170
Musaylimah, 137
National Aeronautics and Space Administration (NASA), 63-64, 67, 69
Necronomicon (Alhazred), 148
1968 (Haldeman), 76-77, 83
1961 (film), 261-262
Neuromancer (Gibson), 220, 257
New Dimensions (anthology series, ed. Silverberg), 251

New Scientist (magazine), 178, 194
Newsweek (magazine), 124
The New York Review of Science Fiction, 124
New York Times, 116, 126
Niffenegger, Audrey, 118
Night Shade Books (publisher), 119
Nine Princes in Amber (Zelazny), 215
Niven, Larry, 71, 236
Nobody's Princess (Friesner), 105
Nobody's Prize (Friesner), 105
No Man's Land (Compton) 176, 177
Norton, Andre, 15, 127
The Notebooks of Frank Herbert's Dune (ed. Herbert), 223
Nourse, Alan E., 189
Odyssey (Homer), 143
Olive Kitteridge (Strout), 147
Omni (magazine), 48
The Once and Future King (White), 124
Only Begotten Daughter (Morrow), 28, 34
Opening Atlantis (Turtledove), 133
Orbit (anthology series, ed. Knight), 18
Orwell, George, 170
Paratime series (Piper), 215
Paul of Dune (Herbert & Anderson), 231
Pavane (Roberts), 134
Pavic, Milorad, 88
Pearson, Lester, 196
Petrovic, Goran, 94
Philip of Macedon, 135
Picard, Barbara Leonie, 143
Piper, H. Beam, 123, 136
Planet of the Apes (film), 190
The Plot Against America (Roth), 257
Poe, Edgar Allan, 91, 92
Pogo (Kelly), 101-102
Pohl, Frederik, 93, 159

Pournelle, Jerry 236
Pratchett, Terry, 101, 111, 207, 222
The Preppy Handbook (Roberts et al.), 99
Presley, Elvis, 43, 68
Principia Mathematica (Newton), 29, 30
Pringle, David, 94
Prisoners of Arion (Herbert), 223
Proust, Marcel, 110, 111, 252
Publishers Weekly, 200
Pulphouse Publishing, 119
Pumilia, Joseph, 249, 250
Pryor, Boori, 56
Pyke, Magnus, 218-219
Quark (TV), 228
Race for God (Herbert), 223
Ragnarok (Compton & Gribin), 180
Ragtime (Doctorow), 257
Ransom, Bill, 237
The Reader (Zivkovic), 96
Reagan, Ronald, 43
Red Dwarf (TV), 259
Reader's Digest, 180
Realms of Fantasy (magazine), 115
Reamy, Tom, 262
The Rebel: an Imagined Life of James Dean (Dann), 59-60
"Reduction in Arms" (Purdom), 153, 156
"Remember the Alamo" (Fehrenbach), 253, 256
Remembrance of Things Past (Proust), 110
Remscela (Frost), 145
Resurrection Inc. (Anderson), 223
The Rest of the Robots (Asimov), 189
The Retrieval Artist (Rusch), 121
Rhinoceros (Ionesco), 188
Rice, Anne, 22
Riddley Walker (Hoban), 121
The Road (McCarthy), 121

Robbins, Harold, 59, 60, 126
Robinson, Kim Stanley, 57, 198
"Rogue Farm" (Stross), 219
Rollback (Sawyer), 200-201
Roth, Philip, 257
Rottenberg, Dan, 168
Rowling, J. K. 107, 222
Ruled Britannia (Turtledove), 134
Russell, Anna, 131
Russell, Eric Frank, 15
Saga of the Seven Suns (Anderson), 223
Salten, Felix, 163
Salvatore, Robert, 228
The Sands of Mars (Clarke), 64
Sandworms of Dune (Herbert & Anderson), 234
Sargent, Pamela, 57
The Satanic Verses (Rushdie), 137
Saunders, Jake (Buddy), 250
Sawyer, Robert, 13
"The Scarlet Band" (Turtledove), 133
Schmidt, Stanley, 18
Schneider, Romy, 182
Schwarzenegger, Arnold, 183
Schweitzer, Darrell, 226
Scithers, George, 97
Scooby-Doo (TV), 143, 151
Scott Meredith Literary Agency, 164, 165, 175
Scudder's Game (Compton), 187
The Search for Tom Purdue (Waldrop), 263
Selected Works of Stephen Vincent Benét, 136
Serling, Rod, 144
SF Voices (Schweitzer), 11
SFWA Bulletin (magazine), 46
Shakespeare in Love (film) 185
Shakespeare, William, 141
Shelley, Percy Bysshe, 33

Shwartz, Susan, 99, 100
Sideways in Crime (ed Anders), 121
Sidney's Comet (Herbert), 223, 228, 247
The Sierra Club, 244
Signet Books (publisher), 227
The Silent (Dann), 42, 49, 57-58
Silverberg, Robert, 45, 120, 157, 158-159, 166, 251
Singularity, 82, 207, 210-211
Singularity Sky (Stross), 215
"The Skin Trade" (Martin), 22
Small Beer Press, 119
Smith, Edward E., 170, 171-172
Solaris (Lem), 91
Son of Tarzan (Burroughs), 171
"A Song for Lya" (Martin), 13
A Song of Ice and Fire (Martin), 22
"The Sound of Thunder" (Bradbury), 254, 255
Space and Time (magazine), 133, 223
The Space Merchants (Pohl & Kornbluth), 76
Space Skimmer (Gerrold), 189
The Sparrow (Russell), 124
Spider's Web (Haldeman), 83
Springer, Jerry, 106
Spinrad, Norman, 45
Spook Country (Gibson), 197
Stalin, Joseph, 195
Stand on Zanzibar (Brunner), 155
Stanton, Harry Dean, 182
The Stranger (Camus), 39
The Starhiker (Dann), 43, 49
Starplex (Sawyer), 197-198
The Stars My Destination (Bester), 154
Starship Troopers (Heinlein), 79
Star Trek (TV), 102, 189-190
The Steel Crocodile (Compton), 178
Stephenson, Neal, 83

Sterling, Bruce, 142, 206
Stockton, Frank R., 87
Stross, Charles, 171
Strout, Elizabeth, 147
Stuart dynasty, 221
"The Stuff of Heroes" (Friesner), 97
Subterranean (publisher), 263
Sudanna, Sudanna (Herbert), 223, 241
Sunset Boulevard (film), 104
Swanson, Gloria, 104
Swanwick, Michael, 146
Synthajoy (Compton), 176, 177, 178, 185
Tabler, Walt, 233
Tachyon Press (publisher), 119
Tain (Frost), 149-150
Tain Bo Cuailnge, 145
Tarr, Judith, 99
Tavernier, Bernard, 182, 183
"The Telephone" (Zivkovic), 93
The Terminal Experiment (Sawyer), 190, 193-194, 198
The Texas-Israeli War (Saunders & Waldrop), 264
Thackeray, William Makepeace, 83
Thatcher, Margaret, 220-221
Thirteen O'Clock (Benét), 136
This is the Way the World Ends (Morrow), 124
Thrilling Wonder Stories (magazine), 66
The Throne of Dune (Herbert & Anderson), 232
Time Gifts (Zivkovic), 86, 91, 93
The Time Machine (Wells), 194
Time Web series (Herbert), 229
T.K. Graphics (publisher), 11
Tolkien, J. R. R., 15, 17, 90, 126, 160
Tor Books (publisher), 51, 192, 196, 200, 201
"Toys" (Purdom), 167
"Treehouse of Horror" (*Simpsons* episode, TV), 255
The Trial (Kafka), 39

The Trinity Paradox (Anderson), 223
The Trouble on Titan (Nourse), 189
Trudeau, Pierre, 196
"Trunk and Disorderly" (Stross), 216-217
Tuttle, Lisa, 20, 249, 250
Twain, Mark, 83, 170, 251
Twilight Zone (magazine), 144
Twilight Zone (TV), 190, 144
The Unfortunate Fursey (Wall), 124
The United States of Atlantis (Turtledove), 133, 138
Unknown Worlds (magazine), 17
The Unquiet Mind (Sargent), 178
The Unsleeping Eye (Compton), 176
Updike, John, 142
"Us" (Waldrop), 257
Utley, Steven, 250, 251
Van Sloan, Edward, 34
Varley, John, 62, 206
Verne, Jules, 177
Vidal, Gore, 141
The Videssos Cycle (Turtledove), 129
Vinge, Vernor, 82, 207
Voices (Le Guin), 184
Voltaire, 161
Von Sydow, Max, 182
Voyage to the Bottom of the Sea (TV), 144
Waiting for Godot (Beckett), 188
Wallace, Bill, 250
Walotsky, Ron, 153
Wake (Sawyer), 201
The War of the Worlds (Wells), 12
War Year (Haldeman), 76
Warner Books, 192
Watch (Sawyer), 201
Webb, Janeen, 50, 56, 59
Webmind (Sawyer), 201

Welcomat (newspaper), 168
Wells, H. G., 12, 177
"What We Really Do at NASA" (Landis), 69
Whipping Star (Herbert), 227
Who Framed Roger Rabbit? (film), 108
The White Plague (Herbert), 226
"'White,' Said Fred" (Friesner), 103
White, Ted, 15
White, T. H., 124, 125
Whole Earth Catalog, 243
Wild Cards series (Martin et al.), 23
Williamson, Jack, 78
Wilson, Robert Charles, 194
The Wind in the Willows (Grahame), 126
Windling, Terri, 145, 146
The Winds of Dune (Herbert & Anderson), 223, 248
Windhaven (Martin & Tuttle), 20
The Witch of Blackbird Pond (Speare), 126
A Wizard of Earthsea (Le Guin), 126
Wodehouse, P. G., 214, 216
Wolfe, Gene, 18
Wollheim, Donald, 155, 165
The Women (Boyle), 141
Wonder (Sawyer), 201
A World of Difference (Turtledove), 133
Worldwar series (Turtledove), 134
Wright, Frank Lloyd, 141
The Writer (Zivkovic), 86, 91
Writer's Digest (magazine), 120, 165
"Write When You Get Work" (Friesner), 98
The X-Files (TV), 227
The Yiddish Policeman's Union (Chabon), 131
Yolen, Jane, 101
Young Warriors (ed. Sherman & Pierce), 105
Zelazny, Roger, 263
Zivkovic, Zoran, 12, 13

Zoo Story (Albee), 188
Zulu Blood (Barnes), 132

ABOUT THE AUTHOR

DARRELL SCHWEITZER is himself an author, editor, and poet, but also by now the most prolific and longest active interviewer in the science fiction field. He conducted his first interview in 1973. Since then he has interviewed at least a hundred authors and editors and the occasional artist. This is his seventh interview book.

www.ingramcontent.com/pod-product-compliance
Lightning Source LLC
Chambersburg PA
CBHW020150090426
42734CB00008B/767